ONE DETECTIVE's
JOURNEY INTO THE ABYSS

Roads Traveled, Lessons Learned, Villainy Exposed

Frederick T. Martens

Published by Sunbury Press, Inc.
Mechanicsburg, PA USA

www.sunburypress.com

For information about special discounts for bulk purchases, please contact Sunbury Press Orders Dept. at (855) 338-8359 or orders@sunburypress.com.

To request one of our authors for speaking engagements or book signings, please contact Sunbury Press Publicity Dept. at publicity@sunburypress.com.

FIRST SUNBURY PRESS EDITION: December 2021

Set in Adobe Garamond Pro | Interior design by Crystal Devine | Cover by Lawrence Knorr | Edited by Lawrence Knorr.

Publisher's Cataloging-in-Publication Data
Names: Martens, Frederick T., author.
Title: One detective's journey into the abyss : roads traveled, lessons learned, villainy exposed.
Description: First trade paperback edition. | Mechanicsburg, PA : Sunbury Press, 2021.
Summary: The author takes his readers on a journey through a fifty-year career investigating organized crime, public corruption, and white collar crime. He provides a compelling argument that upends the investigative rationale that resulted in the conviction of Rubin "Hurricane" Carter and John Ardis. He examines the political cultures of New York, New Jersey, and Pennsylvania that have been subjugated to decades of Mafia domination. He has challenged the rationales that continue to criminalize consensual behaviors. Recognizing the predatory effects of organized crime on the body politic, he has investigated public corruption that has infected the New York Metropolitan Region and Pennsylvania.
Identifiers: ISBN : 978-1-62006-885-4 (softcover).
Subjects: TRUE CRIME / Murder / General | TRUE CRIME / Organized Crime | TRUE CRIME / White Collar Crime.

Product of the United States of America
0 1 1 2 3 5 8 13 21 34 55

Continue the Enlightenment!

In remembrance of three courageous
New Jersey State Troopers
Werner Foerster, Phil Lamonaco, Fred Morrone
who gave all for some

Contents

Preface

Entering the twilight years of a remarkable journey, it is now convenient in the face of this worldwide pandemic to reflect upon the many milestones that allowed me to pursue a career in the New Jersey State Police (NJSP). Since I was ten years old and was selected to be on the school's safety patrol, which the State Police administered, my goal was to be a New Jersey State Trooper. Often passing the Pompton Lakes Barracks, seeing the State Troopers entering their troop cars, I would visualize myself donning that iconic blue and gold uniform.

By the time I graduated high school, I knew that military service would condition me for the most rigorous physical and academic training of any state police organization in the country. Enlisting in the United States Air Force would allow me to choose a career path to prepare me for the State Police.[1] I acquired the necessary skills to apply for and enter the physically demanding and academically challenging State Police Academy through military police training.

Stationed in California, I enrolled in California's progressive education system. It allowed me to acquire a college degree upon returning to New Jersey. It was one of the better decisions in my life.

But there was still another benefit to being in California during those learning years. The Viet Nam War was in its early stages. Stationed at Travis Air Force Base, a departure point for troops going to and returning from Southeast Asia, allowed me to meet and communicate with those on the front lines, fighting a war on the other side of the world. [2]

---

1. The compulsory draft was still in effect during the 60's. Enlistment all but guaranteed a chosen career path.

2. Sheehan, Neil. *A Bright Shining Lie: John Paul Vann and America in Vietnam.* 1988. McMaster, H.R. *Dereliction of Duty: Lyndon Johnson, Robert McNamara, The Joint Chiefs of Staff, and the Lies that Led to Vietnam.* 1997.

Again, attending college in California afforded me another perspective regarding the war, one that was not quite as hospitable to the so-called "Domino Effect" theory—as one country fell to Communism, an adjoining country was in the line for a takeover.

Frequenting the coffee houses and folk music venues throughout Berkeley, San Francisco, and Sausalito, California, I witnessed the anti-war rhetoric, slogans, and protests engulfing the nation. Seeing the young Bob Dylan and Joan Baez performing in Sausalito was part of being Californified.

On the other hand, North Beach in San Francisco held a different vibe, far more avant-garde and wild. Enrico's Café, Finocchio's, the Bunny Room, and the Condor Club were what made this former Italian neighborhood a huge adult Disneyland. I can still remember when my good friend Woody Rasmussen and I purchased our phony IDs to frequent the go-go bars that populated Broadway. I guess you could say that was my initial introduction to California's underworld?

Living among those who personified the military-industrial complex and those identified with the anti-war protests, it didn't take me long to realize that truth was fungible. I was certainly far more curious and skeptical of the government's self-serving claims.

With corpses of American soldiers returning from Viet Nam in the cargo pits of Continental Airlines, I began to question our involvement in a war on another continent. Was America genuinely threatened by a foreign civil war waged for domestic ideological reasons?

Listening to the "Goldwater for President" officers and juxtaposing their views against the students opposing America's involvement in Southeast Asia, I would engage in many lofty debates that allowed me to examine and re-assess my belief system.

As time passed and more information became public, I learned at a very early age that governments routinely deceive, mislead, and dissemble. The false narratives painted by Lyndon Johnson, Robert McNamara, and William Westmoreland were void of the political realities that stared them in their face. It was a sad lesson but served me well as I entered the world of criminal justice, where career aspirations could cloud the search for truth.

Decades later, I was fortunate to have visited Viet Nam. I viewed the intricate tunnels (Cu Chi) carved below the gorgeous landscapes. I shared meals amongst the people of the Mekong Delta. I mingled with the veterans of the war in Ho Chi Ming City and its rural outskirts. I felt the noticeable chill or "edge" in Hanoi, and I spent an entire day in the war museum that featured pictures and artifacts of the *American War*. It is the victors who write history, and their accountings certainly did not comport with ours.

As my parents would often say, the best education in the world was travel. Having been to fifty-five countries over six continents, you learn pretty quickly that America's democracy and promotion of human rights are imperfect but better than many other countries and must not be taken for granted.[3]We live in a country where we can express our distrust of government and are free to travel virtually anywhere.[4]

When the pandemic of 2019 struck, social isolation became the norm, especially at my age. There were fewer years ahead than in the past. But discretionary time was certainly plentiful as I organized my day, filling it with as many meaningful events as I could. Every morning, 7 am to 12 noon was time for reflection, research, and scribing.

In 1967, the year I was selected to attend the New Jersey State Police Academy, *Life Magazine* had published a series of articles that addressed the Mafia's insinuation in practically every political crevice of city, county, and state government.[5] The infamous Newark riots, currently referred to as a rebellion, exposed the extent of corruption that had engulfed the administration of its mayor, Hugh Addonizio.[6]

---

3. Winship, Scott., et. al. *Brookings Institution.* 2021. "Long Shadows: The Black-White Gap in multigerantional poverty." June 10th. Abramitzky, Ran., et. al. *National Bureau of Economic Research.* 2019. "Intergenerational Mobility of Immigrants in the US Over Two Centuries." October.

4. It wasn't until I travelled to Hanoi, China, Russia and Belarus did I realize how precious and fragile freedom was. Being surveilled on a regular basis during my visits demonstrated what we take for granted can evaporate quickly, particularly when despots, demagogues, and authoritarians are in charge. Clearly the terroristic assault on Congress of January 6, 2021 once again demonstrates the evil that can render a government impotent when unprepared.

5. *Life Magazine.* 1967. "The Brazen Empire of Organized Crime." September.

6. Report for Action: Governor's Select Committee on Civil Disorder, State of New Jersey. February 1968. Mumford, Kevin. 2008. *Newark: A History of Race, Rights, and Riots in America.* Williams. Junius. *New Jersey Monthly.* 2017. "The Rebellion in Newark." July 7th. Herman, Max Arthur. 2013. *Summer of Rage: An Oral History of the 1967 Newark and Detroit's Riots.* Hinton, Elizabeth. 2021. *America on Fire: The Untold History of Police Violence and Black Rebellion Since the 1960s.*

These events only reinforced my desire and passion for joining the New Jersey State Police. Unfortunately, believing that I could make a difference gave way to the stark reality that regardless of our founding father's noble intent, justice was an evolving process relegated to human frailties, institutional indignities, and long-held biases.

The New Jersey State Police is one of the most progressive state police organizations in America. Its training and stringent selection processes are second to none, usually taking as much as a year before you were fortunate to be selected to enter the Academy.[7]

Reflecting on my final interview with Detective Thomas Cornelissen in the dining room of my home, I can still remember him cautioning me never to volunteer for anything in the event I was selected to attend the Academy. "One day, I hadn't boxed, and I told the instructor . . . the instructor responded, 'You don't think we know what we're doing . . . put your gloves on and get in the ring' . . . I boxed until the other recruit knocked me out. So never volunteer for anything," Cornelissen gratuitously related. And it truly resonated with me.

What were the chances of me confronting the same situation.? Except I took Cornelissen's sage advice. I did not tell the instructor, Sgt. Phil Berman that I hadn't boxed.

As I was standing at the firing line of the weapons qualification phase of training, Berman's physically imposing silhouette emerged from a row of pine trees. Berman bellowed, "Martens, you didn't box today?" "No, Sir," I replied. "Why didn't you tell us," Berman shouted? "I thought you knew what you were doing, Sir," I foolishly responded. Of course, nothing I said would have mattered. The trap was sprung.

Berman then told me to report to the gymnasium and prepare to box after completing the class at the firing range. Entering the ring with my classmate, Paul Heuser, I boxed until I too was knocked out. Lesson learned—"Damned if you do, damned if you don't." Being second-guessed came with the territory, as I would learn throughout my career.

7. The selection process from written to physical to psychological examinations can begin with several thousand applicants. The beginning class is then whittled down thru injuries, dismissals, and resignations. The graduation rate is approximately 40–60%.

The Academy instructors were experts in the various fields of subject matter that they taught. Berman was a professional boxer. Decades later, his son Joseph told me that his father gave up boxing after being ordered to "throw a fight" if he wished to keep boxing.[8]

Others were experts on the traffic codes, deadly force, Constitutional and statutory law, State Police procedures, and criminal investigation. As a quasi-military organization, its' training parallels the West Point Military Academy model. Instilling a code of conduct that underscored the role of discipline in achieving the organization's goals and objectives defined the unique character that was symbolic of the State Police.[9]

Indeed, the instructors mainly were ex-military veterans who had served during the Korean War or shortly after that. Some were college graduates, although that was not a requirement at the time. Decades later, Col. Justin J. Dintino mandated at least two years of college and two years of military service if an applicant lacked a four-year college degree.[10]

The Academy experience distinguished the New Jersey State Police from the other 521-plus police departments and law enforcement agencies in New Jersey. Remarkably and refreshingly, the State Police was not hostage to the political patronage and nepotism that was often the case with local policing agencies—a practice that is and was antithetical to police professionalism.[11]

Simply put, the New Jersey State Police invested in a well-rounded physical, moral, and academic education for its personnel—enlisted and civilian. Notwithstanding its rigorous six-month training program at the Academy, there were semi-annual in-service training sessions, routine firearms qualifications, lethal force tutorials, ethics, diversity, and gender-awareness seminars.

---

8. *Phil Berman: Legend in His Time.* Conversation with Joseph Berman at the induction in the New Jersey State Boxing Hall of Fame, November 3, 2016.

9. The first N.J. State Police Superintendent, H. Norman Schwarzkopf was a graduate of West Point and retired a general in the Army.

10. Today, the Commandant of the Academy is a law school graduate. Every instructor has at least a baccalaureate degree, with most holding graduate degrees.

11. Janoski, Steve. *The Record* (Woodland Park, NJ). 2020. "How NJ police departments hires officers varies widely. Why it could make reform difficult?" October 27th. Noda. Stephanie. *The Bergen Record.* 2020. "Days After Judge's Ruling Paramus GOP Rejects Police Hires, Including Mayor's Son." November 3rd.

ONE DETECTIVE'S JOURNEY INTO THE ABYSS

In addition, the State Police has made ongoing investments in outsourced training seminars and symposiums taught by the leading experts in their respective fields of expertise.[12] The return on investment has been proven time and again.

Relatively speaking, when compared with its peers and counterparts throughout the state and country, it has met the complex investigative challenges it has confronted. Notwithstanding its so-called "checkered history," it has evolved over the past 100 years into the most educated, diverse, technologically advanced, and institutionally resilient law enforcement agency the state has ever known.[13]

This era in the history of the NJSP was exceptional in so many ways. It was a time when Col. David B. Kelly, followed by Colonel Eugene Olaff, Clinton L. Pagano, and Justin J. Dintino, and their respective staffs transformed the State Police into the premier investigative agency in the State.

Unlike many state police organizations that were primarily traffic-centric, the New Jersey State Police were functionally diversified. Within its' geographic borders, an advanced laboratory for investigating organized crime was available for the pickings. Organized crime is a living and breathing organism, perhaps New Jersey's being the most mature found anywhere in the country.[14]

In the 1960s, the Narcotics Bureau expanded ten-fold. Both an Organized Crime Bureau and Intelligence Bureau became part of its nascent organized crime control initiative. A Major Crimes Unit specializing in advanced homicide and arson techniques was formed. Staffed

---

12. Alone I attended over twenty, one week or longer seminars, symposiums, or training courses to include homicide and arson investigation, organized crime and narcotics investigations, corruption investigative methods and techniques, racketeering tutorials, informant development, intelligence collection and analysis, and management courses.

13. Janoski, Steve. NorthJersey.com. 2021. "Checkered history: At 100, NJ State Police confronts racist past, notes stellar feats." May 11th. Notwithstanding aspects of its sordid past much good has emerged. The N.J. State Police under its current Colonel Patrick Callahan has proven it can handle controversy and truth in a mature, professional, and candid manner. Simply view Callahan's interview with the first Black Trooper, Paul McLemore (February 16, 2021 at NJSP/Facebook) to witness the courage it took to conduct this interview on both Callahan and McLemore's part.

14. Mastrobuoni, Giovanni. *Carlo Alberto Notebooks*. 2010. "Understanding Organized Crime Network: Evidence Based on Federal Bureau of Narcotics Secret Files on American Mafia." September. p. 26.

by detectives who demonstrated an exceptional aptitude for complex, sensitive, and politically precarious investigations, these detectives were often complemented by deputy attorneys general who understood the legal nuances of conspiracy laws. It was uncharted territory. No one knew where and to whom these investigations would lead, nor the collateral damage often left in the wake.

Whether the investigation of political machines in the more urban counties, the infiltration of the notorious Mafia families that plagued the state, or investigating mob-murders, the New Jersey State Police proved that it was up to the task once again.[15] To put it mildly, these were heady and adrenalin-inducing times.

Serving as Lt. Col. Justin J. Dintino's chief of staff, I was privy to some of the most intimate discussions involving any number of high-profile political investigations and those involving the state's ruthless Mafia members. It was an experience that would open my eyes to the dastardly and duplicitous machinations between corrupt politicians, gangsters, and racketeers.[16]

How that all began was again serendipity. Attending an organized crime seminar in Sea Girt, New Jersey, Dintino was at the podium, lecturing. He posed the question, "If drug arrests are going up every year, the purity of the drug sold is improving, and the population using their drug of choice is growing, what does it say about our drug strategy?" I raised my hand. "Yes, detective," Dintino responded.

"Sir, our approach to drug enforcement is failing."

"Correct," Dintino echoed.

---

15. Sullivan. Ronald. *The New York Times.* 1971. "Plot to Fix Criminal Case Laid to Bergen Prosecutor." June 18th. *The New York Times.* 1973. "Tonti Sentenced to 3 Years fined $10,000 on Parkway Extortion Charge." March 14th. Sullivan, Joseph F. *The New York Times.* 1973. "10 in Gang in Jersey Indicted in 5 Killings." November 30th. Sullivan, Joseph. F. *The New York Times.* 1974. "New Jersey Secretary of State indicted on Bid-Rigging Charge." August 1st. Waggoner, Walter H. *The New York Times.* 1975. "State Lists Case Against Crabiel." April 15th. *State v. Joyce, 390 A.2d 151, 160 N.J. Super 419* (1978). *State v. Hacker,* February 19, 1981. Delaney, Bob and Dave Scheiber. 2008. *Covert: My Years Infiltrating the Mob.* February 1st. Considine, Bob. 2010. *Corrupt Jersey Boss Inspires HBO's 'Boardwalk Empire.'* February 16th. Zambito, Thomas. *The Star- Ledger* (Newark, NJ). 2015. "Mob Bust hits family that Inspired 'The Sopranos.'" March 13th.

16. United States Senate: 98th Congress: Committee on the Judiciary. 1983. *Organized Crime in America.* February 16th. pp. 106–299.

After class, Dintino came up to me and asked me where I was assigned? "The Major Crime Unit," I replied.

"Would you consider coming to the Intelligence Bureau," Dintino asked.

"I would love to," I responded. Dintino orchestrated the transfer. I now was a member of the esteemed Intelligence Bureau that reported directly to the Superintendent of State Police. Forty-five years later, Dintino remembered the sequence of events as he lay dying in bed.[17]

"Freddie, I still remember the trade I made with (Major) Baum. Jack Liddy for you. It was the best decision I could have made." Three days later, my friend and my mentor passed away.

Yes, it was quite a journey, one that I never knew where the next road would take me. "Never fear, never quit, and always look ahead" were the words that echoed in my head—words that my mother and father repeated time and again.

They too traveled roads that they never contemplated, fleeing Nazi Germany as Hitler was coming to power. As my mother and father would often say, "Don't think a Hitler cannot come to power in America . . . Germany was a civilized and cultured democracy, and look what happened." These words echo in my head still today. It never occurred to me that domestic terrorists would violently challenge our institutions of democracy as they had on January 6, 2021.[18]

As luck would have it, an opportunity came up that would lead me down yet another road. Contacted by Charles Rogovin, a professor at Temple University School of Law and the first administrator of the Law Enforcement Assistance Administration (LEAA), he asked if I was interested in applying for Executive Director of the Pennsylvania Crime Commission (PCC).[19]

The PCC was dedicated solely to investigating organized crime and public corruption—a thankless task and one that seldom ended well.

---

17. January 21, 2020. On February 1, 2020, Col. Patrick Callahan presided over the funeral of Col. Dintino. It was one of the most memorable displays of pageantry and decorum that exemplified the New Jersey State Police motto; duty, honor, and fidelity.

18. Wikipedia: 2021 Storming of the United States Capitol. Goldman, Adam. *The New York Times.* 2021. "Domestic Terrorism Threat is 'Metastasizing' in U.S., F.B.I. Director Says." March 2nd.

19. See Appendix B.

Approaching my twentieth year in the State Police, which allowed me to retire at 43, I applied. Following a rigorous interview process, I was appointed the Executive Director.

I can still remember when I met with Col. Clinton L. Pagano, handing in my retirement papers. Pagano commented on my future with the New Jersey State Police and how going to Pennsylvania, I would not have the latitude to conduct investigations like here in New Jersey. Knowing better, of course, I said, "I'll take my chances, but I had made up my mind." Pagano's prescient advice was "spot on."

Pennsylvania was an experience I will never forget and one that I often shudder when I do remember. Often perceived in the image of Norman Rockwell's pastoral countrysides and Billy Graham's sermons on wholesome family values, it was hard to reconcile the corruption the infected the body politic. Did I get an education?

While New Jersey was no playground, Pennsylvania proved that corruption was equally insidious, invidious, and pervasive. Without a doubt, every investigation the Pennsylvania Crime Commission undertook confronted political blowback. Investigating the hiring of a Scranton-based mob boss to perform night watchman work at the Philadelphia Industrial Correctional Center, pursuing drug traffickers in the tourist-rich hamlets of Lancaster County, or uncovering corruption in the Office of Attorney General, the political repercussions were swift and endless.

State senators and representatives were constantly inquiring and subtly and not so subtly threatening to defund the Commission.[20] Many have since been incarcerated for corruption-related crimes.

As my days investigating organized crime and political corruption were waning, a true friend and former colleague, Frank Bellis, offered me a position at the Claridge Hotel and Casino in Atlantic City, New Jersey. After decades in the public sector, the private sector provided a new challenge—one that had me reading 10K's and 10Q's, pursuing new financial venues in Belize and Las Vegas, and conducting sensitive internal investigations. Unlike the public sector, these investigations often

---

20. Connolly, Sean. *The Morning Call* (Allentown, PA). 1993. "PA. Crime Panel To Die? Gets House Approval." December 8th; and "Senate Split Over Crime Commission's Future." December 14th.

involved the very people I worked with or for. It, too, proved a professionally rewarding experience.

Time to move on. The world's largest casino company acquired the Claridge, and consolidation and economies of scale were the terms of the times.[21] Again, a former colleague, Joe DeLuca, offered me the opportunity to work in the "Big Apple," conducting corporate investigations on behalf of Fortune 500 companies. One year later, I found myself at the site of what remained of the World Trade Center, post 9-11. Another challenge was ensuring that the rescue and recovery mission was devoid of any Mafia influence or taint.

Reflecting on these milestones and those that followed again reinforced that few things in life are certain or predictable. I have witnessed some of my closest friends and two mentors, Justin Dintino and Charlie Rogovin, pass away in the past couple of years.

I have self-isolated as this pandemic, a once-in-a-lifetime event, has swept across the world, restricting my domestic and international travel. I have learned the value of time spent with my precious family, who was always there throughout my journey.

Hopefully, the vignettes, which can never quite capture the numerous and diverse routines inherent in a law enforcement career, convey a story of justice, injustice, political intrigue and chicanery, corruption, and perseverance.

Unlike some reflective memoirs, I do not claim my exploits are any more or less significant than the thousands of detectives and prosecutors who have entered this treacherous world we call *organized crime.* Without a collective, integrated, and focused approach, law enforcement is disadvantaged in addressing *organized crime.* These brave souls have stories to tell, many of which are more harrowing and informative than mine. Some are even more depressing and certainly more revolting. Perhaps my memoir will encourage others to explore and recollect the events that shaped their respective careers.

---

21. *The Herald News* (Passaic, NJ). 2001. "Caesar's Takes Over Claridge Casino." June 2nd. *Asbury Park Press.* 2001. "Casino Acquisition: Caesars buys Troubled Claridge Casino." May 31st. All-Chips.com. "Bally's Park Place, Atlantic City, NJ. Chip Listing."

There will be those that take umbrage to what I have to say or how I portray an event, an agency, or a person(s). To them, I can only say, "sorry, that is how I remember it. Write your version of history!"

In only three instances, I felt it appropriate to change or camouflage the names of those involved in several investigations. Nonetheless, even in these three cases, a skilled researcher or investigator could uncover the answers to the five basic investigative questions: who, what, where, when, and how? The pseudo-names represent the actual persons and events, which hopefully add to the authenticity of what you are about to experience.

Often I will refer to the Mafia, the mob, or *Cosa Nostra* interchangeably. I will also use the terms tribute, loansharking, numbers, policy, hitman, assassination, and various illegal drugs by colloquial names (i.e., speed, meth, smack, crack, coke, etc.). Through the *Anatomy of Terms,* I have attempted to make sense of underworld jargon.

My memoir includes over 500 actual sources that will validate and corroborate the events as they unfolded. Only by living through this chaotic experience can one appreciate the emotional turmoil and foul political climate that characterized this relatively brief slice of history. I encourage and implore those who wish to understand the human depravity that infected and poisoned the body politic to indulge in the rich, voluminous, and robust research I cited. Only then can you appreciate and understand the physical, mental, and economic toll this takes on society and those who enter the abyss.

As I often tell my friends, *everyone has a story to tell.* It can die with you or, it can promote an appreciable understanding to enhance the greater good.

Hopefully, my journey has?

Acknowledgments

There are several ways to position a memoir. It can be a puff piece designed to erase warts and polish the gems that defined your life. It can be a way of saying thank you, carry on, and goodbye. It can be seen as a contribution to history, addressing that left unfinished, untouched, or unspoken in your lifetime. It can be a written monument to your family and friends. It can add to the universe of knowledge, allowing future generations an insight into what was, what is, and what can be. In my case, it is all the above.

There is one thing that I have learned throughout my career investigating organized crime and public corruption. Nothing is accomplished without a cadre of dedicated, trustworthy, and competent colleagues. Teamwork is the glue that made the career I have chosen to write about an extraordinary journey. It was a lesson I learned in boot camp, re-enforced at the New Jersey State Police Academy, and routinely addressed daily whether at the State Police, Pennsylvania Crime Commission, Claridge Casino-Hotel, or Thacher Associates.

The investigations cited throughout this memoir could not have occurred without teamwork. I was certainly not alone as we plodded through these investigations, nor was I exceptional in experiencing these valuable lessons. Legions of dedicated troopers, detectives, investigators, special agents, analysts, prosecutors, and deputy attorneys general all were part of this once-in-a-lifetime journey. Where appropriate and feasible, I have named them throughout this writing.

Of course, let me begin with posthumously thanking my mother, Ruth, and my father, Fred, who left their homelands to embark on the American dream. Had it not been for their demanding that my brothers and I get an education, my dreams may not have come to fruition.

Coupled with an irrepressible appetite to travel, we never spent a summer that we did not explore some region of this magnificent landscape. To them, I owe my eternal and never-dying love and genuine respect and admiration. They never denied us the wisdom of their experiences, shaping our minds to *embrace* the diversity of people, cultures, and intellect the world had to offer.

It would be an egregious mistake not to follow with the recognition he truly deserves—my mentor extraordinaire, Justin J. Dintino. Early in my State Police career, he took me under his wing. He taught me the art of criminal investigation, particularly involving complex public corruption and organized crime cases. But perhaps the most important lesson I learned from The Colonel was courage—the courage to do what was right under the most trying circumstances.

Investigating public corruption is not a pleasant task. You make many enemies and few allies or friends. You can "go along to get along," as many have done. Or you could address the issues confronting you with the courage and integrity demanded of your oath of office.

Mentored by a person who did the latter, The Colonel never looked back. The Colonel's courage was always front and center till the day he lay in his dying bed. It is a lesson that I was most fortunate to have experienced and one that will remain with me when it's my turn to pass through those "pearly gates." (See Appendix A.)

During the pandemic, my children, Jeffrey, Scott, Heather, Adam, and Robb were my "go-to" maestros. Every Sunday, we would share dinner and stories on the dock, socially distant and avoiding the hugs and kisses that preceded the advent of this dreaded virus. Their continued love over the past decades always served as my beacon of strength that I will never forget but can hardly repay.

Of course, without my ex-wife Karen and their mother, who would join us on the many family occasions, I can only reflect on a sixty-year relationship that, with all its twists and turns, proved the adage, "blood is thicker than water." Never to waiver in jointly raising our children, she was and always will be the willow that withstood the gales and winds that came her way. As the saying goes, "we may not be able to control the winds, but we can adjust the sails." Karen was that most talented and versatile captain.

Having one mentor is lucky enough. But two? That's a charmed life. The accomplished and nationally-renowned Charles Rogovin, lecturer and law professor, was always there to discuss, debate, and synthesize the many issues we confronted.

In Colorado, addressing the effectiveness of their organized crime strike force, Charlie diligently pursued the methods and practices that led to the objections voiced by its critics.[22] In seminars throughout North America or England, Charlie religiously preached the gospel, championing intelligence analysis as the glue that bonded intelligence and organized crime control policies and practices. And when pursuing corruption among the political elites of Pennsylvania, Charlie always made the case cogently and resoundingly. He was my *capo di tutti capi*. (See Appendix B.)

The late Thomas "Toby" Thacher, Frank Bellis, and Joe DeLuca were instrumental in stewarding my career through paths and alleyways that I would never have imagined.[23] Whether it was resisting Mafia influence at the site of the World Trade Center post 9-11; exposing waste and corruption inflicted by Hurricane Katrina in New Orleans; pursuing the serial killer Bobby Durst in Texas; investigating prospective casino applicants in Belize, Australia, and Las Vegas; and addressing the aftermath of "The Troubles" of Northern Ireland, it was a journey no amount of money could have bought.[24] Thank you for those indelibly-etched and incredible memories.

When bombarded by the corrupt forces that resulted in the Commission's demise, my colleagues at the Pennsylvania Crime Commission, an agency that proved to be "the little engine that wouldn't quit," always stood tall. Michael Reilly, Charles Rogovin, Jim Manning, Arthur Coccodrilli, Allen Hornblum, Glenn Walp, and Arlin Adams proved their medal when the chips were down.[25] And of course, John Ryan, Alan Bailey, Willie Byrd, Joe Dougherty, Ed Recke, Jim Kanavy, Nancy Kushner, and Paul Spear, and yes, so many others, never once lamented the fact

22. Rogovin, Charles H. and Frederick T. Martens. *An Assessment of the Colorado Organized Crime Strike Force*. 1984. Denver, Colorado. Levinson, Arnold. *Rocky Mountain News*. 1984. "Report Blasts strike force as unprepared, ineffective." September 16th.
23. Roberts, Sam. *The New York Times*. 2017. "Thomas Thacher, Who Fought Construction Fraud, Dies at 71." November 22nd.
24. Wikipedia: Robert Durst
25. Wikipedia: Glenn Walp. Wikipedia: Arlin Adams.

that the Commission was going down in flames. "We did our job," it was "the right thing to do," was their simple message to those who questioned our collective and fateful decision.

As a child who grew up with a disability—dyslexia—I was fortunate to have Mrs. Isabel Pace as my eighth-grade English teacher. Her unwavering patience in teaching me the lost technique of diagraming allowed me to break this crippling disease. Reading and writing, ever since, became a passion.

While several university professors shaped my views of the world, Dr. Edward Cook stands out.[26] Trained as a philosopher, Dr. Cook demonstrated how the Socratic art of debate, persuasion and, logic could untangle the most twisted and perverse arguments. As he proved time and again, nuance lies in the details. Never avoid reading the details, for that is where the devil hides.

Thirty-one years ago, my first station commander, Major Joseph Rogalski, prematurely passed away.[27] As I reflected on August 28, 1967, I remember standing in front of this giant of a man. Six foot four, ramrod straight, meticulously groomed, and looking every bit a "Troopers' Trooper," he perused my personnel file. He commented, "college-educated, eh . . . you will get an education here and not quite like those liberal professors taught you." He then proceeded to articulate *Rogalski's Rules*. It was a most fortunate assignment that provided me with an unvarnished introduction into the State Police culture. Given Rogalski's satirical mockery of the investigative branch, I suspect some of what I have to say today would not sit well with his uncompromising moral compass. But he was never one to ignore a rational argument and arrive at a credible opinion. His incisive intellect enriched those that had the distinct privilege of sharing in his wisdom.

Last, my best friends throughout my life, Jules, aka Butch and Leanne Pellegrino, were always there through thick and thin. To remain friends with someone over 68 years is a gift that few can ever experience. I was most fortunate to know that they always knew who I was, what I was, and where I was, even when we did not always agree. Thank you!

---

26. Emeriti Faculty. Fairleigh Dickinson University. Rutherford, New Jersey.
27. *The Courier-News.* 1990. "Joseph A. Rogalski, 62, Former State Policeman." July 30th. p. 8.

In polishing off this most incredible journey, my South African and Australian friends Sharon Geake and Gwynne Craven had an unwitting influence on me. Sharon, who never quite knew how she reignited my interest in her life living under Apartheid and Gwynne, who championed our visit to the Nelson Mandela Museum in South Africa, allowed me to fully appreciate and understand how the rule of law oppressed the masses. Thank you, Sharon and Gwynne, for sharing these experiences and insights with me during this most dark and horrid period in the history of South Africa.

It would certainly be an egregious error if I did not thank my publisher, Lawrence Knorr and his most able assistants Marianne Babcock and Crystal Devine for a herculean effort to make this final chapter in my life a reality. They held my hand and were a constant inspiration throughout this most arduous process.Now join me on my journey. Hopefully, you will come to understand why you should never *blindly* trust your government and always remain vigilant. *Peaceful* protests and *peaceful* demonstrations designed to expose the corrupt and misinformed government policies need not be discouraged or crushed for fear of telling ugly truths.

Veritas liberabit vos!

Anatomy of Terms

Bookie: A person who accepts illegal bets from persons seeking to capitalize on a sporting event.

Cosa Nostra: Sometimes referred to as *La Cosa Nostra*, it is a secret criminal organization comprised of persons of Italian ethnicity. In Italian, it means "Our Thing."

Capo: A Mafia or Cosa Nostra member who commands a crew of ten or fewer soldiers.

Coke: Cocaine

Crack: Free-based cocaine that comes in the form of a hardened substance.

DSFC: Detective Sergeant First Class

DSG: Detective Sergeant

Flaking: Planting illegal paraphernalia on an innocent person.

Godfather: The boss of a crime family or one who offers protection to criminals.

Hash: Hashish, a derivative of marijuana.

Hit: A murder or assassination.

Informant: Usually, a person who was arrested or had an arrest record that agrees to provide information or assist the police in an investigation.

Loansharking: To lend money at interest rates that are deemed illegal by the government.

LSD: A psychedelic, mind-altering drug.

Mafia: A criminal organization of Italian-American descent that engages in racketeering activities defined by the RICO statute. Often used interchangeably with the term Cosa Nostra, mob, or outfit. Nowadays, refers to any secret criminal organization.

Meth: Methamphetamine, an illegal drug that induces a heightened state of anxiety and paranoia. Referred to as "speed" or "crystal."

Mob: Refers to the Mafia, usually comprised of persons of Italian ancestry.

Money Laundering: Exchanging money derived illicitly for clean money to camouflage the source.

Numbers: The last three numbers of the revenue generated at a pre-determined race track or, sometimes, the legal lottery.

Organized Crime: The broad generic term referring to a form of criminality that is rationally executed and seeks exclusivity and monopoly control over illicit or, at times, licit markets.[28]

Pad: A routine pay-off scheme usually to the police to avoid criminal prosecution.

Policy: Same as the numbers racket, in which the bettor bets with a bookie on the last three numbers of the daily revenue at a predetermined horse racing track.

Quaaludes: A semi- hypnotic drug that lowers anxiety and leads to a state of drowsiness.

RICO: Racketeer Influenced Corrupt Organization Act.

Source(s): People who provide information to the police but wish to remain anonymous.

Speed: Refers to methamphetamine.

Smack: Heroin

Tribute: The payment of monies to the reigning Mafia or crime czar in an entire region under their control.

Vice: An activity that is a consensual act but is deemed illegal by the state. It represents the moral ambiguity in the law. Gambling, narcotics, prostitution, pornography are routinely referred to as vice.

---

28. For a discussion of this term, see Steffensmeier, Darrell and Fred Martens. *International Encyclopedia of the Social and Behavioral Sciences.* 2001. *Crime: Organized.* pp. 2928–934. Sergi, Anna. 2018. *MAFIAROUND. Fighting Italian Mafias Outside of Italy.* November 29, 30th. Abadinsky, Howard. 2016. *Organized Crime.*

1

A Triple Murder, A Mob-Hit, A Missed Opportunity?

It was June of 1966. I had just returned home from California after completing a four-year stint in the United States Air Force. A triple murder believed to have been committed by Rubin "Hurricane" Carter was splashed across the headlines of the major newspapers. It consumed the political discourse throughout Passaic County, New Jersey, and beyond.[1]

Stopped by the Paterson Police in the vicinity of the Lafayette Bar and Grill where the triple murder occurred earlier in the evening, Carter and his driver, John Artis, were questioned regarding their alleged involvement in killing a bartender and two patrons. The three victims were white, and Carter and Artis were Black. A perfect prescription for all sorts of Machiavellian shenanigans in a city known for its penchant for corruption, brutality, and organized crime's influence and control.

After being detained and questioned by the police, Carter and Artis were returned to the crime scene. After being seen by the witnesses, they were released from police custody.[2] No charges were filed. No bail was set. And most notably, no restrictions were placed on their movements.

They could have but did not abscond as others had. They remained readily available for further questioning and investigation. They testified

---

1. See *The Butler's Child; Hurricane: the Miraculous Journey of Rubin Carter; Rubin "Hurricane" Carter and the American Justice System; Hurricane Carter: The Other Side of the Story; The Hurricane Tapes by the BBC; Doubts, Errors and Unknowns Still Haunt the Case of Artis and Carter* [*The Bergen Record*, Mike Kelly, June 17, 2019]; and *Media Meddlers: The Real Truth About the Murder Case Against Rubin "Hurricane" Carter,* for a robust discussion of this investigation, prosecution and judicial debacle.

2. The practice of corrupting the witnesses by placing the suspects at the scene of the crime has been discredited and is incompatible with best practices.

before the Grand Jury. They were administered polygraph tests and passed. Indeed not the typical behavior of two Black males suspected of an act of unimaginable human carnage. Nor was it a typical response by the police who believed they had in custody the assailants who had committed a triple murder.

However, three months later, they were charged with the triple murders, mainly on the eye-witness testimony of a serial criminal and chronic liar, Alfred Bello and, his cohort in crime, Dexter Bradley.

To paraphrase the words of Bob Dylan, this is a story about the "Hurricane"—a story that is relevant in light of our current examination of systemic racism and its effects on the administration of justice.[3]

Relitigating the Past

My decision to address a triple murder and the mob murders that happened fifty-four years ago was inspired by the recent publicity surrounding the publication of Vincent DeSimone's memoir and the BBC's riveting investigation.[4] Admittedly, the suspects, Rubin Carter and John Artis, were set free on two occasions. Carter, Artis, and DeSimone, the lead detective, have since passed away. The only eye-witness, Alfred Bello, has been thoroughly discredited by DeSimone.[5] Other witnesses have since expired.

Minds have been made up, and positions solidified regarding Carter's and Artis's guilt or innocence. No amount of dredging up the history of this ill-fated prosecution will change any opinions or add any substance to what is already known.

All that was true before 2019.

The publication of DeSimone's memoir, *Media Meddlers,* has undoubtedly opened up *Pandora's Box*. Until 2019, all we learned about

3. *Hurricane* was a Bob Dylan protest song released in 1976 that championed the cause of Rubin "Hurricane" Carter.

4. DeSimone, Vincent J. and James V. DeSimone. 2019. *Media Meddlers: The Real Truth About the Murder Case Against Rubin "Hurricane" Carter.* April 17th. Hammer, Joel and Steven Crossman. *BBC: The Hurricane Tapes.* 2019.

5. DeSimone, Vincent J. 2019. *Media Meddlers* p. 198–99. It should be noted that Justice Clifford of New Jersey's Supreme Court remarked, "Never before could defendants argue so persuasively that Bello was in all respects a complete, unvarnished liar, incapable of speaking the truth." *State v. Carter, 449 A .2d 1280* (N.J. 1982) Supreme Court of New Jersey. August 17, 1982.

DeSimone's mindset during this investigation was what he testified to in court. Now we have been afforded his unvarnished and unedited inner thoughts and actions, shielded from public scrutiny for decades. And what his memoir says and equally as relevant, what it doesn't say should re-open a robust and spirited analysis of the investigation and prosecution.

Furthermore, mindful that those involved in the investigation and the prosecution voluntarily participated in the recent BBC Podcast, *The Hurricane Tapes*, new *evidence* has been uncovered. This *evidence* seriously undermines the credibility of Alfred Bello as well as his "handler" and a principal witness, Detective Robert Mohl.[6]

With the release of a recent nationwide study of 2,400 exonerations, the investigation of this triple murder and the prosecution of Carter and Artis is not only relevant today but equally as problematic. "Misconduct by the police, prosecutors, and other law enforcement officials is a regular problem . . . [as is] concealing exculpatory evidence," the study concluded.[7] These findings reflect squarely on the investigation and prosecution of Carter and Artis.[8]

Moreover, we have now entered an era where justice and the processes to achieve justice are meticulously scrutinized. We have witnessed a consensus, fragile as it may be, around the notion that justice has been

---

6. Hammer, Joel and Steven Crossman. *British Broadcasting Corporation.* 2019. *The Hurricane Tapes.* Episode 3 @27:13. Hammer, Joel and Steven Crossman. *BBC World Service* 2019. *The Hurricane Tapes: Robert Mohl, Rubin Carter & Telling the 'other side' of the story.* January 21st. Also see *State v. Yough, 49 N.J. 587* (1967) in which Donald F. Young, who was subsequently arrested by the New Jersey State Police for taking payoffs from the Genovese Mafia Family, is a critical witness in a disputed Miranda warning proffered by Mohl. *The New York Times.* 1973. *A Detective Chief Among 5 Indicted.* June 23rd. *The New York Times.* 1974. *Captain Cleared of Bribe Charge.* June 7th. *State v. Joseph F. Esposito, 148 N.J. Super. 102* (1977) February 9th.

7. *Government Misconduct and Convicting the Innocent: The Role of Prosecutors, Police and Other Law Enforcement.* September 1, 2020. As the New Jersey Supreme stated in reversing the guilty verdict, "The withholding of material evidence favorable to a defendant is a denial of due process and the right to a fair trial . . . in the present case . . . both the October 11 tape and the promises made to Bradley clearly possessed the capacity to have affected the jury's evaluation of the credibility of Bello's and Bradley's identification testimony . . . We conclude . . . that the defendants right to a fair trial was substantially prejudiced so that the judgment of conviction must be vacated and a new trial ordered." *State v. Carter, 69 N.J. 420* (1976).

8. Chokshi, Niraj. *The New York Times.* 2017. "Black People More Likely to Be Wrongfully Convicted of Murder, Study Shows." March 7th. *The National Registry of Exonerations.* Meissner, Christian A. and John C. Brigham. *Psychology, Public Policy and Law.* 2001. "Thirty Years of Investigating The Own-Race Bias in Memory For Faces." vol. 7, no. 1, pp. 3–35.

routinely and structurally denied to those who often lack the financial or political assets that could and would level the playing field.[9]

However, there may be a more compelling reason, one that has escaped any critical discourse.

South Africa, after Apartheid, made the conscious decision to revisit the practices of its national security services during this brutal era. It established a *Truth and Reconciliation Commission* that sought the testimony of those responsible for the brutal execution of Apartheid. This *Commission* added to the historical record and demonstrated that a form of justice, imperfect as it might be, can be achieved absent the constraints imposed by a criminal trial.[10]

New Jersey and Passaic County should consider a similar tribunal to address these murders and others that were part of the Mafia's control of the rackets in Paterson during the 60s and 70s and until this very day.[11]

Passaic County and Paterson, circa the 1960s and Beyond

To fully appreciate the explosive mix of race and criminal justice, it is essential to gain an appreciation for the corrupt milieu that infected the administration of justice in Paterson and Passaic County during the 60s and apparently into the 21st century.

Born in Paterson and attending school there, several of my classmates had joined its police force. Their disdain and considerable resentment toward the constitutional protections afforded by Miranda, Escobedo, and other Constitutional protections were viscerally-palpable.

---

9. *Brennan Center for Justice.* 2020. "Lost Earnings: How the Criminal Justice System Deepens Inequality." September 15th. Vaidyanathan, Brandon. *The Public Discourse.* 2020. "Systemic Racial Bias in the Criminal Justice System Is Not a Myth." June 29th.

10. *Truth and Reconciliation Commission Website. Promotion of National Unity and Reconciliation Act, No. 34 of 1995.* The State of Maryland has established via legislation, a Truth and Reconciliation Commission which specifically addresses lynching. It should be noted that the statute of limitations has tolled on all the crimes committed during the Carter-Artis investigation with *the exception of the crime of murder.* Canada also undertook a similar approach. See Wikipedia: Truth and Reconciliation Commission/Canada.

11. Sources indicate that this practice has continued into 2021, with video poker machines populating bars and social clubs throughout Paterson, and police officers being paid as much as two thousand dollars a month. "The more things change, the more they stay the same."

DeSimone captures the tenor of the prevailing attitude quite succinctly, reflectively opining, "Mention Miranda to a policeman, and it's like spitting on his mother grave . . . [its] the ultimate obscenity for law enforcement officials and prosecutors."[12]

Upon being assigned to work undercover in Paterson in the early seventies as a newly-minted State Police detective, we were routinely warned to avoid the Paterson police if at all possible. Known to "flake" suspected drug dealers or those they "had it in for," the Paterson Police Department suffered from chronic integrity challenges.[13]

Its' feared and infamous "Goon Squad" was essentially used to brutalize and extract confessions from those they believed committed a crime. Summary justice practiced with virtual impunity.[14]

Using "stand-ins (i.e., persons amenable to being arrested for monetary or other benefits) to admit to crimes they did not commit routinely occurred. Often this was the case when it involved politically sensitive investigations.

As the third-largest city in the State, Paterson proved to be a lucrative target for state investigators. The federal government was consumed with Essex and Hudson counties, which were bereft of corruption.[15]

Directed from the highest levels of State government, the State Police were dispatched to investigate the rackets in Paterson in the early 70s. With the newly formed organized crime and intelligence bureaus, access to electronic surveillance, and a state grand jury, the State Police were

---

12. DeSimone, Vincent J. 2019. *Media Meddlers.* p. 83. Miranda was the Supreme Court decision that required the police to advise a suspect that he/she had the right to remain silent, have an attorney present during questioning, if indigenous would bet provided an attorney, and if he/she does agree to being questioned, anything he/she says can be used against him/her (384 U.S. 436 [1966]). It was decided on June 13, 1966, four days (June 17, 1966) prior to the triple murder.

13. "Flaking" is a term which connotes the planting or secreting of illegal paraphernalia on a person. It could be drugs, numbers slips, guns, ammunition, etc.

14. *The New York Times.* 1968. "Paterson Inquiry on Police Ordered; Prosecutor Hears Several Charges of 'Riot' Brutality." July 9th. *The Morning Call* (Paterson, NJ). 1969. "Indicted Paterson Police Deny Brutality Charges." January 4th. *CBSNEWYORK* 2013. "Surveillance Video Captures Alleged Paterson, N.J. Police Brutality." July 1st. *WNYC.* 2019. "Feds Investigate Allegations of Violence and Corruption in Paterson's Police Department." April 5th.

15. *Report for Action* aka Lilley Commission. 1968. Wikipedia: Angelo DeCarlo. Wikipedia: Simone DeCalvalcante. Hoffman, Paul. 1973. *Tiger in the Court.* Stern, Herbert J. 2012. *Diary of a DA: The True Story of the Prosecutor Who Took on the Mob, Fought Corruption, and Won.* September. Jerde, Sara. *The Star-Ledger* (Newark, NJ). 2015. "Lawyers Recall Corruption Trial That Changed New Jersey Politics." June 15th.

prepared to confront what we thought were the waning vestiges of "home rule"—a political reality that made political fiefdoms sacred territory.[16]

Concurrently, a renowned anthropologist from Columbia University, Francis A.J. Ianni, had developed an interest in the study of organized crime. Publishing a book on Italian-American organized crime in 1971, Ianni decided to examine what he believed was the ethnic-succession process in organized crime.[17] Blacks, he argued, were the next racial group to extend their influence into organized crime.[18]

Ianni found Paterson was in the grips of an Italian-American crime syndicate, exercising control over the gambling rackets, compromising the police, and maintaining long-held relationships with politicians. Blacks were attempting to wrest power from the Italian-American syndicate but were often hampered by the police, whose salaries were handsomely subsidized by the racketeers.[19]

By 1971, about the time Ianni initiated his study of the Paterson rackets, the New Jersey State Police were enmeshed in their investigations of the rackets in Paterson. "Wires" were strung on the phones of several local racketeers. These wires led to the phones of several Paterson Vice Squad detectives and into the inner sanctum of the Passaic County Prosecutor's Office.

Throughout the State Police investigation, efforts were made by the corrupt detectives to redirect the State Police toward arresting the Black-run numbers operators. The intent was to deflect attention from the organized crime syndicate that dominated the Paterson rackets—The Genovese Mafia Family.

Arresting those who comprised competitors of the Mafia was a common practice and was well-known to the State Police. By eliminating the competition, the Mafia exercised exclusive control of the rackets. This practice was one of several *modus operendi* used by the Mafia.

Unbeknownst to the Paterson detectives, the State Police were well aware of their motives. The State Police purposely and selectively initiated

---

16. See Appendix A.

17. Ianni, Francis A.J. 1972. *A Family Business: Kinship and Social Control in Organized Crime.*

18. Ianni, Francis A.J. 1974, *Black Mafia: Ethnic Succession in Organized Crime* (hardback) and 1975 (paperback).

19. Ibid., pp. 72–104, 353–55.

raids of Mafia-sanctioned gambling syndicates. These raids would generate conversations between the Mafia operators and the police who were protecting their operations. True to form, incriminating conversations were recorded.

Complaining to the vice squad detectives that they were not receiving the protection they were paying for, the bookmakers and their controllers provided the verbal evidence needed to charge the police with various corruption-related offenses. Two vice-squad detectives, Joseph Esposito and Donald Young, and a politically connected county detective, Raymond Kordja, were ultimately charged.[20] Young, given immunity from prosecution, testified against Esposito and Kordja. Both Esposito and Kordja were convicted and sentenced to prison.

Initiated twenty years later was another *state* investigation into Paterson's underworld. This time, the targets were the lucrative video poker operators who again were protected by members of the Paterson vice squad. Three vice squad detectives were charged with taking payoffs from a mob-controlled syndicate. Two were convicted. The third forfeited his job to avoid retrial.[21]

And as sure as the sun will rise tomorrow, in 2019, eight Paterson police officers were charged by the FBI with a variety of corruption-related offenses—extortion, theft of money and drugs, selling drugs, and physical assaults.[22]

---

20. *The New York Times.* 1973. *A Detective Chief Among 5 Indicted.* June 29th. Young was afforded immunity and testified against Esposito and Kordja. Young was also a crucial witness in a previous case in which he acted as a notary in a contested confession of a person convicted of murder. See *State v. Yough, 49 N.J. 587* (1967).

21. Mendez, Ivette. *The Star-Ledger.* 1991. "Differing Portraits open trial of 3 cops." October 9th. Mendez, Ivette. *The Star-Ledger.* 1991. "Cop partly cleared in gamble case." November 2nd. *The Star-Ledger. 1992.* "Paterson Cop Resigns, is spared new trial." April 4th. *The Bergen Record* (Hackensack, NJ). 1989. "Vice Detectives Arrested on Corruption Charges." July 12th. Kunkle, Fredrick. *The Bergen Record* (Hackensack, NJ). 1989. "To many, top vice cop was above suspicion." July 14th.

22. *The Star-Ledger.* 2019. "Seven Paterson cops arrested in FBI probe: Who are they?" March 26th. Malinconico, Joe. *Paterson Press.* 2021. "The FBI's Paterson police corruption case remains at a COVID standstill. What comes next?" Sources have verified that as of this very day, payoffs amounting to two-thousand dollars a month are being made to members of the Paterson Police Department.

The sordid history of this police department and its enablers demonstrates an ongoing pattern of *systemic* corruption and how it was part and parcel of a cultural ethos in Passaic County. Some members of the vice squad essentially served as the enforcement arm of the Mafia. It was against this seamy, tawdry background that the investigation and prosecution of Carter and Artis took place.

Racial Unrest and Animus Consumed the Body-Politic

Time often brings clarity to events that may have had no significance in the heat of the moment. With the publication of DeSimone's memoir in 2019 and a fresh look at the triple murder investigation by the BBC, the convictions of Carter and Artis rightfully deserve still another colonoscopy.[23]

Once again, the threads of this ill-fated but crudely-orchestrated investigation and prosecution can be methodically dissected. What emerges is a much more sinister plot than had been exposed by the defense attorneys, the media, and the researchers' decades prior.[24]

In some respects, we can thank those who took part in this investigation and prosecution for inadvertently and unintentionally shining a light on the corrupt underbelly of a criminal *justice* system that perverted, contorted, and shielded a systemically corrupt government.

With Carter and Artis convicted on two separate occasions, only to have their convictions overturned both times, once by the New Jersey Supreme Court and a second time by the Federal judiciary, the nagging and certainly polarizing question is "what went wrong?"[25]

---

23. DeSimone, Vincent J. 2019. *Media Meddlers.*

24. There were two Black mob-related murders that took place in 1969 in New Jersey that defined the "war" that was occurring between the Mafia and the Blacks. The first involved Robert "Bobby" Harris who was murdered by Tino Fuimara, a soldier in the Genovese Family. The second was Alton Hughes who was murdered by Frank Miceli, a soldier in the Gambino Family. Both Harris and Hughes were vice czars; Harris in Paterson, and Hughes in Newark.

25. *State v. Carter, 354 A.2d 627* (1976). Rubin Carter and John Artis v. John J. Rafferty, 781 F2d 993. (3rd Cir. 1986).

There were many moving parts to this investigation and prosecution that went off track.

The belief that the triple murders at the Lafayette Bar and Grill were racially driven shaped the contours of this investigation. There was no doubt to DeSimone that the murder of Roy Holloway, who was Black by Frank Conforti, who was White, set the stage for the triple murder of three White Patersonians. The motive was apparent, at least to DeSimone and his acolytes.[26] Racial revenge, plain and simple. Ultimately, this rush to judgment proved to be a missed opportunity.

With this heinous crime occurring during the administration of its self-anointed "law and order" mayor Frank X. Graves, public outrage demanded a quick and tidy resolution to this triple murder. Graves announced a reward of $10,000 [$80,000 by today's standard]. The incentives for solving this triple murder could not have been more galvanizing. Graves generously provided unlimited resources.[27]

Racial unrest had begun to percolate throughout many of our urban centers. The Harlem riots of 1964, followed by others in Paterson, Philadelphia, Chicago, and Los Angeles, signaled the beginnings euphemistically referred to as "the long, hot summer." Black power was met with White resistance. The police were naturally the arm of the White establishment. Polarization of the races was at an all-time high.[28]

Paterson was no exception to this roiling wave of Black power and White resistance. Graves called for "meeting force with force" and issued "shoot to kill" mandates.[29] "Law and order," with an emphasis on "order," set the stage for what was about to evolve into one of the most celebrated

---

26. DeSimone, Vincent J. 2019. *Media Meddlers*. pp. 24-25, 52.

27. Wice, Paul B. 2010. *Rubin "Hurricane" Carter and the American Justice System*. pp. 15–16. Hirsch, James S. 2000. *Hurricane: The Miraculous Journey of Rubin Carter*. pp. 31–41. Bello with the assistance of the investigating detectives, made an attempt to collect this reward, notwithstanding their obvious conflict of interests in pursuing these monies.

28. *The Morning Call* (Paterson, NJ). 1964. "Young Negroes Riot in Paterson, Mob Police, Bus, Smash Windows." August 12th. *National Advisory Commission on Civil Disorders*. 1967. *The Kerner Report*. Bentley, Stuart. 1968 and 1972. *Report For Action: An Investigation into the Causes and Events of the 1967 Newark Race Riots*. Governor's Select Commission on Civil Disorders, State of New Jersey. Branch, Taylor. 1988. *Pillars of Fire: America in the King Years 1963-65*.

29. *BlackPast.org*. 2017. "Paterson, New Jersey Uprising (1964)." December 13th.

and internationally-renowned criminal prosecutions in the state's history: The State of New Jersey vs. Rubin "Hurricane" Carter and John Artis.[30]

Indeed, the public seemingly witnessed a classic textbook example of two worlds colliding—the upper and underworlds. How the pieces fit together to create a chain of events that enveloped the guilty, not-so-guilty, and perhaps even the innocent is a piece of urban history that demands a sober and critical analysis.

The Motive that Eluded the Investigators

Initially, my fascination with this investigation was encouraged by my friendship with Francis A.J. Ianni, aka "Fritz," the credentialed anthropologist on the faculty of Columbia University.[31] Ianni, a resident of both New York City and West Milford, New Jersey, had published *A Family Business* in 1971. He addressed the evolution of Italian-American organized crime, suggesting that the Mafia or Cosa Nostra was invariably inter-related networks weaved together through kinship relationships.

I, in turn, was initiating my research examining the topic of organized crime homicides. In researching many mob-related homicide cases, I met with several sources I had developed in Paterson.[32] These meetings and my research ultimately led me to Ianni, who proved to be intimately knowledgeable about Paterson's under and upper worlds.

Meeting with him in his office at Columbia University, he invited me to dinner at his home in West Milford, New Jersey. There I met his warm and dynamic wife, Liz Ianni, who sought to understand the culture of urban policing in her own right.[33] Many conversations from that day forward ensued.

---

30. Raab, Selwyn. *The New York Times*. 2014. "Rubin (Hurricane) Carter, Boxer Found Wrongly Convicted, Dies at 76."

31. *The New York Times*. 2013. "Dr. Francis A.J. Ianni." December 10th.

32. Marks, Peter. *The Star-Ledger*. 1981. "State Police Intensify Mob 'Hit' Probe." April 21st. Martens, Frederick T. *John Jay College of Criminal Justice*. 1973. *A Study of Organized Crime Homicides in the State of New Jersey: 1960-1973*. Martens, Frederick T. *Federal Probation*. 1990. *African-American Organized Crime: An Ignored Phenomenon*. December, pp. 43–50.

33. *Two Cultures of Policing: Street Cops and Management Cops*. 1983. Elizabeth Reuss-Ianni.

Of course, my familiarity with Paterson and Ianni's interest in the Paterson rackets intersected. We discussed in detail the role of the Italian-American syndicates in Paterson. Ianni shied away from using the term Mafia or Cosa Nostra for reasons far too academically obtuse to discuss at this time.

We spoke of the corruption that he uncovered. We ruminated about the Black gambling operators, their controllers, and their ability to operate under the protection of the Genovese Mafia Family. I discussed my knowledge and conversations with one of the most prominent Black syndicate leaders in Paterson.

"Lil Hutch," as he was known, represented one of Paterson's most sophisticated Black gambling enterprises. He was wholly beholden to the LaPlaca faction of the Genovese Mafia Family.[34] He was protected by the police, primarily because of his illegal business relationship with the Genovese Family.

"Lil Hutch" proved to be an invaluable source of information for me as I attempted to untangle the myriad of relationships between the vice czars, racketeers, the police, and the political structure.[35] Time and again, "Lil Hutch" would pontificate on the fragile state of affairs between the upper and underworld.

In discussing ghost arrest, "Lil Hutch" became visually animated. The police, he would opine, needed to appear as if they were vigorously enforcing the gambling laws. They would arrange for "Lil Hutch" to set someone up for a "bust." It often was a competitor, someone willing to take a "fall" (i.e., arrest) for money, a "wanna-be" who wished to ingratiate himself with the bookmakers, an indebted bookmaker, or a recalcitrant policy operator. Independents were fresh, raw meat.

---

34. Wikipedia: Genovese Crime Family New Jersey Faction: Gatto Crew. In 1991, the Genovese and Luchese Families were intimately involved in illegal video poker gambling in Paterson, N.J. See *State Commission of Investigation, Video Gambling.* 1991. September, pp. 21–25; "I would make payments to the police officers in Paterson . . . they would take a payoff each week . . . and they would tell me if anything was going to come down beforehand so I could pull my machines out . . .", p. 28.

35. Martens, Frederick T. *Federal Probation.* 1990. "African-American Organized Crime: An Ignored Phenomenon." December, pp. 43–50.

The bench was quite deep and never lacked willing and not-so-willing candidates. These arrests would serve the interests of both the police and the Genovese Mafia Family, who were continuing to tighten their grip on the gambling rackets in Paterson.[36]

Ultimately, in 1974 Ianni published *Black Mafia*, which described in vivid detail what he believed was the ethnic-succession process.

Ianni's findings were spot-on concerning the underworld in Paterson:

> . . . the Paterson network is an example of a larger network once
> entirely controlled by the local Italian syndicate but now broken
> into two competing networks whose contacts are based largely on
> conflict . . . In organized crime, this can be a violent process, as was
> the case here.[37]

This finding, of course, served as the predicate for my ongoing interest in the Carter-Artis investigation and its prosecution. If what Ianni had uncovered and concluded was true, coupled with what I had learned from "Lil Hutch," could the investigation and prosecution of Carter and Artis be reflective of this "fragile relationship between the upper world and the underworld" that "Lil Hutch" spoke about?

Indeed, what was overlooked or ignored by both the detectives and prosecutors investigating the Holloway assassination and triple murder at the Lafayette Bar and Grill was a more violent contemporary history puncturing the Mafia's control of the numbers and vice rackets throughout the country.

"The Mafia is not an equal opportunity employer . . . From East Harlem to Cincinnati, blacks who had challenged white syndicates were murdered by gangsters or arrested by corrupt law enforcement officials . . . ,"

---

36. Light, Ivan. *American Sociological Review.* 1977. *Numbers Gambling Among Blacks: A Financial Institution.* Steffensmeier, Darrell and Jeffery Ulmer. *American Sociological Review.* 2006. "Black and White Control of Numbers Gambling: A Cultural Assets-Social Capital View." February, pp. 123–56.

37. Ianni, Francis A.J. 1975. *Black Mafia: Ethnic Succession in Organized Crime.* p. 80 (paperback)

the prolific organized crime journalist Nicholas Gage wrote in 1967—one year after the triple murder and the public execution of Holloway.[38]

Acutely aware of disproportionate power exercised by the Mafia over the rackets in Black communities, delegates of the Congress for Racial Equality in 1967 declared, "Blacks should take control of the operation of the vices in their community."[39]

Two years later, The Black Economic Conference for African-Americans called for the divesture of Mafia-owned vice rackets in the Black community. "Racketeering, prostitution, and the numbers . . . must be put in the hands of the Black community . . ." argued the esteemed economist and social activist Robert Browne.[40]

Decades later, I met with and discussed this case with Selwyn Raab, *The New York Times* reporter who, to the chagrin of the Passaic County authorities, impugned the eyewitness testimony of Bello and Bradley.[41]

Our discussions went on for hours, convincing me that insofar as Carter and Artis *may have had some involvement in the triple murder*, the manner they were investigated and prosecuted raised many unanswered and troubling questions?[42]

---

38. Gage, Nicholas. *Wall Street Journal.* 1967. "Bias in the Mafia: Negroes are barred from 'Executive' Posts in Organized Rackets." October 26th.

39. Cressey, Donald R. 1969. *Theft of the Nation.* p. 196.

40. Browne, Robert S. *New York Public Library.* 1969. "Inter-Religious Foundation for Community Organizations Papers," Box 15, Folder 5, Schomburg Center for Research in Black Culture. April 25th. Cobb, Charles E. Jr., et. al. 2008. *No Easy Victories: African Liberation and American Activists Over a Half Century: 1950-2000. Robert S. Browne: A Voice of Integrity.* See also Steffensmeier, Darrell and Jeffery T. Ulmer. *American Sociological Review.* 2006. "Black and White Control of Numbers Gambling: A Cultural Assets-Social Capital View." pp. 123–56. Vaz, Matthew. 2020. *Running the Numbers: Race, Police, and the History of Urban Gambling.*

41. Raab, Selwyn. *The New York Times.* 1976. "An Ex-Associate of Rubin Carter Charges Pressure by Prosecution." October 14th.

42. Allegations of police and prosecutorial misconduct challenged the case throughout its history. Planting of evidence, exculpatory evidence with-held, witnesses intimidated, and rights abused were the dominant themes that permeated the prosecution of Carter and Artis—allegations that are more relevant today.

Having several "connected friends" from Paterson, I often heard the name Frank Conforti bandied about among this circle of "friends." His bar, The Waltz Inn, was a well-known vice denizen which the Genovese Family controlled. This location was known by the State Police and to those familiar with the rackets in Paterson. My sources and "Lil Hutch" were quite knowledgeable about Conforti's involvement in the gambling rackets in Paterson.

According to the official and likely sanitized version of events, Conforti murdered Elwood Holloway over a business dispute involving the sale of the Waltz Inn.[43] Had the argument been simply over money, a seemingly thorough investigation would have rightly concluded that Conforti had other extra-legal means available to him to resolve this alleged business dispute. The execution of Holloway was over much more than that.

Murdering Holloway in plain view of others certainly would not bode well for escaping an arrest and prosecution. It would, however, send a chilling and ominous message to others who may have been contemplating escaping the Mafia's grip. And it certainly was consistent with the Mafia's *modus operendi* during the 60s.

Notably, Bobby Harris, one of Paterson's more successful Black numbers operators, was brutally beaten, tortured, and shot multiple times.[44] Publically paraded around the Black neighborhoods of Paterson, his body dumped in the Bergen County Meadowlands.

At the time, the Paterson Police Department boldly proclaimed, "We want to solve this one so bad we can taste it."[45] At the same time, the

43. Harvey. Everett. *The Morning Call* (Paterson, NJ). 1967. "State Concludes Conforti Prosecution." February 28th.

44. *The Morning Call* (Paterson, NJ). 1969. "Clifton Gambler Slips Away." December 17th. *The News* (Paterson, NJ). 1969. "10 In Area Among Indicted." December 17th. *The Herald News* (Passaic, NJ). *1969.* "Not 'Indifferent,' Says Lowe of Murder Probers." April 4th. Scarpo, Ed. 2014. *Decades of Violence Behind the Waterfront Case: Grisly Murder Credited to Fuimara.* December 21st. Ianni, 1975. *Black Mafia.* pp. 80–86.

45. In an identical murder/motive, Alton Hughes of Newark, N.J., a Black numbers and vice czar, was found murdered in Howell, N.J. The killer was Frank "Butch" Miceli, a soldier in the Gambino Family. This murder remains unsolved as well. *Asbury Park Press.* 1970. "Two '69 Shore Slayings Unsolved." January 4th. *Asbury Park Press* 1969. "Victim Identified as Newark Man." July 23rd.

Passaic County Prosecutor, John Thevos, refused to take jurisdiction for the investigation, announcing, "They have the turkey, not us. The statute reads that the murder investigation belongs where the body is found." The message was clear: no resources to solve this Mafia hit were provided, and none were.[46]

Arguably the questionable explanation by Conforti for killing Holloway served as a convenient and too many, the likely motive for the triple murder at the Lafayette Bar and Grill which immediately followed?[47]

Knowing that the Lafayette Bar and Grill and the Waltz Inn were well-documented numbers and vice locations controlled by the Genovese Family never tickled the investigator's probative instincts. Or if it had, it was summarily dismissed or ignored.

Nor did it occur to any of the detectives investigating these homicides that the Waltz Inn and the Lafayette Bar and Grill were part of Emil "Bonsei" Esa's gambling network. Esa, who answered to the Genovese Mafia Family, was one of several vice czars who were paying off members of the Paterson Police Department's Vice Squad and at least one member of the Prosecutor's Office.

Lacking any credible motive for Carter and Artis to have engaged in this horrendous act of human carnage, racial revenge became the governing *theory* that framed the investigation from day one. It was based entirely on the race of the victims and the alleged offenders. Whether this motive represented a conscious effort to divert attention from the territorial wars between the Genovese Family and the Black vice operators who formed the "Association"; or was simply implicit bias being visited on Carter and Artis may never be known.[48]

---

46. *The Morning Call* (Paterson, NJ). 1969. "Bullet Found in Body of Gambler." April 1st. Zuckoff, Murray. *The Morning Call* (Paterson, NJ). 1969. "Just a Hood to Police, Bobby Stood Tall in the Fourth Ward." April 1st.

47. Wice, Paul B. 2000. *Rubin "Hurricane" Carter and the American Justice System.* New Brunswick: Rutgers University Press. pp. 15–16. *The Hurricane Tapes.* 2019, Episode 2 @32:00.

48. The "Association" was a collage of Black numbers and vice operatives who had bandied together in order to, among other things, divest the Mafia of control over their illegal activities. Implicit bias refers to the attitudes and stereotypes we bring to situations through our unconscious actions.

Remarkably, immediately following Holloway's murder, Eddie Rawls, Holloway's step-son, brazenly confronted the Paterson detectives investigating the Holloway execution, threatening retaliation if Conforti escaped prosecution.[49] Rawls was well aware of the corrupt relationship between the Waltz Inn, Conforti, and the city's vice squad. He suspected or knew that a cover-up was likely to be initiated. He also knew the underlying motive for Holloway's murder. And it was not the version constructed by Conforti and conveniently accepted by the police.

The "Association," a confederation of Black vice entrepreneurs that Rawls belonged to, struggled to wrest control of their numbers racket from the Mafia. Rawls was personally invested in this ongoing subterranean war.[50]

Accordingly, the defense attorney Lewis Steel representing Carter, and an independent researcher, Paul Wice, came to the same conclusion: the triple murder at the Lafayette Bar and Grill was likely the result of a Mafia-related dispute.

As Wice points out, "supposedly James Oliver [the bartender at the Lafayette Bar and Grill] was the target of the shooters whereas the other victims were eliminated to silence them. Oliver, it was rumored, had failed to pay protection money to the organized crime group controlling gambling in Paterson."[51]

---

49. DeSimone, Vincent J., 2019. *Media Meddlers.* p. 24.

50. It should be pointed out that this phenomenon—divesture of Black numbers operations—was not unique to Paterson, N.J. See Cook, Fred J. *The New York Times.* 1971. "The Black Mafia Moves Into The Numbers Rackets." April 4th. Vaz, Matthew. 2014. *Racial Politics, Illegal Gambling, and the Rise of Government Lotteries in the United States, 1960-1985.* June 2014. pp. 71–96; George, Felicia B. 2015. *Numbers and Neighborhoods: Seeking and Selling the American Dream in Detroit One Bet at a Time.* Wayne State University Dissertations. pp. 202–31. Cooley, Will. *Journal of Urban History.* 2011. "Stones Run It': Taking Back Control of Organized Crime in Chicago, 1940-1975.* pp. 911–32. Albini, Joseph L. 1971. *The American Mafia: Genesis of a Legend.* pp. 284–85; Fine, Sidney. 1989. *Violence in the Model City.* Cressey, Donald R. 1969. *Theft of the Nation.* p. 119; Carlson, Gustav. 1949. *The Argot of Numbers Gambling.* October. *Pennsylvania Crime Commission.* 1991. *Organized Crime in Pennsylvania: A Decade of Change.* March 30th. pp. 29–31, 228–30. Lombardo, Robert M. *Crime, Law and Social Change.* 2002 *The Black Mafia: African-American Organized Crime in Chicago 1890-1960.* pp. 54–57. Sealey, Pat. *The Miami Herald.* 1968. *Negroes Get Rung on Mafia Ladder.* March 12th.

51. Wice, Paul. 2000. *Rubin "Hurricane" Carter and the American Justice System.* p. 197. Martens, Frederick T. *Rutgers University. Criminal Justice Criminal Law Book Reviews.* 2020. *Media Meddlers.* March.

This motive was echoed by Steel, who claimed the triple murder "could have been the result of a mob hit on a numbers bar that had withheld the take."[52]

An opportunity was lost when the detectives fixated on the racial revenge motive and ignored compelling information to the contrary. A *theory* devoid of facts dictated the course of the investigation. Had the investigators uncovered what Ianni had discovered and what "Lil Hutch" knew, the investigation may have taken another trajectory. And it would have provided the prosecution with a credible motive, but one that likely would have taken the investigators on a politically hazardous journey.

Conforti was charged with first-degree murder. He was convicted of second-degree murder, a verdict that implied passion and provocation was the basis for the killing. He never took the witness stand, however, to advance this defense.[53] Naturally, Conforti's involvement in the policy and numbers rackets was never explored. In retrospect, Rawl's initial concerns were well-founded.

The prosecuting attorney Vincent Hull was adamant and prescient that the racial revenge *theory* advanced by the investigators would *not* be proffered at the trial of Carter and Artis—and for a good reason. It lacked an evidential fact pattern. The court likely would see this line of questioning as prejudicial and would be reluctant to sanction such a racially explosive motive.[54]

What DeSimone's memoir conveniently disregards is why Eddie Rawls, Holloway's stepson, was not thoroughly investigated.[55] Both Hull and the newly-appointed prosecutor, Burrell Ives Humphrey, raised this

---

52. Steel, Lewis M. 2016. *The Butler's Child.* p. 220. *The News* (Paterson, NJ). 1973. "Esposito, Kordja Arraigned." June 29th.

53. *The Morning Call* (Paterson, NJ). 1967. "Conforti Guilty of Murder." March 4th. p. 3. Leopold, Evelyn. *The Morning Call* (Paterson, NJ). 1967. "Conforti Murder Case Slated For Jury Today." March 3rd. p. 10.

54. Hammer, Joel and Steve Crossman. 2019. *BBC: The Hurricane Tapes.* Judge Haddon Lee Sarokin, Rubin Carter and a massive fish. Episode 9. March 4th.

55. In what was an almost identical event, the defense attorney in the trial of Harold Matzner, et. al. raised the same question, asking the jury why the Passaic County Prosecutor, John Thevos, had exonerated John Ventura, the vice-lord of Paterson, after he took the 5th before a grand jury? "Why wasn't Ventura investigated . . . maybe it was a shield put up by the prosecutor's office . . ." a defense attorney opined before the jury. (*The Home News.* 1969. "DeFranco Death a Gangland Execution." February 4th. p. 19.)

issue with DeSimone, only to be ignored. No one had more motive than Rawls.

Consequently, an independent investigation ordered by then-Governor Brendan Byrne named Rawls and Elwood Tuck the responsible parties for the triple murder.[56] Rawls failed a polygraph examination; both Carter and Artis passed theirs. Curiously, DeSimone summarily absolved both Rawls and Tuck in his memoir.[57]

In retrospect, there may have been a good reason to have ignored Rawls' involvement in the triple murder. It likely would have led to the corrupt relationships with the Paterson Vice Squad, Prosecutor's Office, and the Genovese Mafia Family. It would only add more noise and clutter to an already messy investigation. This was, of course, Passaic County, where stubborn details were conveniently ignored.

Carter and Artis Retried for Being Black

With exculpatory documents withheld from the defense, the New Jersey Supreme Court had no choice but to reverse the jury's verdict. A decision was imminent as to whether a retrial was practical or even warranted.

In the intervening years between the initial trial and the Supreme Court's decision, more information unearthed created considerable doubt about the investigative findings that resulted in their initial conviction.

First and foremost was the recantation by Bello of his original testimony. Without Bello as the eyewitness, the case was essentially dead. With Bello and the different reiterations during several interviews over the intervening years, his credibility would suffer from a withering cross-examination.

Dexter Bradley, Bello's accomplice on the night of the triple murder, refused to testify if the state decided to retry Carter and Artis.[58]

Lacking a credible motive that conclusively implicated Carter and Artis, the state took an untenable position. With the prosecuting attorney,

---

56. Hawkins, Eldridge. 1975. *Report to the Hon. Brendan T. Byrne: The Rubin 'Hurricane' Carter and John Artis Investigation.* December 10th. pp. 6–7.

57. Ibid. DeSimone, 2019. *Media Meddlers.* p. 197.

58. In the first trial, Bradley denied seeing Carter and Artis at the scene. DeSimone, Vincent J. 2019. *Media Meddlers.* pp. 166, 204.

Hull, studiously avoiding the racial revenge theory in the first trial, the prosecutors had a personally agonizing decision.[59]

Fortunately, DeSimone addresses the thought process that led to advancing the racial revenge motive in the retrial of Carter and Artis. "Under New Jersey law, it is not necessary to prove motive in order to obtain a conviction . . . since the beginning . . . it had been our contention . . . Rubin Carter and John Artis massacred white people at the Lafayette tavern as revenge for the murder of LeRoy Holloway, a black man, by Frank Conforti, who was white . . . After weighing these facts and others, we decided we had a strong enough case to get a conviction without motive . . . Ten years later . . . we elected to show the revenge motive . . . ," DeSimone wrote in his previously undisclosed but now legally relevant memoir.[60]

A respected civil libertarian and a member of the NAACP, Burrell Ives Humphreys was appointed prosecutor by Governor Byrne. Byrne's reputation for integrity was burnished when he was the prosecutor in neighboring Essex County.[61] Referred to as "the man who couldn't be bought," Bryne was committed to ensuring the integrity of his administration. He tasked Humphrey's with cleaning up the corruption and racial prejudice that had "still plagued the Paterson police."[62]

Humphreys had a dilemma. Does he dismiss the indictments against Carter and Artis, or does he prosecute a case that lacks investigative integrity?

Recognizing the obstacles confronting him in a second trial, Humphreys requested and received assistance from the State Police and experienced homicide investigators from the Essex County Prosecutor's Office. Perhaps with a fresh set of eyes, evidence overlooked or information in dispute earlier might prove helpful in the event of a retrial?[63]

Humphreys was hostage to or under-estimated the internal bureaucratic politics and inertia confronting these newly-assigned investigators

59. DeSimone, Vincent J. 2019. *Media Meddlers.* p. 52.
60. Ibid.
61. Simone "Sam the Plumber" DeCalvalcante in the infamous tapes publicly released, stated "you can't get to him" (referring to Byrne). "He can't be bought."
62. Wice, Paul B. 2000. *Rubin "Hurricane" Carter and the American Justice System.* pp. 99–100.
63. DeSimone, Vincent J. 2019. *Media Meddlers.* pp. 209–10.

and detectives. DeSimone was not about to relinquish his oversight nor his authority.[64] He remained in charge.

The Byrne Administration was under pressure to resolve the situation that had become an international embarrassment by this time. Byrne was contemplating pardoning Carter and Artis.[65] His attorney general, William Hyland, was dubious of the prosecution after the Supreme Court's unanimous rebuke. DeSimone voiced his strenuous opposition to dismissing the indictments or pardoning Carter and Artis. He threatened to resign.[66]

Indeed, Humphrey's had to consider the local fall-out if he decided against a second prosecution. The families of the victims were denied justice. The public would be outraged. His staff, prosecutors, and investigators would be demoralized. And perhaps, more than anything, Mayor Frank Graves would be incensed.[67]

Hyland requested a prosecution memorandum outlining the strengths and weaknesses of the case in light of the recent developments. Humphreys made a calculated decision to embrace the racial revenge motive that was simply a theory at this point.

Opining in a letter and memorandum to Hyland and Robert Del Tufo, the Director of Criminal Justice, Humphrey's wrote, "In view of the fact that only a few hours earlier a black bar owner had been shot dead by a white, a revenge motive may be postulated for the Lafayette Grill homicides."[68]

---

64. State Police Detective Thornell Gregg was assigned to the Prosecutor's Office. During conversations with Thornell, in his inimical jocular manner he would criticize the investigation they were asked to conduct. He recognized that nothing they could do that would change the trajectory of the case. He and those assigned from Essex County simply were window dressing. It was clearly optics over substance.

65. *The New York Times.* 1975. "Byrne Clears Way to Pardon Carter." October 16th.

66. DeSimone, Vincent J. 2019. *Media Meddlers.* p. 199.

67. Wikipedia: Frank Xavier Graves. Hirsch, James S. 2000. *Hurricane: The Miraculous Journey of Rubin Carter.* pp. 31–41. Of course Graves "law and order" mantra was on full display when one of his vice squad detectives was arrested for taking payoffs. As Graves foolishly opined, "had he been charged with narcotics corruption, I would have been livid." Kunkle, Frederick. *The Bergen Record* (Hackensack, NJ). 1989. "To many, top vice cop was above suspicion." July 14th.

68. *Confidential: Attorney's Work Product for the Eyes of the Attorney General,* Director of Criminal Investigation and Their Authorized Agents. April 14, 1976. p. 11. In fact, the New Jersey Supreme Court sustained Humphrey's decision to advance the racial revenge motive for the triple murder at the Lafayette Bar and Grill. *State v. Carter, 91 N.J. 86* (1982).

Bolstered by Carter's testimony before the Grand Jury referring to "talk that there would be a 'shaking' in Paterson as a result of the death of the black bar owner," Humphreys had now accepted the racial revenge motive, "hook, line, and sinker."

As far as Bello's inconsistent testimony, Humphreys knew that rehabilitating him would be difficult. Humphreys declared, "Obviously, the case is a very difficult one for the state. The credibility of Bello . . . will be sharply attacked by the defense . . . [however] the totality of the evidence plus considerable discrepancies in the defendants' version combine to give the state a *prima facie* and persuasive case resulting in a reasonable chance for a conviction."[69]

The state acquiesced to the prosecution's judgment. It proved, in the end, a tragic decision in so many respects.

The case would be re-tried before Judge Bruno Leopizzi, a well-regarded defense attorney in his earlier life. Engaging in a series of judicial gymnastics, Leopizzi allowed Humphreys to pursue his racial revenge motive to Carter's defense attorneys' dismay and vehement objecttions.[70]

Once again, Carter and Artis were convicted of the triple murder. Appeals through the State's court system afforded Carter and Artis no relief.[71]After serving 15 years, Artis was paroled from prison.

Carter, sentenced to a life behind bars, had one last option. Carter (and Artis) challenged their convictions by filing a *writ of habeas corpus*, a legal motion seldom granted. A federal court granted the *writ*.

The federal judge hearing the case would be Haddon Lee Sarokin. He methodically and meticulously dissected the issues raised by Carter in this *writ*.

---

69. Letter from Humphreys to DelTufo dated April 14, 1976.

70. For a lacerating analysis of Leopizzi's decision, see Lewis M. Steel, 2016. *The Butler's Child.* pp. 206–46.

71. In a 4-3 decision by the New Jersey Supreme Court, the Court found, "The evidence offered by the State against Carter and Artis was admissible not because they are blacks, but because they were members of the particular local community involved and had a special relationship to Holloway and his stepson Rawls . . . Fueled by racial undertone, the defendants may have been motivated to avenge the death of Rawl's stepfather." The dissent ignored the issue of racial animus but did agree that exculpatory evidence denied the defendants, prejudiced the defendant's right to a fair trial. See *State v. Carter, 91 N.J. 86* (1982).

In a scathing 70-page opinion, Sarokin eviscerated the racial revenge motive and the theory behind it.[72] Daunting and ruthlessly, Sarokin's eloquent prose summed up his decision: "The extensive record clearly demonstrates that petitioner's convictions were predicated upon an appeal to racism rather than reason and concealment rather than disclosure."

Notwithstanding for the *second* time, exculpatory evidence was withheld from the defense by the prosecution, Sarokin wrote,

> "Underlying the prosecutor's theory and the summation is the insidious and repugnant argument that this heinous crime is to be understood and explained solely because the petitioners are black and the victims are white . . . for the state to contend that an accused has the motive to commit murder solely because of his membership in a racial group is an argument which should never be permitted to sway a jury or provide a basis for conviction."[73]

Sarokin gave no deference to the New Jersey's Supreme Court.[74] Sarokin opined, "This court is convinced that a conviction which rests upon racial stereotypes, fears and prejudice violates rights too fundamental to permit deference to stand in the way of relief . . ."

Sarokin was ahead of the times when he rendered his decision, as was Vincent Hull, the prosecuting attorney who initially rejected advancing this racially explosive motive.[75] With the prosecution being rebuked a second time and witnesses having passed away or memories faded, the decision to try Carter and Artis a third time would prove problematic.

---

72. *State v. Rafferty, 621 F.Supp.533* (November 7, 1985) DeSimone had passed away in 1979, six years prior to Sarokin's decision to free Carter and Artis.

73. *State v. Carter, 91 N.J. 86* (1982).

74. Ibid., Seldom do federal courts over-rule state supreme courts. The issue must be so egregious that the federal judiciary has no other choice than throw deference to the wind.

75. In a study conducted by two law schools and a think-tank, the investigators found that "ineffective leadership by police commanders . . . and chief prosecutors" led to 54% of false convictions in 2,400 exonerations. In 35% of those exonerated, *witnessing tampering, misconduct in interrogation, and fabricating evidence* were found to exist. The most common type of misconduct was *concealing exculpatory evidence.* See *National Registry of Exonerations.* 2020. "Government Misconduct and Convicting the Innocent: The Role of Prosecutors, Police, and Other Law Enforcement." September 1st. DeSimone, Vincent J. 2019. *Media Meddlers.* p. 52.

Donald Belsole, the new Director of the Division of Criminal Justice, strongly recommended dismissing all charges against Carter and Artis.[76] The indictments reluctantly were dismissed.[77]

While Carter and Artis were never exonerated, their convictions were reversed on two separate occasions by two different courts. The murders of Hazel Tanis, James Oliver, and Fred Nauyaks remain unsolved—or a cold case in today's vernacular.[78] Naturally, all sorts of speculation, innuendo, and conspiratorial musings continue to stir passionately among both the believers and the nay-sayers.

For this, DeSimone's judgment finally did prove prescient.[79]

Loose Lips Sink Ships[80]

Promoted by Humphrey as "A man of enormous courage, implacable determination, and unswerving integrity," DeSimone's storied legacy is unabashedly captured in his memoir.[81] Both alarming and illuminating, we are treated to his candid inner thoughts as this investigation and its prosecution was winding its way through the criminal justice system.

Under oath, DeSimone testified that he administered the *Miranda* rights to Carter and Artis. Both Carter and Artis denied they were afforded their rights. Miranda had only been decided four days earlier. Few agencies had codified this ruling into acceptable protocols so recently after the Supreme Court handed down its decision.

Nonetheless, the trial judge accepted DeSimone's sworn testimony.

Would the judge have been as charitable had he known of DeSimone's utter disdain for the high court's ruling?

According to DeSimone, "The Miranda case has been watered down somewhat by the high court rulings in the past ten years, but the guts remain. Recently the United States Supreme Court almost wiped it from

76. Hirsch, James S. 2000. *Hurricane: The Miraculous Journey of Rubin Carter.* pp. 637–38.
77. Ibid., pp. 636–38.
78. Wice, Paul B. 2010. *Rubin "Hurricane" Carter and the American Justice System.* p. 188.
79. DeSimone, Vincent J. 2019. *Media Meddlers.* p 323.
80. From one military veteran to another veteran.
81. *The Herald News* (Passaic, NJ). 1979. "'The Chief' Dedicated Lawman." October 31st.

the books, but the liberal members of the bench still prevailed by a nar-row margin. Most of us in law enforcement are hoping that the nation's highest court will continue its conservative trend and will eventually obliterate this black mark against law and order."[82]

DeSimone was diligently working on his memoir during both the first and second trials of Carter and Artis. Recordings were also made by DeSimone, reflecting his actions and judgments during the investiga-tion, the prosecution, and the judicial decision-making. The contents of his memoir and the recordings are and were exculpatory. And they were likely done on the taxpayer's dime and time.

We now know that DeSimone had secreted his memoir and record-ings in an office file cabinet. The prosecution never turned these exculpa-tory documents over to the defense. For the *third* time, Carter and Artis were denied exculpatory material by the state that, without any question, would have changed the trajectory of this investigation, its prosecution, and the judiciary's rulings.

DeSimone astonishingly admits to having little use for the principal eyewitness, Alfred Bello. Referring to Bello as "an opportunist, look-ing for the best he could be offered . . . engaging in gargantuan false-hoods . . . and exotic fantasies," DeSimone never voiced his misgivings to the court.[83]

Evidently, the prosecutors were unaware of DeSimone's distrust of and disdain for Bello, which in and of itself raises many troubling questions?

Also, we now know why and perhaps how Paterson Detective Robert Mohl, a critical witness for the prosecution, was able to *convince* Bello to return to New Jersey from "a city out west" to testify at the retrial of Carter and Artis.

According to DeSimone, "it didn't take much salesmanship on the part of Bob Mohl . . . to convince Bello to return to New Jersey . . . he has a way of winning the respect of people he arrests. He is calm, me-thodical, firm, and reasonable. He knows how to sell himself to suspects.

82. DeSimone, Vincent J. 2019. *Media Meddlers.* p. 84.
83. Ibid., pp. 195–99.

If you ever have to face arrest, Bob Mohl is a good choice to be arrested by, if you want to get everything off your chest."[84]

By Mohl's own recorded admission or confession, he regales in physically assaulting the principal eye-witness, Alfred Bello, on at least one occasion.[85]

Notably, Bello had assaulted one of the detectives guarding him. DeSimone had told Mohl to "go up there and straighten things out . . . I [*Mohl*] knocked on the door, Bello answered, I gave him one shot and knocked him out," Mohl proudly reflects in a recently-taped interview with the BBC.

This criminal assault against the state's principal witness would have likely impeached the credibility of Mohl and Bello.

But something even more sinister may have triggered what, in retrospect, was a flawed investigation from its very beginnings.

The Carter-Artis investigation cannot and should not be seen as a one-off. Instead, it must be viewed within the historical context of the ongoing underworld unrest that encroached on the long-standing domination of the Genovese Mafia Family's financial and political investments in Passaic County.

The murder of Gabriel DeFranco[86] on October 6, 1966, four months after the triple murders at the Lafayette Bar and Grill, and the subsequent murder of Robert "Bobby" Harris, the Black numbers czar, two and one-half years later were all part and parcel of the Genovese Mafia Family's ongoing struggle to maintain and solidify its control of the gambling rackets in Paterson.[87]

---

84. Ibid., p. 30, 216.

85. *The Hurricane Tapes*, 2019, Episode 3 @27:13. Kelly, Mike. *The Bergen Record* (Hackensack, NJ). 2019. "Revisiting the Hurricane Murder Case: Son resurrects his detective father's memoir." June 17th.

86. Krajicek, David J. *New York Daily News.* 2016. "Unsolved 1960's "New Jersey phantasmagoria' murders linked by wild tale of counterfeiting, four way sex." October 9th. *The Record* (Hackensack, NJ). 1966. "DeFranco Death Link to '52 Slaying Seen." October 7th. *The Herald News* (Passaic, NJ). 1966. "Suspect in Counterfeit Ring Slain in Paterson." October 6th.

87. Zuckoff, Murray and Louise Esteven. *The Morning Call* (Paterson, NJ). 1969. "Grim Details Revealed in Gambler's Killing." April 2nd. *The News* (Paterson, NJ). 1969. "10 In Area Indicted." December 17th. Scarpo, Ed. 2014. *Mafia News in New York and America: Decades of Mob Violence Behind Waterfront Case.* December 21st. It should be pointed out that Alton Hughes, a Black vice czar from Newark was murdered and his body found in Howell, N.J. The alleged killer was Frank "Butch" Miceli, a member of the Gambino Mafia Family. *Asbury Park Press.* 1971. "Crime Flourishing." November 2nd.

Had the ongoing territorial war between the "Association" and the Genovese Mafia Family been credibly investigated, the likely motive for both the Holloway and the triple murders would have emerged. There was an underworld war for control of the lucrative numbers and vice-rackets. Conforti, Holloway, and James Oliver, the Lafayette Bar and Grill bartender, were ensconced in this war. Rawls and Tuck were as well. Whether or not Carter and Artis were, remains an open question?

Regardless, had this investigative avenue been pursued, the motive for the triple murders and the assassination of Holloway would have offered the prosecution a viable and sustainable investigative hypothesis.

Absent that, Humphrey's had little choice but to embrace the racial revenge motive or dismiss the case.[88] He was confronted with the classic Gordian knot.

The political implications of dismissing the indictments would have been dire and likely hindered any chance for career advancement. *Senatorial courtesy*, a time-honored tradition in New Jersey, could have denied judicial appointments or promotions to those central to this investigation.[89]

Richard Caruso surely understood this. An experienced Essex County detective seconded to the Passaic County Prosecutor's Office, he concluded, "There was something really wrong . . . prosecutors and police not only stonewalled attempts to examine the case with a fresh eye but deliberately manipulated evidence." [90]

Whether the investigation and prosecution of Carter and Artis were the consequence of ineptness, naiveté, over-zealous advocacy, willful blindness, or more sinister motives, fundamental and material deceptions and inconsistencies trailed this investigation throughout and were consciously ignored. Consequently, in a last-ditch effort to secure

---

88. DeSimone, Vincent J. 2019. *Media Meddlers*. p. 52.

89. Mayor Frank Graves had been elected a senator at this point and held the careers of prospective judges in his hands. *Morning News* (Paterson). 1979. "Romei Named to Bench." February 1st. *The News* (Paterson, NJ). 1979. "An Easy Choice." March 14th. *The Record* (Hackensack, NJ). 1979. "Breaking a Deadlock." June 11th. *The Record* (Hackensack, NJ). 1979. "Humphreys Passes First Test." December 11th.

90. Kelly, Mike. *The Bergen Record* (Hackensack, NJ). 2019. "Doubts, errors, unknowns still haunt the case of 'Hurricane' Carter, John Artis." June 17th.

convictions, the search for truth was brutishly compromised, as were the reputations of those who blindly followed this tortured path.

But the real tragedy of this entire debacle was the families of the three victims who never received a *truthful reconciliation* for their pain and suffering. The guilty killers and their conspirators escaped. That is the only reasonable conclusion given the dismissal of these indictments.

Ironically, the person responsible for dissembling this search for justice and advancing the careers of the many who foisted this ill-conceived prosecution on the taxpayers of Passaic County was denied an appointment to the Division of Motor Vehicles. The Genovese Family tentacles proved, in the end, their omnipresence.[91]

Just one more episode in the continuing saga of *JERSEY JUSTICE.*

---

91. *Button Guys of the New York Mafia: Gerardo Vito Catena—the Acting Boss.*

2

The Crime of Vice

Attending New York University (NYU) in the 1970s opened my eyes to understanding just how critical the role of law-making is to the administration of criminal justice. NYU had, at the time, retained some of the more well-known criminology professors. Edwin Schur, Paul Walton, and Jock Young stick out in my mind because I was one of their students.

As a lawyer and a sociologist, Schur wrote extensively on the sociology of law and how legislation was shaped by competing social movements. In particular, his approach to the term *victimless crime*, or crimes without victims, demonstrated how our resort to morality and moral panics often mold how the law is legislated and enforced.[1]

Why would he ask, do we criminalize gambling when both the gambler and his bookmaker agree to partake in the activity? Ditto for prostitution, when the prostitute agrees to engage with the "john?" Or the drug user who willingly buys from the drug seller?

These are consensual agreements that deserve to be protected by the state, not criminalized. Thought-provoking, to say the least, but certainly not quite as nuanced as I had experienced working the street.

The summer of 1975 saw Paul Walton, one of the authors of *The New Criminology*, listed in the University's catalog as a visiting professor from London.[2]

---

1. Schur, Edwin M. 1965. *Crimes Without Victims: Deviant Behavior and Public Policy.* Schur, Edwin M. and Adam Bedau. 1974. *Victimless Crimes: Two Sides of a Controversy.* Sheldon, Randall G. *Resurrecting Radical Non-Intervention: Stop the War on Kids.*

2. Walton, Paul and Jock Young. 1998. *The New Criminology Revisited.*

With his colleagues, Jock Young and Ian Taylor, they challenged traditional criminological orthodoxy, upending the likes of the more conventional criminologists. I, along with a State Police colleague, Jack Cole, took their seminar.

Law and its promulgation were in their world, simply the powerful subjugating the powerless to a life of exploitation and denigration. It was a classic Marxist argument that certainly harkened me back to my days at the coffee houses of Berkeley, Sausalito, and San Francisco.

Steeped in the ground-breaking research of Richard Quinney and Bill Chambliss (i.e., *Critical* and *Conflict Criminology*), the law was more than an objective instrument or reflection of society's values.[3] According to these fledging genres' of criminologists, it purposely protected the economic advantage of a few at the expense of the masses.[4]

At the same time as these converging criminological theories were consuming the academic world, the "war on drugs," a term that is often associated with former President Richard Nixon, was ramping up. Running on a "law and order" platform and recognizing how drugs were inundating white middle-class communities, Nixon declared drugs "public enemy number one."[5]

The year was 1971, four years after I had graduated from the New Jersey State Police Academy. It was the year that popular culture was imbued with the likes of the mob-busting detective John Shaft in the movie *Shaft,* "Popeye Doyle" in The *French Connection,* and of course, the iconic Clint Eastwood of *Dirty Harry* fame. To say that these were euphoric times would be a gross understatement.[6]

Intent on advancing my career in the investigative branch, I applied for a position in the Narcotics Bureau. Interviewed by several of the ranking officers in the Bureau, I was informed weeks later to report to

---

3. Quinney, Richard. 1970. *The Social Reality of Crime;* Chambliss, William J. 1982. *Law, Order and Power.* Sloan, Karen. *The Recorder.* 2020. "UC Law Deans Unite to Defend Critical Race Theory Amid Trump Attacks." September 14th.

4. These criminologists were referred to as "the crits" for their embrace of critical race theory which was developed by a number of civil-rights advocates and scholars.

5. Locke, Alex. *Business Insider.* 2019. "Top Nixon Adviser reveals the racist reason he started the 'war on drugs' decades ago." July 31st.

6. Morris, Wesley. *The New York Times.* 2020. "'Shaft' 'Dirty Harry' and the Rise of the Super-cop." November 5th.

Division Headquarters in West Trenton, New Jersey. I was selected to become a warrior in this noble war against drugs. I was assigned to the North Unit—Northern New Jersey, the most populous region of the state and another suburb of the Big Apple—New York City.

Before "hitting the bricks," all those selected had to undergo a two-week training course in Sea Girt, New Jersey. I was only 27 years old, listening to the war-weary veterans who had worked every phase of narcotics investigations; I was looking forward to working undercover.

For those who have never experienced the so-called "adrenalin rush" or the thrill of undercover investigations, every day was new, exciting, challenging, and dangerous.[7] Learning how to conduct yourself on the street among users and "pushers" was the real deal.[8]

However, it was nothing like *Miami Vice*, which years later romanticized and fictionalized the swashbuckling and sartorially- dressed Don Johnson and Phillip Michael Thomas. This was down and dirty, living, sometimes sleeping among those who were looking to buy their daily fix, as well as those looking to accommodate them. However, most of the time, they were the same—users were sellers to pay for their addiction.

During our training, we learned the language of the street, often laced with profanity and politically offensive epitaphs. We were taught about the costs of the different drugs, what they looked like, and the euphoria they produced. We were instructed on informant development and maintenance. How to avoid ingesting the illegal drugs you were buying, mainly when a seller was testing your street creds, proved to be one of the more prickly subject matters.

Told to maintain contact with our "cover or surface agent," this agent was usually an older, more experienced detective who interceded in dicey situations. It could involve being tossed by the local police, being arrested, or having a physical altercation.

---

7. Girodo, Michel. *Proceedings of the Aylmer Conference on Stress in Law Enforcement.* 1984. *Conventional and Exceptional Stress Reactions in Undercover Agents.*

8. Almonte, Robert. 2005. *Covert Operations Management.* Girodo, Michael. 1984. *Narcotics Officer: Psychological Factors in Undercover Narcotics Agents.* pp. 59–62.

We would call and meet with the cover agent before hitting the bricks and terminating the day or evening's events. The phone booth was our mobile office and safety zone. Beepers and cell phones were decades away.

Body language often said more than words. A squint, a roll of the eyes, a smirk, an offensive or defensive move, the inflection or tone of your voice, or a stutter (which I found highly effective) could impute more than verbal exchanges. Similarly, what was *not* said and deflected or avoided could be equally predictive and telling.

How you carried yourself, how you approached a situation, your reaction to a stressful situation, and your diction could either "sell you, tell you, or fell you."

It was essential that you understood the people you were interacting with, knew the language of the street, dressed accordingly, and never displayed fear. Either you had it, or you didn't. Instincts often prevailed over formal knowledge and training. Being a discerning listener was an attribute that proved life-saving time and again.

Patience in this line of work was undoubtedly a virtue. Rushing a drug deal could be deadly. Blunders were inevitable. Ensuring that all your avenues were covered and having an exit strategy was often the difference between a successful deal going down and the deal falling apart. Or even your life. It often was a game of chess as opposed to checkers.

Testifying in court was an art form that required verbal dexterity, polished articulation skills, and an intuitive awareness regarding the defense attorney's legal strategy. Before being asked, knowing the question became a skill learned by suffering withering cross-examination by opposing counsel. It was not unusual for the defense attorney to question your credibility by implying that your persona on the street was one big lie—a constructed fiction.[9]

If you could deceive the defendant, you were equally as adept at misleading the jury. Why should you be believed in the courtroom when

---

9. In a profound self-reflection of one's life in pursuing justice, Robert Ansell a renowned criminal defense attorney opined, ". . . I have to think about whether the absence of reality in my life is a function of my personality or my character, or is it the result of what I do? Am I so used to dealing with scripts, fabricating truths, manipulating reality, that I end up doing that in my life because I'm so used to doing that all day in court." Mitchell, Paige, 1976. *Act of Love: The Killing of George Zygmanik.* p. 241.

you led a double life on the street? It was the classic conundrum that an undercover detective faced when testifying in court.

Shielding the informant's identity was of utmost importance. As is the case with most informants, they seldom have a spotless criminal record. Additionally, their motives are often suspect and open to an array of motivations—revenge and self-survival being the more prevalent. And they can be terrible witnesses on the stand.

Accordingly, it was strongly encouraged that the undercover agent remove the informant from witnessing or being involved in any drug transaction. This decision obscured the informant's identity and ensured their safety.

"Entrapment," or encouraging or promoting a criminal act when the defendant had no intent to commit a crime, can at times represent a defense attorney's only line of inquiry. It usually was unsuccessful.[10] It required the defendant to admit to the crime and then contend that "the man made me do it." Who said what to whom first often is the determining factor in deciding whether the defendant entered into the transaction voluntarily or was encouraged, manipulated, or enticed by the undercover agent. Accumulating multiple "buys" was one way of undermining this defense.

The testimony of the undercover agent is critical to a conviction or acquittal. Convincing twelve jurors that your covert actions were legal and within the bounds of fair play were essential for conviction. Seldom, however, did the defendant testify because their criminal history was subject to cross-examination by the prosecutor. Thus, most cases resulted in plea bargains.

There are times that a jury cannot come to a unanimous decision. Referred to as a "hung jury," the case was either dismissed or retried.

A hung jury happened only once to me. It involved a Viet Nam War veteran who was a double amputee. I shall simply refer to him as

---

10. Interestingly, in one of the more infamous narcotics cases, John DeLorean, the former General Motors executive, was acquitted of trafficking in multi-kilos of cocaine, convincing the jury that he was set-up by the D.E.A. *BBC News.* 1984. "DeLorean cleared of drug charges." August 16th.

"Joey C."[11] He had *accommodated* the sale of marijuana to me. He was a passenger in a car driven by Steven Scharaldi. He had merely passed the ounce of marijuana from Steven to me, knowing, of course, that it was illegal to dispense marijuana. At the time, I had no idea that "Joey C" was a double-amputee and a war hero. It was only later that I was appraised of this by Detective Michael Feura. Nonetheless, we felt it our obligation to charge "Joey C" as well as Scharaldi.

"Joey C's" arrest made national headlines. It was an embarrassment and indelible stain of his otherwise exemplary record. The circumstances surrounding his unselfish act of enormous self-sacrifice seared into my psyche. It was not a prosecution that I was proud of or comfortable with. But as we were taught, "the law is the law . . . juries decide guilt or innocence . . . not the police."

Offered a very lenient plea bargain that would have spared him jail time, "Joey C" bravely and rightfully refused. His courage, honor, and dignity demanded a trial.

I testified that after negotiating with the driver of the vehicle, Steven Scharaldi, the purchase of an ounce of marijuana, "Joey C" had passed the marijuana to me through the passenger's window of a vehicle. I then handed the twenty dollars to "Joey C," which I witnessed give it to Scharaldi. That was the extent of "Joey C's" involvement.

Taking the witness stand in his defense, "Joey C" admitted to taking part in the transfer of the marijuana. His testimony focused on the fact that he was merely accommodating the sale on behalf of his friend, Steven.

"Joey C" then related how he had used marijuana as a result of his time in Viet Nam. He spoke to the catastrophic and life-altering war injuries he sustained while attempting to save a fellow Marine.

The judge instructed the jury that the law required a conviction if the defendant demonstrated criminal intent to distribute the marijuana.

---

11. *The Daily Record* (Morristown). 1971. "Hero's Arrest, Parents' Sobs Show Tragedy of Drug Raid." May 18th. *Des Moines Tribune* (Iowa) 1971. "Arrest War Hero in Drug Raids." May 20th. See also *Spokane Daily Chronicle,* May 20, 1971, p. 18; *Tampa Tribune,* May 21, 1971, p. 51. *Akron Beacon Journal,* May 20, 1971, p. 16. *Kansas City Star,* May 21, 1971, p. 21; *Daily Advertiser* (Lafayette, Louisiana), May 23, 1971, p. 49; *The Daily Journal* (Vineland, NJ), May 20th; and *St. Joseph-News-Gazette,* May 20, 1971, p. 30. *The News* (Paterson, NJ), February 2, 1972, p. 27.

It was a relatively straightforward standard, but one that "Joey C" had challenged with an emotionally wrenching story of his tour in Viet Nam.

After several hours of deliberations, the jury returned. They could not arrive at a unanimous decision. At least one juror had held out. It was a hung jury.

When asked by the prosecutor whether I wanted to retry the case, my answer was absolutely NOT! That the jury failed to reach a unanimous verdict was a blessing for both "Joey C" and me.

In retrospect, it was a prosecution that I wish I had never pursued. Was this distribution of marijuana arrest worthy of prosecution, especially knowing what we know today?[12] Was marijuana indeed that gateway drug to heroin?[13] Or was this just another fiction that enveloped us in another unwinnable war?[14]

Sadly, "Joey C" suffered from the collateral damage of two politically invented wars—both of which demonstrated his relentless courage, resilience, and determination to survive.

After my training, I took a fictitious name that I would remember if challenged. Mine was Marty Grimes, with an address of 111 Broadway, Paterson, New Jersey.

I was issued an automatic weapon as opposed to your standard police-issued .38 police revolver. And the registration on my undercover vehicle reflected my fictitious identity.

At times, my authenticity was questioned. To gain his, sometimes her trust, they demanded you ingest the drug you were buying. If it was heroin, they wanted to see you stick the needle in your arm. Marijuana

---

12. New Jersey has joined 14 other states legalizing the use of recreational marijuana. Rense, Sarah. *Esquire.* 2020. "Here Are All The States That Have Legalized Weed in the U.S." Nov. 4th. Oregon recently decriminalized heroin, cocaine, methamphetamine, and an assortment of other psychotropic drugs. Fuller, Thomas. *The New York Times.* 2020. "Oregon Decriminalizes Small Amounts of Heroin and Cocaine. Four States Legalize Marijuana." November 4th. Erb, Kelly Phillips. *Forbes.* 2020. "House Passes Bill to Legalize Marijuana for Federal Purposes." December 4th.

13. White, John. *CNBS: The Definitive On-Line Cannabis Resource.* "The History of Marijuana." Stutman, Robert. *The Hill.* 2020. "A Retired DEA agent's plea: Time to reschedule marijuana." December 28th. Mosher, Clayton and Scott Atkins. 2019. *In The Weeds: Demonization, Legalization, and the Evolution of Marijuana Policy.*

14. For a compelling albeit controversial treatise on the legalization of all drugs that are currently illegal, see Carl L. Hart, *Drug Use for Grown-Ups: Chasing Liberty in the Land of Fear.* 2020.

was simply "taking a toke." Methamphetamine, or "speed," as it was called, could create a delicate situation. But as we were taught, your keen judgment, your words, and your behavior often dictated the drug dealer's response.

Never were you to partake in using any drug, regardless of the situation. Not only could it impair your judgment, but it could impeach your testimony at the subsequent trial. This mandate was a career-defining no, NO.

I still can remember several attempts to buy from one of the most prominent "speed" dealers in Morris County, Stephen Belyea.[15]Like most meth dealers, he was super-paranoid. He trusted no one. Ultimately, I was introduced to him by an unwitting informant, Gary Granito. But Belyea remained ultra-suspicious of me. He would often comment that he had never seen me indulging in the "meth" I was purchasing from him.

For whatever reason(s), Susan, his paramour, took a liking to me. Several times she made sexual advances toward me, perhaps testing me. Knowing if I were an undercover detective, as Belyea suspected, not indulging her overtures would be a tell-tale sign. I made it clear that I had no interest in a sexual relationship. "I get off on speed, not pussy" was my classic go-to line. "Nothing beats the rush I get from speed."

Working up from small bags to ounces of "speed," I became one of Belyea's most valued clients. It became a weekly event, solidifying my standing with Belyea. While I am sure he questioned never witnessing me ingest the "meth," the money he was making from me, and the false sense of security he felt while not being arrested only re-enforced my street "creds" with him.

To further bolster my standing with Belyea, we decided to arrest him, Susan, and me in a pre-arranged raid. Our goal was to learn from Belyea who his source was. Perhaps we could instill enough paranoia in Belyea that he would believe his supplier had "set him up."

On April 28, 1971, the New Jersey State Police arrested the three of us for possession of "speed" and LSD. Booked at the Riverdale Police Department headquarters, we spent several hours together in a jail cell.

_____
15. *Daily Record* (Morristown, NJ). 1971. "Huge Drug Bust Hits Dover Area." May 18th.

We contemplated on who might have set us up? But Belyea never mentioned his supplier, who I intermittently suggested might have been an informant for the police.

Bailed out, I continued buying "speed" from Belyea, attempting to learn his source.[16] He was never forthcoming.

Weeks later, Belyea and Susan again were arrested in early morning raids. With the arrest of 58 drug dealers from whom I had purchased every drug imaginable, I had to personally confirm the identities of those booked as a result of the undercover investigation.[17] Now, I was dressed in a suit and tie, not my worn and torn street garb.

Seeing me standing there at the Dover National Guard Armory awaiting the arrival of those arrested, Belyea lunged, yelling, "I knew you were a fucking narc . . . I knew it . . . I'll take care of you mother-fucker." At that point, Detective Sergeant Leon Adams, my supervisor, took Belyea into the men's room and read him the riot act. There were no further outbursts from Belyea.[18]

Rather than stand trial, Belyea and Susan forfeited their bail and remained fugitives for several years. Finally turning themselves in, they were sentenced to less than a year in jail, allowed to enter a work-release program, and given several years' probation. Not quite the sentence you would expect for fugitives from justice who were, at the time, the largest meth dealers in the county.

Naturally, every city had its vibe, and you had to learn to adjust to it. Dover was different from Newark or Paterson. Lyndhurst was different from Netcong or Newton. Similarly, the persona you acquired had to be consistent with the drug you were buying. Sometimes you had to act outrageously—crazy, maniacal, and even violently vicious, mainly if you were a "speed freak." Other times you remained docile, under the weather, or doped up, especially if you were a heroin addict.

---

16. *The Herald News* (Passaic, NJ). 1971. "Three Seized in Drug Raid." April 28.

17. *The Herald News* (Passaic, NJ). 1971. "58 Nabbed in Morris Drug Raid." May 18th. *Paterson News.* 1971. "Record Indictments in Morris: 36 Indicted in Drug Raids." August 11th. Berardelli, Vic. *The Daily Record.* 1971. "Says Raid Just Beautiful" and "The Big Drug Roundup." May 19th.

18. *Daily Record* (Morristown, NJ). 1976. "Morris Fugitives Now In Custody." June 13th and October 17th.

Every situation demanded a different act, and every act had different outcomes. You were simply playing a role on a large but ultimately lethal stage. Only you had to be convincing, could not forget your lines, and always be aware of your safety.

Indeed, safety was paramount when working undercover. Simple issues as never allowing someone to sit behind you in the car. Always have your back to the wall when in a diner, bar, or restaurant. Be aware of your surroundings while on the street, especially planning an escape route or two. Never be surrounded by a group of people. Arrange a time and place to meet with your cover agent when "the buys" were completed.

While these rules are relatively benign, the actual implementation on the street was not as convenient nor straightforward as you may suspect.

One evening, while I was working the streets of Dover, one of the "pushers," William White aka Billy, whom I befriended, began questioning my roots in Paterson, New Jersey. Billy started asking me names of people that I should have known if I was from Paterson.

One name he casually brought up was "Sonny" Sonntag.[19] I attended high school with Sonny and knew him primarily by his reputation. Sonny was a tough kid who hung out with a rough crowd. Anybody who was somebody knew of Sonny. So when Billy asked me if I knew him, I was sure he was attempting to determine if I was the real deal and, indeed, whether I grew up and lived in Paterson.

Without thinking, I acknowledged attending Central High School with Sonny.[20] Billy immediately responded, "I'm sure Sonny would like to see you. Why don't we go see him?" "Sure," I immediately and foolishly responded.

There would be no way Sonny would know I was a State Police detective. The class of 1962 was quite large, and Sonny and I did not consort

---

19. *Courier Post* (Camden, NJ). 1979. "4 Indicted in Kidnap & Sexual Torture of Woman. "October 25th, p. 14. *Asbury Park Press*. 1980. "Trio Convicted in Sexual Torture of Young Woman." June 7th, p. 38. *Federal District Court, State of New Jersey.* 2009. *Sonntag v. Powers.* January 23rd; *Asbury Park Press*. 1980. "Trio Convicted of Sexual Torture of Young Woman in Asbury Park." June 7th, p. 38; Swann, Barbara. *The News* (Paterson, NJ). 1980. "3 Get Stiff Jail Terms in Woman's Sex Torture." September 9th, p. 4.

20. The beat poet Allen Ginsburg's father, Louis taught English at Central High School.

with one another or associate in the same crowd.[21] Nor with the years that passed would Sonny know where I had been, what I had done, nor for whom I worked? The chances of being recognized or known were infinitesimal. It was a chance worth taking.

We drove in my car to a house located in Lake Hopatcong, about 20 minutes from Dover. Getting out of the car, we walked up the stairs. I left my off-duty automatic weapon under the seat of my car. Billy knocked on the door. Someone answered, and we entered the house. Sitting around the table were four males. All four had guns lying on the table, one in front of each of them.

Immediately I recognized Sonny. He was bi-racial. "Sonny," I said, "How are you?" He looked at me and replied, "I don't know you mother-fucker." With that, the other three sitting around the table picked their guns up and started banging them on the table, chanting, "He don't know you mother-fucker, he don't know you mother-fucker."

Realizing this would not end pleasantly, I quickly exited the house, leaving Billy to fend for himself. Had I brought my gun into the house, the outcome would have been much different. I would not be telling this story today, knowing what I know now.

Later, I met with Billy. We discussed what occurred. He was not thrilled that I left him there. I made it clear that he was setting me up, and it was him or I. He then related that they "beat the shit out of me for bringing you there." My response was equally as terse. "I should beat the shit out of you for setting me up, you mother-fucker . . . now get the fuck away from me, you no good bastard."

At this point, Billy realized that he had better cut his losses and left.

The next time I saw Billy was in court. There we exchanged some pleasantries and nostalgically reflected on that evening. I had decided to cut him a break. Meeting with the prosecutor trying the case, I recommended a lesser sentence, to which Billy pled guilty.

He had suffered enough, even though I still harbored animosity toward him for setting me up. But in the end, all Billy was doing is what I would have expected. Making sure I was not a narc.

---

21. I transferred from Central High School to Manchester Regional High School in 1960. Sonntag's interaction with me would have been extremely limited, if at all.

Sonntag was charged and convicted of a most heinous crime seven years later—sexual torture and kidnapping. He was sentenced to 112 years in prison. The acts of human depravity were so despicable that the judge refused to cite them in his decision denying Sonntag's motion for *habeas corpus.*[22]

Cleopatra, A Mob Enforcer, and the Ultimate Sting

Drug trafficking is purely a cash-only business. The state provided us access to a relatively generous budget. It was certainly an aspect of working undercover that made the more undesirable aspects of the job more palatable. You were able to eat in the finer restaurants, drive the newer cars, and engage in an unconventional lifestyle with a certain degree of impunity and immunity.

When pursuing the larger wholesale dealers and distributors, we would use "flash money." The Federal Reserve in Elizabeth, New Jersey, was our bank.

Its moniker, "flash money," was derived from the fact that you would "flash the money." The dealer would then produce the product—heroin, cocaine, marijuana, or speed. Once seeing the kilos, the surveillance team would be alerted either via an on-body transmitter or a pre-arranged physical signal. The arrest(s) was immediate.

This approach differed from that used in conducting retail level enforcement. The goal was to improve the quality of life within the communities targeted for an enforcement initiative. Removing as many drug pushers from the street was the tactical objective. Under this investigative strategy, the undercover agent would simply purchase the drug for a nominal cost, obtain a name or other identifying characteristics, and effect the arrest *months later.*

Employing this *modus operendi* allowed the undercover agents to continue working the street, building their street creds with other

---

22. *Sonntag v. Powers.* 2009. *U.S. District Court.* January 23rd. "Due to the heinous and depraved nature of the assaults Petitioner and his co-defendants inflicted on L.B. the details of the assault have been omitted from this Opinion," Judge Dennis Cavanaugh wrote.

dealers. After several months, large-scale, early morning raids maximized the shock value.

To ensure the safety of the arresting agents, raiding teams would assemble in the early-morning hours and simultaneously disperse, arresting those previously identified by the undercover officer. The element of surprise was to the benefit of the detectives whose safety was of utmost importance.

It took very little time for the word to spread throughout the community. This enforcement methodology would create paranoia among the "druggies," making the availability and purchase of drugs more difficult. At least, that is what we believed.

It was always quite rewarding to see the community's positive reaction after 50 or 60 drug dealers were arrested and removed from the streets. Community leaders would have nothing but praise for ridding their neighborhood of these "pushers" who were accosting their children on the way to school, in the playgrounds, and in the parks.[23] We were their knights in shining armor. Or so I thought at the time.

We indeed were not the oppressors of whom Walton and the radical and critical criminologists spoke. Nor were these laws without victims, about which Schur wrote. Victimized day in and day out, the police were their only recourse absent vigilante justice.[24]

A proactive police presence seemed to reinforce the notion that those economically challenged communities benefited from community-driven policing. "Quality of life" enforcement was not just for the more

---

23. Narvaez, Alfonso A. *The New York Times*. 1986. "Mayor of Passaic Leads Drug Rally: Heads March of Pupils After 117 Arrests Are Made in Schoolyard Sales." September 12th. Ladd, Scott. *The Star-Ledger*. 1986. "Neighborhood Outcry prompts drug sweep." February 7th. Berkowitz, Nathan. *The New York Times*. 1989. "Effectiveness of Drug Law is Questioned." April 9th. Senator Frank X. Graves and mayor of Paterson sponsored the law which enhanced the penalties for selling drugs within 1000 feet of a school zone.

24. With the recent efforts to defund the police, community leaders Black and White have challenged the narrative, arguing, "We want radical police reform, where all citizens are treated fully human by all cops, and not just the 'good ones' we all know well . . . we will not sacrifice the safety of our community in pursuit of . . . lofty goals with no plan to back them up . . . the drug trade has been revived in two homes, to unprecedented levels, with conflicts resulting in fights and shootouts." Samuels, Sondra and Don Samuels. *The Star Tribune*. 2020. "Why We Northside Neighbors are suing Minneapolis." August 24th. Worthy of discussion is a 2021 Netflix documentary, *Crack: Cocaine, Corruption & Conspiracy*, produced by Stanley Nelson.

affluent communities, which often surrounded the cities.[25] No one, rich or poor, chose to live in drug-infested neighborhoods.[26]

Today we now know that this proactive enforcement approach ultimately incarcerated an overwhelming number of minorities.[27] Seen as doing more harm than good, communities of color have borne the brunt of the "war on drugs."[28] Mass incarceration of minority males and the attendant consequences have delegitimized the police and the institutions of criminal justice in the very communities most affected by rampant drug trafficking.[29]

The legislation that established mandatory minimums and "three strikes and you're out" created a policing dilemma that only exacerbated the dire consequences of the "war on drugs."[30] Successive political administrations have done little to remedy this situation.

Once again, it demonstrates the conflicting and often self-defeating consequences of enforcing laws that criminalize mutually consenting behavior. The moral ambiguity of these laws has placed the police in an untenable position. It has exacerbated the distance between the police and the community. It's the classic example of "under-policing" and

25. Moore Mark H. and Mark A.R. Kleiman. *National Institute of Justice.* 1998. "Perspectives on Policing: The Police and Drugs." September. Wilson, James Q. and George L. Kelling. 1998. *Broken Windows: The Police and Neighborhood Safety.* Mazerolle, Lorraine Green. 2005. "A Systematic Review of Drug Law Enforcement Strategies." February. *National Institute of Justice.* 2015. *Practice Profile: Street-Level Drug Enforcement.* October 27th. Newburn, Tim and Joe Elliott. *Crime Detection and Prevention Strategies.* 1998. *Police Anti-Drug Strategies: Tackling Drugs Together Three Years On. Policing Drugs: The Costs and Benefits of Law Enforcement Strategies.* 2015.

26. Stanmyre, Matthew. *The Star-Ledger.* 2020. "He Went From Class President to Drug Dealer, then dead at 16. My Desperate Personal Search for Answers." December 20th. While certainly anecdotal, it is illustrative of the conflict that confronts law enforcement as it struggles to address the dire consequences of the illegal drug trade that has and continues to ravage communities across the United States. See documentary, Profit, Alan. 2012. *The Frank Matthews Story.*

27. *Stanford Law and Policy Review.* 2009. "Race, Drugs, and Law Enforcement in the United States." June 19th.

28. Grillo, Ioan. *The New York Times.* 2020. "End the War on Drugs Now." November 20th.

29. Neely, Mason. 2004. *Pennington Post.* "Retired Narcotics Officer takes intellectual tact to war on drugs." January 22nd. *Common Sense for Drug Policy.* 1999. "A Police View On the War on Drugs: Chief Hubert Williams." March 25th. Small, Deborah. *Journal of Social Research.* 2001. "The War on Drugs is a War on Racial Justice." Fall. Mauer, Marc. *The Sentencing Project.* 2009. "The Changing Racial Dynamics of the War on Drugs." April. McWhorter, John. *Cato's Letter.* 2011. "How the War on Drugs Is Destroying Black America." Winter.

30. Vaidyanathan, Brandon. *The Public Discourse.* 2020. "Systemic Racial Bias in the Criminal Justice System is not a Myth." June 29th.

"over-policing"—a phenomenon that accents minor violations of the law and ignores the more serious violent confrontations.[31]

Sir Robert Peel, the father of modern policing, wrote in 1829, "Police, at all times, should maintain a relationship with the public that gives reality to the historical tradition that police are the public and the public are the police . . . the ability of the police to perform their duties is dependent upon public approval of police actions."[32] These principles are as relevant today as they were then.

Of course, enforcing the laws proscribing vice required the police to enlist the aid of informants. As a rule, no one reports purchasing drugs, nor does anyone report selling drugs. Only through an elaborate process known as informant procurement, development, and maintenance can the police infiltrate the drug subculture.

My mentor Justin Dintino repeatedly said, "give me one good informant, and I will give you ten detectives . . . Informants are the bread and butter of a criminal investigation, whether it involves a burglary, a murder, or a drug cartel." He was one of the few that valued, nurtured, and promoted informant development.[33]

To this day, this mandate is embedded in my investigative DNA. And one that I have repeated to those who choose criminal investigations for their career path.

Over the last several decades, the literature is replete with the dangers inherent with informants. Let there be little doubt; it is a dirty business. Informants are essentially criminals. They lie, steal, cheat, kill, and are untrustworthy and disloyal. They readily turn on their colleagues, some of whom may be their best friends. In short, they are not people that you would generally seek out or befriend.

Of the many I have encountered over my career, you learn very early that you enter the relationship cautiously and with a great deal of

---

31. Leovy, Jill. 2015. *Ghettoside.* January 27th.

32. *Law Enforcement Action Partnership (LEAP). Sir Robert Peel's Policing Principles.* Wikipedia: Peelian Principles. Oliver, Willard M. 2017. *August Vollmer: The Father of American Policing.*

33. Natapoff, Alexandra. 2008. *Snitching: Criminal Informants and the Erosion of American Justice.* N.Y.U. Press. Alu, Mary Ellen. *The Morning Call* (Allentown, PA). 1994. "Informant's Role Isn't a License to Steal." Shamas, Diala. *Brooklyn Law Review.* 2018. "A Nation of Informants: Reining in Post-9/11 Coercion of Intelligence Informants." vol. 83, no. 4, pp. 1175–226.

suspicion. Paraphrasing a famous phrase, "never trust and always verify," should be the governing principle that defines the relationship.

The informant can protect you from harm or deliberately put harm in your way. They can paint a roadmap that encapsulates some and shields others. Informants often are specialists in certain crimes. They know their environment, certainly better than you.

That is why intelligence plays a critical role in both recruiting the informant and providing you, the undercover agent, with a general understanding of the landscape you are about to encounter.

Performing proctology on the informant is not only desired but is obligatory. Knowing their history, habits, friends, relatives, associates, and prior criminal behaviors are central to the recruitment process. Informant development represents a critical piece of any organized crime control program.[34]

This was certainly the case when I learned about the arrest of "Big Louie" on the New Jersey Turnpike for a weapons violation.[35] Having investigated his father in the early seventies, I immediately recognized that "Big Louie" might be worth a visit.

His father was considered a significant player in Paterson's underworld.[36] According to "Lil Hutch," "Big Louie's" father was one of several conduits to the Paterson vice squad, paying them off as well as setting up competitors and others for arrests.[37] There was little doubt in my mind that "Big Louie" also knew quite a bit about the rackets in Paterson, if through nothing more than *osmosis*.

Dispatching Detectives Vince Modarelli and Larry Churm to interview "Big Louie" at the Middlesex County correctional facility, it was

---

34. Karchmer, Clifford L. *The New York Times*. 1981. "Keeping Informants Under Control." p. 15.

35. *United States v. Pablo Fernandez*. 1997. No. 440, Docket 96-1023. July 28th. Mladinich, Robert. *The Sweet Science*. 2005. "Size Matters." October 3rd.

36. *The Evening News* (Paterson, NJ). 1979. "Reputed Numbers Boss Arrested: Another Man Charged in $60G drug bust." April 5th.

37. *The Evening News* (Paterson, NJ). 1973. "Esposito, Kordja Arraigned." June 29th. p. 1. *The News* (Paterson, NJ). 1974. "Esposito Tells of Monitor Trap." May 24th. p. 3. *The Herald News* (Passaic, NJ). 1977. "Firing of Cop Upheld by State." February 8th. p. 11. *The Herald News* (Passaic, NJ). 1982. "Drug Kingpin Gets 20 Years." June 17th. p. 51.

apparent that he would play hardball and refuse to cooperate. But jail time has a way of softening even the most hardened criminal.

Weeks passed, and finally, "Big Louie" reached out to Modarelli. He wanted to talk, but not about Paterson and the rackets. Instead, "Big Louie" had a proposition. He would provide information on a bi-coastal cocaine operation in return for dismissing his charges. He would not, and *absolutely would not*, provide any information on Paterson's mob-infested underworld or police corruption.[38]

Although we were in the business of drug enforcement, I was not necessarily receptive to "Big Louie's" demands. Plus, several obstacles needed to be resolved before we could move forward.

"Big Louie" had a criminal record.[39] A weapons violation would not be looked at kindly by the prosecutor or the court. Guaranteeing "Big Louie" a suspended sentence would be tricky and delicate, particularly given a history of violence. He was a boxer as well as a nightclub bouncer and enforcer for the mob.

Moreover, we had no idea who "Big Louie" was going to give up. Was it worth the trade-off, or was it merely another mule in the endless chain of drug couriers? We needed more information as well as some assurances, other than simply his word.

Providing us with the name of the courier was a start. In one of several debriefings, "Big Louie" provided us with the name of Stephen Kalt. According to "Big Louie," they met in college in the early 70s in Florida. They dealt in drugs, mainly cocaine and Quaaludes, while in college and continued their relationship throughout the seventies. Kalt had developed his connections and was trafficking in kilos of cocaine, according to "Big Louie."

Naturally, we had to conduct a background investigation on Kalt. We learned that he was living in Knoxville, Tennessee. He had a criminal

---

38. Scott, Janny. *The Record* (Hackensack, NJ). 1981. "Good Words Are Few at Sentencing." December 18th. Hallett, Bruce. *Daily News* (New York). 1975. "Paterson Cop in Court Again." February 4th. *Daily News* (New York). 1975. "Ex-Paterson Cop Draws 1 Year." April 12th.

39. Mladich, Robert. *The Sweet Science*. 2005. "Size Matters." October 3rd; *The Bergen Record* (Hackensack, NJ). 1979. February 28th. p. 24. *The Evening News* (Paterson, NJ). 1981. July 11th. p. 5.

record for possession of drugs. A consensually recorded conversation would solidify our interest.

We had "Big Louie" contact Kalt telephonically. Kalt had indicated that he was dealing in kilos of cocaine and could service "Big Louie" with as many kilos as he needed or wanted. We instructed "Big Louie" to arrange a meeting with Kalt. He agreed.

On October 25, 1985, Kalt met with Modarelli and "Big Louie" in New Jersey to discuss purchasing ten kilos of cocaine. Looking to establish an east-coast outlet, Kalt stated that he was selling kilos of cocaine for approximately $35,000. He had any number of kilos Modarelli could afford.

Over the next several months, Modarelli remained in telephonic communications with Kalt, nurturing his relationship and establishing his street creds as a major distributor and potential east coast connection.

In early 1986, Kalt contacted Modarelli and indicated that he would be in the New York metropolitan area in or about the third week of January. Modarelli told Kalt that he would be available, but he needed a heads-up to arrange for his investors to collect the monies. They settled on a price of $34,000 per kilo and an initial purchase of three kilos.

In a surprise telephone conversation on January 21, 1986, Kalt told Modarelli that he was at the Helmsley-Madison Hotel in mid-town Manhattan. Realizing that we only had hours before we met with Kalt, we arranged to collect and inventory the money from the Federal Reserve, assemble three surveillance teams, and strategize the intended transfer of cash for kilos.

However, a tactical legal issue confronted us. The New Jersey State Police had no jurisdiction in New York City. We could not affect an arrest in a jurisdiction outside of New Jersey. If anything went awry, we could be charged with any number of criminal offenses, as well as administratively disciplined. We also knew the suits in West Trenton would not have our backs if something went wrong.

We considered notifying the New York City Police Department or the Drug Enforcement Administration, which would have transferred jurisdiction to one of the two agencies. Any chance of working up the ladder would be within the sole province of another agency. In short, we would have been left high and dry after diligently and patiently infiltrating this narcotics network.

Relying upon the extraordinary undercover skills of Modarelli, the decision was made to meet with Kalt in New York City but execute the arrest in New Jersey. Modarelli would have to convince Kalt to come to New Jersey if Kalt wanted $102,000.

Upon arriving at the Helmsley-Madison hotel, Kalt told Modarelli to meet him in Suite 1555. It was there that Kalt would make the transfer of the three kilos of cocaine for the cash. It was here that Modarelli had to apply his exceptional skills working undercover. Modarelli had my complete confidence.

There was, of course, one more hitch. If Modarelli went to Suite 1555, there might have been others in the room, increasing the probability of a "rip-off" (i.e., robbery). Completely alone, Modarelli's safety was now an issue. Should he go to Suite 1555 carrying $102,000, or should the deal be called off? Modarelli would have to make a split-second decision.

Modarelli decided to go to the room and "flash" the $102,000. He would refuse to consummate the transfer unless he could test the purity of the cocaine in a make-shift laboratory he had established at his apartment in New Jersey.

Kalt, seeing the money, agreed. Greed always prevailed, especially among money-hungry drug dealers.

In Modarelli's undercover car, unaware of what was about to occur, Kalt was driven to New Jersey, closely followed by the surveillance teams.

Kalt was placed under arrest in the lobby upon arriving at the Hasbrouck Heights Sheraton Hotel, a favorite location for drug traffickers who flew into Newark or Teterboro airports.

Kalt initially refused to cooperate. He was staring at decades in prison. Finally agreeing to cooperate and debriefed over several days, his arrest was never publicized. This accentuated his ability to persuade his co-conspirators into flying from California to New York to collect their share of the money.

There is, of course, nothing more rewarding than working up the distribution chain. From Kalt, we would now get his supplier and hopefully the importers.

My years investigating organized crime prepared me for the time and patience necessary to undertake complex long-term investigations. These investigations relied upon the enterprise theory, patiently assembling the pieces to a puzzle known as RICO.[40]

From my earlier days working the streets of Paterson, Newark, Dover, and the many suburban towns surrounding the metropolitan area, this new approach—an enterprise approach—was what we had come to believe would have the most impact on the availability of drugs.

While retail-level buys and busts were enthusiastically welcomed by those communities overwhelmed by drug dealers, the availability of drugs was not affected. One dealer replaced another; the market continued to supply the demand, and the cost of doing business remained relatively unscathed. In other words, we were spinning our wheels, getting nowhere.

Kalt was more than forthcoming. He discussed in intimate detail how his introduction into the world of drug trafficking. Of course, it was not quite the story "Big Louie" had told us. But truth varies according to who is telling it.

"Big Louie," according to Kalt, was his supplier of cocaine in the early 80s. "Big Louie" was obtaining his cocaine from a Columbian supplier in Miami. He was dealing in multi-kilos.

To develop Kalt's credibility, we had him contact his supplier. We consensually recorded the call to his supplier, Reed Wallace, who lived in Los Angeles, California. Thirty-one years of age, Wallace was dealing in multi-kilos of cocaine, most of which sold for thirty thousand dollars or more a kilo.

Wallace was considered a significant player in the cocaine market. Kalt was selling the cocaine to "Big Louie" that he had bought from Wallace on consignment. This arrangement clarified and validated how "Big Louie" knew he could coordinate a deal that would spring him from jail.

At this point, we realized that to pursue this to its ultimate conclusion, we would have to enlist the Drug Enforcement Administration (DEA). We contacted the Newark office.

---

40. McFeely, Richard A. 2001. *F.B.I. Law Enforcement Bulletin.* "Enterprise Theory of Investigation." vol. 70, issue 5, pp. 19–25.

Assigned to the case was Special Agent Brian Collier. Having worked with Collier over the years, he was the perfect agent to methodically and patiently investigate a complex criminal conspiracy. He was not wedded to the traditional "buy and bust" mentality. Racking up metrics was not his specialty. He understood that time and tenacity were essential in pursuing an enterprise-based prosecution. And he possessed the skill-sets to assemble the pieces to complete this intricate jig-saw puzzle.

With Kalt cooperating, Wallace was the next rung up the proverbial ladder. Summoned to New York to collect his money, the DEA arrested Wallace on January 31, 1986. Wallace had prior cocaine and a wire fraud conviction. The conspiracy started to unravel, with Wallace, much like Kalt, agreeing to reduce his criminal liability.

We didn't know at the time that Wallace was living with Victoria Sellers, the daughter of the iconic and renowned British actor Peter Sellers. Anytime a drug case involves a celebrity, the stakes exponentially are raised. Usually, they retain the best attorneys, and all legal avenues are exhausted.

To top things off, Sellers had made her maiden appearance in a 10 page spread in the April issue of *Playboy Magazine,* scantily-clad as Cleopatra. But could we prove that she was involved in the conspiracy to import drugs?[41]

According to Wallace, his connection for cocaine was a Columbian national, Andres Polido-Zorrilla. The network involved many Californians. They were engaged in beatings, robberies of drug traffickers, weapons trafficking, and murder. And as suspected, Wallace implicated Victoria Sellers in this conspiracy, providing us with a tape recording he had made.

In this recording, a drug dealer identified as "Richard" verbally confronted Sellers after being viciously assaulted and hospitalized and his vehicle stolen.[42]

---

41. *Los Angeles Times.* 1986. "'Enforcer' in Sellers Drug Case Sentenced to 10 Years." July 15th.

42. *The Orlando Sentinel.* 1987. "Sellers Testifies in Drug Case, She Tells of Guns, Cash With Former Girlfriend." March 12th. *Associated Press.* 1986. "Defendant Convicted in Sellers Drug Case." June 3rd.

RICHARD: Victoria, this is Richard.
VICTORIA: How are you doing, Richard?
VICTORIA: What do you want, Richard?
RICHARD: I want to know where my car is?
VICTORIA: It's at the shop at Santa Monica and Doheny.
RICHARD: You know Victoria, I spent three days in the hospital . . . I just got out . . . My chin is broken . . . your good friend Reed [Wallace] beat me up with billiard cues that night you invited me over . . . He wanted $10,000 restitution for your name . . . why did you call me over to get beat up?
VICTORIA: I left when you came in . . . Reed asked me to bring you over.
RICHARD: Darling, you told me to come over to your house . . . you damn well knew what Reed was going to do.
VICTORIA: You deserved it, and if my father found out what you fuckin did . . . don't even talk to me about the hospital . . . I hope your body is broken . . .

The recording implicated Seller's role in this bi-coastal and international drug distribution network.[43]

Indicted on March 12, 1986, Wallace and Sellers were charged with conspiracy to distribute cocaine.[44] Wallace was denied bail. Sellers was released on one-hundred thousand dollars bail.

Upon learning that Sellers had retained the former attorney general of New Jersey, Irwin Kimmelman, a motion was made by the federal government to have Kimmelman removed from the case.

As Attorney General, Kimmelman oversaw the State Police during the earlier phases of this investigation. He was conflicted. Kimmelman could no longer represent Sellers. In his stead, Sellers retained prominent criminal defense attorney John Barry, husband of federal judge Maryanne Trump-Barry, the sister of former President Donald J. Trump.[45]

---

43. *The Los Angeles Times.* 1986. "Seller's Daughter Admits Cocaine Guilt, Will Testify." May 28th.

44. *New York Post.* 1986. "Peter Sellers' Daughter On Drug Rap." March 13th. *Star.* 1986. "Tragic Drugs Downfall of Peter Sellers' Daughter." April 1st.

45. *Supreme Court of the State of New York, County of New York.* 2020. *Mary L. Trump v. Donald J. Trump, Maryanne Trump Barry.* September 24th.

Sellers, a British citizen, was subject to deportation. Recognizing the delicate situation Sellers was confronting. Barry arranged a rather generous plea-bargain for Sellers. She would plead guilty to participating in an international drug distribution network, would cooperate, testify in court, receive a three-year suspended sentence, and any efforts to deport her suspended.[46]

On the other hand, Wallace would receive a ten-year sentence for his international drug distribution enterprise involvement.[47]Kalt, for his cooperation, would be sentenced to five years.

Naturally, celebrity and social status bring certain privileges. In Seller's case, both her mother and father's iconic status among the Hollywood elites.[48] It was her access to the famed music mogul Lou Adler and his political connections throughout the entertainment industry and its well-heeled benefactors.[49] And it was retaining John Barry as legal counsel, who was well-respected among the federal judiciary. The value of an endless reservoir of money and connections was on full display.

Which simply highlights the obvious and glaring disparities that routinely undermine the "war on drugs."

On February 17, 1986, three weeks earlier, we had an opportunity that was just too outlandish to pass up. We initiated a ludicrous sting operation that once again demonstrated how the insatiable demand for cocaine had fostered a wild-west frenzy among drug dealers.[50]With cocaine inundating the New York-metropolitan area, we would often quip that purchasing cocaine was easier than delivering a pizza.

While speaking with my assistant Vic Irrizzary, he told me of a relationship he had developed with two Columbian drug dealers, Gustavo Lopez and Juan Guillermo Castano. Through a series of meetings, he convinced

46. *The New York Times*. 1987. "Victoria Sellers Gets Suspended Jail Term." March 12th.
47. *Los Angeles Times*. 1986. "'Enforcer' In Sellers Drug Case Sentenced to 10 years." July 15th.
48. Victoria's mother Britt Ekland was featured in the James Bond series, *The Man With The Golden Arm* (Rollings, Grant, *The US Sun*, 2020. "WANTING MOORE: Ex-Bond Girl Britt Ekland says next 007 should be more like Sir Roger Moore." March 10th.). Married to Peter Sellers, who starred in *The Pink Panther*, both Britt and Peter were icons among Hollywood's movie moguls. Wikipedia: Britt Ekland; Wikipedia: Peter Sellers.
49. Lou Adler was married to Britt Ekland, Victoria's mother. Adler and Eckland had a son together, Nic Adler. Adler was a giant in the world of music and film. Wikipedia: Lou Adler.
50. *The News* (Paterson, NJ). 1986. "Suspects Nabbed in Sting." February 20th.

them to meet with Juan Mattos, our undercover agent. They agreed. Mattos portrayed himself as a disc jockey for a local radio station—1921 on your radio dial. To solidify his story, the two drug dealers followed him to the Hackensack Barracks, which housed the Narcotics Bureau. There were no signs displayed indicating it was a State Police facility. There was a prominent radio tower in the parking lot, which Mattos misrepresented as the radio station antenna—WNJSP, as in New Jersey State Police.

Sitting in the State Police parking lot, Mattos negotiated a deal with them, agreeing to purchase a kilo of cocaine for $31,000 the next day. They would meet him at his sound booth inside the building, which housed the North Jersey contingent of narcotics and organized crime detectives.

On February 18, 1986, Lopez and Castano arrived unannounced in the Hackensack State Police Barracks parking lot. Immediately greeted by Mattos, they were escorted to my office, carrying a kilo of cocaine secreted under an overcoat. Upon seeing me, they threw the cocaine on my desk. Placed immediately under arrest, they were handcuffed and taken to the Bergen County Jail.

A year later, they pled guilty to the charge of distribution of narcotics. Both were sentenced to 5-7 years in state prison by Superior Court Judge James Madden.[51]

Madden said he was "fairly certain that the two had received the cocaine that was 82-percent pure, from organized crime." He was "outraged that major drug dealers were recruiting couriers who had no criminal records in hopes that the courts would be lenient with them."

They, of course, had no one to offer up to mitigate their sentences. They had no famous mothers or fathers. They were simply mules for a larger criminal enterprise. They were undocumented aliens. And they had no access to prominent criminal defense attorneys who would have the ability to arrange an attractive plea bargain with a sympathetic prosecutor and compliant judge.

Just another compelling anecdote in the "war against drugs."

---

51. *The Record* (Hackensack, NJ). 1987. "Drug Dealers Sentenced After Radio-Station Sting." May 3rd.

Investigating the Low Hanging Fruit

There is an old saying, "luck is the residue of design." Perhaps that was the case when I requested California for assignment after graduating from the Air Force's military police school in San Antonio, Texas.

Stationed a few short miles from Berkeley, San Francisco, and Sausilito, I witnessed first-hand the evolution of the Free Speech Movement, the beatniks and hippies that populated Haight-Ashbury, and the use of hard drugs and psychedelics that inundated the counterculture of the sixties. It was an education that ultimately prepared me for a career in the State Police and simultaneously allowed me the mental flexibility to work undercover. In retrospect, it made for a seamless transition.

Witnessing the dire consequences of the war in Viet Nam and its flawed rationale, an equally-as-faulty justification for the "war on drugs" was now being proffered. Perceived as the gateway drug to the more hard-core drugs—heroin, meth, LSD, and cocaine—arresting those who indulged in marijuana was the answer to preventing more severe addictions. Arguably, the "Domino Theory" was being re-imagined to define the "war on drugs."[52]

The symbolism certainly struck home one evening in Wayne, New Jersey—a white, middle-class community bordering Paterson.

Having just purchased heroin, PCP (i.e., angel dust), marijuana, Quaaludes, and methamphetamine (i.e., speed) in the open-air drug-infested market of the T-Bowl shopping center, a young boy no older than 14 approached me. He asked whether I could purchase him a bottle of wine from the liquor store—a controlled dangerous substance that was legally available.

Here was a 14-year old child who could purchase a shopping cart of any illegal drug in an unregulated market but was obligated to enlist someone over 21 years of age to buy him a bottle of wine in a licensed

---

52. Marijuana was the second-most common use of drugs after alcohol by troops in Viet Nam. It was reported that 34% of the troops deployed to Viet Nam had used marijuana. Menninger, Roy W. and John C. Nemiah. 2008. *American Psychiatry After World War II (1944-1994). November 1st.* Westheider, James. 2011. *Fighting in Vietnam: The Experiences of the U.S. Soldier.* p. 173.

liquor store. It served as an epiphany, making me question the utility of drug enforcement and its attendant lifetime debilitating effects.[53]

However, that is not where I began. It was where I arrived after witnessing both the short-term and long-term consequences of drug enforcement.[54] As is often the case in formulating public policy, the sin is not in admitting error but rather remaining wedded to the senseless policies of those who refuse to acknowledge their destructive consequences.[55]

When I first began working the street in the blue-collar city of Dover, New Jersey, there was little doubt in my mind that arresting drug dealers would diminish the availability of drugs. Ultimately this approach would dissuade potential users from imbibing in these physically debilitating and emotionally harmful substances.

My informant, Willie Rinaldi, a drug user and seller himself, agreed to introduce me to his clients and colleagues for a self-serving reason. He did not want his sister to become addicted to drugs. He believed that the more people arrested for selling drugs would eliminate the temptations that might induce his sister to experiment with drugs.

What, of course, Willie and I ignored was a simple law of demand begets supply. Within weeks of arresting over 58 drug dealers, many of which were addicts, the streets returned to normal.[56] Drugs were everywhere. Dealers were a bit more cautious but certainly not shy. So long as demand existed, someone would take the risk to address the supply. Until or unless demand evaporated, supply would always exist.

---

53. Hari, Johann. 2016. *Chasing the Scream: The First and Last Days of the War on Drugs.* Bloomsbury Press. March 1st. McCormack, Robert. *Law Enforcement News, John Jay College of Criminal Justice.* 1987. "Interview of Frederick T. Martens." November 10th. Andrews, Paul. C. Longfellow, F.T. Martens. *Federal Probation.* 1982. "Zero-Sum Enforcement: Some Reflections on Drug Control." pp. 14–18. Neely, Mason. *Pennington Post.* 2004. "Retired narcotics officer takes intellectual tact to war on drugs." January 22nd.

54. Schulte, Lucy. *The Star-Ledger.* 1986. "State Police 'Host' Drug Deal, Snare Two." February 19th.

55. Former Defense Secretary Robert McNamara's *mea culpa* was featured in *The Fog of War,* a documentary in 2003 in which he admits to his mistakes in executing the war in Viet Nam. He passed away 6 years later. Wikipedia: The Fog of War.

56. *Daily Record* (Morristown). 1971. *Huge Drug Bust Hits Dover Area.* May 18th. *Daily Record* (Morristown). "Police List Narcotics Defendants." May 19th. *The Paterson News* (Paterson, NJ). 1971. "36 Indicted in Record Indictments in Morris County." August 11th. *The Paterson News* (Paterson, NJ). 1972. "Morris Grand Jury Indicts 25 Persons." February 2nd.

After Dover, I worked in Paterson, a completely different milieu and demographic. Whereas there were very few Black distributors in Dover, Paterson had its share and more. In a city with relatively large segregated Black neighborhoods that were generally off-limits to those who did not reside there, strangers, especially Caucasians, were perceived in less-than-a-favorably light.

Nonetheless, when it came to scoring in Paterson, it was like "shooting fish in a barrel."[57] There was an endless supply of drugs and an accommodating cadre of those from the suburbs looking to capitalize on the insatiable appetite surrounding this economically depressed city.

However, unlike Dover, where the market was quite fluid and open, Paterson's drug markets were shaped by territories where notable drugs dealers were *licensed* (i.e., permitted) to sell. Whether this was a consequence of territorial allocations between competing gangs or the product selective police enforcement or non-enforcement was not relevant to me at the time.

In retrospect, an answer to this arrangement may have provided the Narcotics Bureau with a better understanding of just who we were arresting and who we were ignoring. And it definitely would have answered the million-dollar question: were we, through our random-based arrests, organizing a relatively benign retail drug market?

But there was also another factor that was at play. Known for "flaking," the Paterson Vice Squad was quite aggressive in stopping and searching vehicles that appeared to be looking to score, especially if the car was a newer model, registered outside the city, and driven by someone White. Our supervisors instructed us to be especially vigilant as it was not unusual to have drugs planted in your car or on your person.

As an undercover agent, you had to move quickly and cunningly to avoid being tossed by the police. The last thing you needed was the vice squad learning of the undercover operation the state was conducting. Not only was your safety at risk, but there were likely noticeable changes in the drug distribution networks.

---

57. Ladd, Scott. *The Star-Ledger.* 1986. "27 Netted in Operation 'Silk City.'" February 7th. Wright, Chapin. *The Star-Ledger.* 1986. "Drug Trade thrives 6 months after raid." August 17th.

I can still remember visiting my father in a suburb of Paterson after purchasing several decks of heroin. My dad was in the kitchen. He had been chosen to sit on a jury in Paterson but refused to say anymore. "The judge instructed us not to discuss the trial outside the jury room," he seriously and sternly related.

Chosen as a juror after telling the judge and defense attorney that I was in the State Police and worked undercover was simply incomprehensible. I suspected when the judge or defense attorney asked if he could be impartial, his answer was yes—not at all surprising to me. But to the judge or the defense attorney?

A week or two later, I again stopped to see my mother and father. I asked him the verdict. He stated that it was a drug case, and they found the defendant not guilty. Truly unfathomable, I thought.

"Why," I asked. "We felt that the cops planted the drugs on him," was his answer. Apparently, the reputation of this police department was well-known even among the "law and order" citizenry that my Dad ardently represented.[58]

After racking up another 50 or more buys in less than a couple of months, raids swept the city.[59] Paul Friedman, a grammar school classmate, was one of those I arrested for selling heroin.[60] I often wondered how this relatively docile, kind, and gentle soul could have found his way into this chaotic and, at times, violent world? Drugs were indeed non-discriminating.

Lyndhurst, New Jersey, was our next targeted area for investigating a wide-scale drug distribution network. It had permeated the schools, both grammar and high schools. Lyndhurst was a predominantly white middle-class community, mostly of European descent.

Here the demographics were primarily school-aged children, mainly high school. Being quite a bit older than those I was buying from, I reinvented my persona.

---

58. Not much has changed over the last fifty years, although claims of police misconduct are now being taken much more seriously. Closson, Troy. *The New York Times*. 2021. "A Detective Was Accused of Lying. Now 90 Convictions May Be Erased."

59. *Paterson Evening News*. 1972. "Drug Raids in City Yields 19 Arrests." March 21st.

60. *The News* (Paterson, NJ). 1972. "Seven Sentenced in Drug Cases." May 18th.

Posing as a burnt-out Viet Nam-War hippie who merely wanted to get high every day, citing poetry that Allen Ginsberg and Bob Dylan popularized, and engaging in anti-war tirades, I was able to convince eighty-plus high school students and two eighth-graders that I was a confused and aimless drug fiend.

It was so easy that as the months passed, I became a bit careless. I would show up; usually, late afternoon, hang around appearing to be half-doped up, just looking for my next score. One minute I was buying marijuana, the next minute heroin, the next minute speed or meth, PCP, then a methadone tablet or two, LSD of course, a little hash(ish), and finish off my shopping spree with Quaaludes. This buying spree was a huge no-no. You were either a junkie, speed freak, a spaced-out dead-head, or a pill popper. It was doubtful you were all of the above; it was impossible unless you were a "narc."

While purchasing LSD from one of the high-school "pushers," I drowsily asked him his name? He asked me, "Why do you want my name?" My cavalier response was, "I need it for the police report." He laughed and sold me LSD. It was that simple and easy.

Taking time out from the hectic pace of the street, my partner Detective Lou Trowbridge and I decided to go to the local pub, grab a bite to eat, and shoot a little pool/billiards. Known for distributing Quaaludes, one of the pool players, Ron O'Gara, offered me some Quaaludes. Not one to pass up a drug deal, I obliged. Upon exchanging the money for the Quaaludes, he ordered me to "pop" a Quaalude as he watched.

Realizing that he was on to me, I knew this was not going to end well. "Take it, you mother-fucker," handing me a Quaalude. Readying my pool cue for what was going to be classic slug-fest, I responded, "hey mother-fucker, you take it, or I'll beat your fucking head in," acting maniacal and crazed. Classic bi-polarity at its best.

At this point, Lou walked over. Lou's 6-1, 210-pound frame quelled the situation. "Back off mother-fucker, or I'll shove this pool cue up your ass." Everything calmed down. Lou and I left. We later saw O'Gara in court, arrested for distributing Quaaludes.

I realized the ease with which we could burn through people selling drugs made me far too arrogant and confident. I let my guard down.

Fortunately, this wasn't Paterson or Newark. There the consequences could and likely would have been much more severe and deadly.

On June 13, 1972, 88 retail-level "drug dealers" were arrested in a five-square-mile town. Mystified by the sheer number of teenagers arrested over four months, the mayor commented, "I knew we had a few, we weren't completely clean, but I didn't think there were so many." [61]

Perhaps the most prophetic words came from one of those arrested. Commenting on the magnitude of the arrests and the arrest of two eighth-graders, "What good will it do? They'll all be fined and sent home again, and everything will be the same. They can't put all of us in jail."

And he was spot on. All received suspended sentences and probation.

Nobody went to jail. Lyndhurst was not Paterson, or Newark, or Trenton. This suburb was a predominantly white, blue-collar, middle-class community.

This teenager in 1972 knew what most adults feared to acknowledge in 2021.

Over the last 50 years, the war on drugs has cost the United States at least one *trillion* dollars—which indeed says something about the voracious American appetite for illegal drugs.[62] But even more egregious and revealing was the systemic racism that was exacerbated and showcased for all to see.

Rebranding the Oldest Profession

For those embarking on a career investigating public corruption, my advice is simple: enlist as informants, a stable of prostitutes who are well-positioned in the criminal underworld.[63] There are no better sources than those who corral politicians and political elites in the so-called "honey

61. Cook, Joan. *The New York Times. 1972.* "Drug Roundup Is Shock to Divided Town." June 18th. *The New York Times.* 1972. "2 Pupils Among 88 Arrested in Jersey as Sellers of Drugs." June 13th.

62. Pearl, Betsy. 2018. *Ending the War on Drugs: By the Numbers. Center for American Progress.* June 27th. Wright, Chapin. *The Star-Ledger.* 1986. "Drug Trade Thrives 6 months after Raid." August 17th.

63. Pollock, Kent. *The Philadelphia Inquirer.* 1975. "Wiretapping Case Set Precedent." August 5th.

trap."[64] And they certainly can alert you to the chatter on the street that will aid you in solving any number of other crimes.

As any street-wise detective will tell you, most prostitutes are in it solely for money. It may be to pay their rent, put food on the table, contribute to child-care costs, or advance their quest for a better quality of life. A smaller segment of the market is drug addicts who simply sell their bodies to maintain their addiction.

Every major city has its so-called tenderloin or red-light district. It is generally a city section that allows for a safe retreat to local motels or hotels. There is a relatively minimal police presence unless, of course, the town elders are demanding a police crack-down, usually for politically expedient reasons.

The police are all-too-familiar with the locations. Often they have made arrangements with hotel or motel management, which will alert them to the appearance of prostitutes and their more notable clients. If it involves public officials, it never hurts to have salacious material used for extortionate purposes. The so-called "honey trap" can often serve as the invisible mediator and adjudicator in dicey and politically precarious situations.

I learned the value of cultivating prostitutes at my first State Police assignment in 1967. The Fort Dix State Police Barracks territory included two military bases, Fort Dix Army and McGuire Air Force Bases. With soldiers and airmen always looking for a good time that usually involved women, Wrightstown and the motels that populated the area were havens for prostitutes.

Night clubs such as the Satellite Lounge and the Rex Lounge were magnets attracting prostitutes up and down the east coast.[65] All were searching for the cash-flush GI and for someone with whom to *share* it. With your traditional crimes such as breaking and entries, assaults, and robberies primarily investigated by the State Police, credible and reliable information sources were often critical to successful investigations.

---

64. Wikipedia: John le Carre' aka David John Moore Cornwell.
65. *Burlington County Times.* 2013. "Fire at Old Satellite Lounge is Suspicious." February 18th. Moran, Mark. *Weird NJ.* 2015. "Time Forgets the Satellite Lounge." November 8th.

My first station commander was SFC Joseph Rogalski. Upon reporting for duty with my classmate Tom Grabowski on August 28, 1967, Rogalski made it abundantly clear that you would have hell to pay if you violated the three rules he laid down.

The first was money. Don't take payoffs. Your career will be over before you know it.

The second was alcohol. No drinking on duty or hours before you reported to duty. And not while driving home, after a 48-hour shift.

Third, stay away from women who will entice, avail, or throw themselves at you for any number of reasons. That uniform and the authority it represents are natural aphrodisiacs.

These were *Rogalski's Rules*. Violate them at your peril. What Rogalski was signaling, of course, was the temptations that are endemic to the police environment, especially in this particular epicenter of vice and iniquity. One of many lessons I learned that Rogalski earlier opined was not part of my college education.

The station detectives were Jimmy Dowd and Lou Parisi. Living in the area, Dowd knew all the miscreants that made up the criminal underworld. If a building suspiciously burnt down, he knew who to contact to determine if arson was the cause. A body lying in the woods, usually someone within Dowd's or Parisi's orbit, could point them in the right direction. And breaking and entries were so commonplace that the newly-assigned recruits would do the initial investigation. Dowd or Parisi would follow up, usually with an arrest.

Of the hundreds of detectives that I had worked with over the decades, Jimmy and Lou instinctively understood the value of informants. "Work smart kid, and then working hard will come easy," was one of Parisi's favorite expressions to the younger Troopers.

Prostitution was rampant. These were primarily women who were living on the margins of society. It was an industry, albeit illegal, ripe for all sorts of corrupt and nefarious shenanigans. Absent a complaining victim; prostitution was impossible to police. Elaborate sting operations periodically were executed but merely clogged up an already over-burdened court calendar.

Which, of course, led to the next best thing: recruiting a stable of informants that you could call upon when there was a violent or politically sensitive crime. It's where I first learned about the value-added skill that prostitutes brought to the table.

As my career advanced, the lessons learned in this hub of human degradation and vice proved indispensable in investigating organized crime and public corruption. Whether it was Paterson, Dover, Newark, or the adjoining suburbs, you knew that the prostitution rackets were a viable source of valuable intelligence—providing any number of investigative leads.

Naturally, with any information garnered from criminals, the detective must critically evaluate the credibility and honesty of the source. To fall prey to the guile and cunning skills of a prostitute can result in self-deception, missed opportunities, and above all, sexual misdeeds. It was *essential* to corroborate all you were told, usually with documentary records, phone calls, and multiple independent sources.

Accordingly, when I was appointed the Pennsylvania Crime Commission Executive Director, one of my first mandates was to reassess our informant procurement and maintenance program. Realizing that we had a rather large geographic area and a limited staff to address the multitude of organized crime and public corruption issues, incentivizing the agents would be the only viable approach.

Informant management would be a priority. Who would be promoted or afforded additional compensation or favored perks was often a consequence of their investigative acumen. It was the only sensible way to augment and exponentially enhance our investigative capabilities.

Allentown, Pennsylvania, was a city that enjoyed a rather historical and rich reputation for prostitution.[66] Because of the inter-and intrastate highway system, a substantial amount of cargo flowed through Allentown. Motels and go-go lounges catered to the truckers, who often provided a viable client base for the prostitution rackets. Allentown was a prostitute's nirvana for many reasons, this just being one.[67]

---

66. Jenkins, Philip. *Pennsylvania History.* 1998. "A Wide Open City: Prostitution in the Progressive Era: Lancaster." vol. 65, no. 4, pp. 509–26.

67. I have relied to a large extent on FBI Agent Raab and Fritz, PCC Special Agent James Kanavy, Schultz, and Spear's superb investigative skills and memory on the Parenti era. *1990 Report: A Decade of Change.* 1991. *Pennsylvania Crime Commission.* March 30th. pp. 86–88, 222.

The reigning lord of vice in this city was John Parenti, a Russell Bufalino Mafia family member.[68] Parenti was high profile, flashy, and cultivated a publicly visible profile with politicians and law enforcement officials. It burnished his cachet, or so he believed.

Parenti was the "man to see" in Allentown if you needed something resolved. His sphere of influence ran the gambit, from legitimate businesses to gambling, loansharking, prostitution, and extortion.

Like his counterparts in other cities, Parenti would use the police to arrest the independent bookmakers and prostitutes unless they or their pimps were willing to pay tribute (i.e., protection) to him. Parenti had an outsized and brazenly-irreverent persona, which in large part, provoked his downfall.[69]

Ultimately Parenti was arrested and convicted of tax evasion and illegal gambling. A decision by the Bufalino Mafia Family (Scranton), the Genovese Mafia Family (New York), and the LaRocca Mafia Family[70] (Pittsburgh) restructured control of the rackets in Allentown. This restructuring resulted in partner-sharing arrangements that afforded the various local criminal groups a share in the loot that the vice rackets generated.[71]

With Allentown attracting prostitutes from other locales, the ability to operate with impunity and without generating unwanted attention from law enforcement could prove problematic unless you could acquire protection from law enforcement. Protection was usually accomplished

---

68. Russell Bufalino was one of the original mob bosses to attend the now infamous Appalachian Conference in 1957. Birbeck, Matt. 2013. *The Quiet Don: The Untold Story of Mafia Kingpin Russell Bufalino. Pennsylvania Crime Commission: 1970 Report*. 1970. July 2nd. p. 32.

69. *The Morning Call* (Allentown, PA). 1972. "Brief Filed For Appeal by Parente." June 27th. p. 11. *The Morning Call* (Allentown, PA). 1977. "Jury Finds Parenti, Fedock guilty in bookmaking." September 29th. p. 32.

70. *The New York Times*. 1984. "Figure in Pennsylvania Crime Dies at 82 in His Bed At Home." December 5th. Ove, Torsten. *Pittsburg Post Gazette*. 2000. "Mafia Long History Here, Growing From Bootlegging Days." November 6th. Wikipedia: John Sebastian LaRocca. Martens, Frederick T. 1988. *Pennsylvania Chiefs of Police Association Bulletin: Some Pennsylvania Mafia Folklore*.

71. *Pennsylvania Crime Commission*. 1991. *Organized Crime in Pennsylvania: A Decade of Change*. March 31st. pp. 86–87, 113, 138. *The Pittsburgh Press*. 1951. "$2,500 Champagne Bracelet Spouts from Spring on Bluff." July 10th. p. 1. *Pittsburgh Post-Gazette*. 1951. "Two Sentenced in Racket Case." April 26th. p. 5.

by working for a pimp or connecting with the police or the political power brokers. The Eastside of Allentown possessed all the attributes necessary to operate relatively unscathed.

Motels and go-go lounges owned or operated by local racketeers who paraded as legitimate businessmen and political operatives were located minutes off the main thoroughfares. Infamous for prostitution were the Airport Road motels and go-go lounges easily accessed from the principal highway—Route 22.[72]

According to "Shannon," one of our many credible sources, "there were tricks (prostitutes) and johns (their customers) driving through the parking lots like it was a supermarket . . . It was fairly common knowledge that the Airport Road motels were protected from raids by the police."

Insofar as the police conducted raids, they were often the result of information provided by the "connected" pimps or those looking to consolidate the market by arresting the independents who naively offered their services to unsuspecting clients. Exclusivity was garnered by those who subjugated themselves to the local powers-that-be, often so-called "legitimate businessmen."

These raids effectively allowed the police to take credit for enforcing the laws against prostitution while simultaneously allowing local racketeers to stabilize and organize the prostitutes through protection and extortion. *It was the classic distinction between vice enforcement and organized crime control*—and one often lost on those enforcing the laws against vice.[73] Or more to the point, the difference between organized crime and *Organized Crime*.[74]

---

72. *The Morning Call* (Allentown, PA). 1984. "7 Arrested on Drug, Prostitution Charges." March 8th. p. 18. *The Morning Call* (Allentown, PA). 1988. "Prostitutes Use Airwaves." April 10th. p. A1. *The Morning Call* (Allentown, PA). 2008. "3 Arrested in Internet Prostitution Sting." July 12th. p. 1. *The Morning Call* (Allentown, PA). 2010. "Allentown pimp admits running ring." April 29th. p. 7. *The Morning Call* (Allentown, PA). 2013. "Three women charged with promoting prostitution after sting at motels." November 29th. p. A13. *The Morning Call* (Allentown, PA). 2015. "Human Trafficking Convictions 2008-2012." May 10th. p. 12.

73. McCarthy, Bill and Mike Mallowe. 1983. *Vice Cop: My Twenty-Year Battle With New York's Dark Side.*

74. Dintino, Justin J. and Frederick T. Martens. 1983. *Police Intelligence in Crime Control: Maintaining a Delicate Balance in a Liberal Democracy.* pp. 33–57.

Select district court justices who were elected (vis-à-vis appointed) relied on local racketeer's political war chests. Campaign donations often laundered through local business associations assured their election or re-election. Their allegiances to these corrupt alliances were thus, secured.

Certain members of the police department, particularly those assigned to the vice squad, were well aware of these insidious and corrupt alliances. Those who were on the payroll of the vice lords who controlled the rackets saw this as an opportunity to ingratiate themselves with the political power-brokers, reaping the extra-legal benefits, of course.

Simply put, prostitution in Allentown was and remains the most stable, durable, and resilient business—bar none. It is a well-oiled machine that has defied periodic police crackdowns and suppression efforts.[75]

When independent prostitutes attempted to share in the spoils associated with the trade, they were arrested. Bail bond agents arranged for their bail, usually in concert with the local district justices.[76] For symbolic reasons, some would be jailed. Others would agree to work for a pimp, who would protect them from arrest and prosecution.[77] Sexual favors were given to select politicians, police officers, district justices, common-plea court judges, and prominent local businessmen. The system was corrupt from top to bottom.[78]

"Denise" was another of our "go-to" sources on the Eastside of Allentown. Conversant with the prostitutes that worked the Airport Road motels and go-go lounges and having established long-term relationships with their pimps and the racketeers, "Denise" was a fountain of

---

75. *The Morning Call* (Allentown, PA). 2014. "Lehigh Valley Prostitution Arrests in the Past 10 Years." July 13th. p. A13. *The Morning Call*. 1985. "2 L.V. Officials Seek Prostitution Solution." September 20th.

76. *The Morning Call* (Allentown, PA). 1979. "District Magistrate tied to federal corruption probe." December 9, 1979. p. 3.

77. *The Morning Call* (Allentown, PA). 1980. "Corruption Investigation Focuses on Prostitution." January 20th. *The Morning Call* (Allentown, PA). 1989. "Allentown Plans prostitution task force." September 2nd. *The Morning Call* (Allentown, PA). 1997. "Brader Murder is Still Under Investigation." July, 27th. p. 8.

78. In an exhaustive study of organized and corruption in Europe, the research found that "police corruption is the most common used throughout the European Union to facilitate prostitution. Along with drugs, the prostitution market is the key driver of corruption within the police." Gounev, Philip. *Center for the Study Of Democracy.* 2010. "Examining the Links Between Organized Crime and Corruption." September 15th. p. 135.

information. She had engaged in sexual relations with any number of district justices, police officers, and businessmen. As she would often say, an insurance policy allowed her to demand and receive VIP treatment when the situation commanded a favor or two.

Her meticulous records and incredible memory were validated repeatedly. The Commission sought the sworn testimony of those she had provided specific, irrefutable information during our periodic debriefings.

The more the Commission investigated, the more political blowback would come our way. Successive public officials, prominent attorneys, and local businessmen were not shy in their desire to defund the Commission. What began as an investigation into the prostitution rackets had morphed into open political warfare.[79]

On several occasions, the Commission was bluntly told that its funding would be denied if it continued investigating the vice rackets.[80] The FBI had initiated several investigations into corruption involving the district justices and their relationships to racketeers. They, too, were subjected to flurries of political intrusions and legal impediments.[81] Political retribution and intimidation had forestalled any substantive enforcement initiatives that would have imperiled the reign of the local vice operators and their political benefactors.

The vultures of vice were adept at warding off sustained initiatives that would upend this culturally embedded prostitution racket that seemingly defined Allentown's illicit political economy.[82]

---

79. *The Morning Call* (Allentown, PA). 1993. "Crime Report Comes Under Attack, Ritter, Preate Rap Tactics." April 29th. p. 7.

80. Carpenter, Paul. *The Morning Call* (Allentown, PA). 1993. "Crime Panel: It is difficult to pull strings. April 30th." *The Morning Call* (Allentown, PA). 1994. "It's A Crime That We'll Lose the Exposure." April 19th. In one instance the mayor's brother during a private hearing, warned that the funding for the Commission would be eliminated if we continued our investigation into the Allentown rackets. *Pennsylvania Crime Commission: 1992 Report*. pp. 30–38.

81. *The Morning Call* (Allentown, PA). 1981. "Witness Testifies in Joseph Trial." June 16th. *United States District Court, Eastern District, Pennsylvania. CR-81-0978 July 1981. USA. v. Joseph A. Joseph.*

82. In 2013, the New York District Attorney Office brought a case against a renowned prostitution network centered in Allentown, Pennsylvania, which miraculously escaped prosecution in Pennsylvania? *The New York Times.* 2013. "Father and Son Pimps Are Sentenced to 3 to 9 Years in Prison." July 8th.

Paterson, New Jersey, was no different.[83] The evolutionary pattern was much the same. Mafia members exercised control over the local rackets. Independents were arrested and extorted.

One of the principal vice operators in Paterson was John "Johnny" Ventura, owner of the La Vie en Rose, a renowned Mafia-meeting venue.[84] Ventura was indebted to the Genovese Mafia Family.[85] He was implicated in the Mafia-inspired murder of Paterson bookmaker Gabriel DeFranco—another cold case that remains unsolved today.[86]

Ventura exercised his Fifth Amendment privilege before a grand jury regarding this murder.

Ventura's illegal activities were well-known to the police and politicians. In testimony before the State Commission of Investigation, a video poker operator testified, "if I was going to operate in Paterson, I had to pay the right people," referring to Ventura.[87]

In one of his last run-ins with the law, Ventura was arrested for gambling and extortion with Lt. Raymond Zdanis of the Paterson Vice Squad and two other detectives.[88] Zdanis was the chief architect targeting prostitutes—mostly Black—that was operating independently in Paterson.

A co-defendant with Ventura and Zdanis was Raymond Kordja. Kordja was convicted in 1974 of protecting a Genovese Family gambling

---

83. *Paterson Press* (New Jersey). 2019. "50 Arrested in Paterson Prostitution Operation." July 4th. *The Star-Ledger*. 2019. "N.J. go-go bar owner, 8 others arrested in undercover prostitution bust, cops say." November 20th. *Paterson Press*. 2017. *The Record* (Hackensack, NJ). 1979. "Paterson Takes on Hookers." October 21st. p. 2; "Paterson Police Arrest 30 in prostitution sweep." June 26th. *The News*. 1971. "Arrest 10 in crackdown on Tavern Prostitution." October 23. *The News*. 1971. "Vice Squad Zooms in On Prostitution." March 24th. *The News* (Paterson, NJ). 1971. "Indictment Hits Motel Manager." December 30th.

84. New Jersey *State Commission of Investigation: Video Poker*. 1991. pp. 21–22.

85. *The Herald-News* (Passaic, New Jersey). 1991. "Paterson Cop Bribe Trial Delayed." September 6th.

86. *Asbury Park Press*. 1969. "Ventura Wasn't Suspect Prosecutor Tells Court." January 23rd. p. 6. *The News* (Paterson, NJ). 1969. "DeFranco Testimony Closes as Artist Rebuts Bar Story." February 1st. p. 9.

87. *New Jersey State Commission of Investigation: Video Poker*. 1991. pp. 21–22.

88. *The Bergen Record* (Hackensack, NJ). 1989. "Vice Cops Arrested for Payoffs." July 12th, 14th. *The Herald News* (Passaic, NJ). 1991. "Paterson Cop Trial Delayed." September 6th. p. 13. *The Record* (Hackensack, NJ). 1992. "2 Cops Get 7 Year Prison Terms." p. 1. Mendez, Ivette. *The Star-Ledger*. 1992. "21 Arraigned in sweep of mob-linked video gambling." June 25th.

enterprise while a detective in the Passaic County Prosecutor's Office. Finally, in 2008, Kordja was arrested for operating a prostitution ring.[89]

"Millie," a source I had developed over several years, knew the prostitution rackets in Paterson and its various "players." She knew everything about Ventura's nefarious relationships with the Paterson Vice Squad. She was well-aware of efforts to maintain the prostitution racket within the control of the Mafia. It was a classic case of the police being used to organize the prostitution rackets.[90] Either they paid Ventura and Zdanis for protection, or they were arrested.

Millie had no qualms discussing the murder of DeFranco. It was believed that DeFranco had become an informant and was about to expose Ventura's vast network of political connections. Co-operating with law enforcement usually resulted in a death sentence.[91] This was long before a witness protection program was enacted.

In what can only be described as a bizarre, convoluted, and ethically challenged investigation conducted by the Passaic County Prosecutor's Office, three people were charged with DeFranco's murder: a newspaper publisher, a police detective, and a bookmaker. Despite all of the hoopla, fanfare, and hysteria surrounding this case, no one was convicted.[92]

As one of the defense attorneys in the trial exonerating the three defendants pointed out, "Why Ventura wasn't investigated . . . Nobody ever investigated Ventura . . . This gangland part was never brought out . . . Was this put under the rug? [93]

89. Marko's. Kibret. *The Record* (Hackensack, NJ). 2008. "Dad, daughter charged in prostitution scheme: A very extensive operation authorities say." January 23rd.

90. Misse, Michel. *Estudos Avancados*. 2007. "Illegal markets, protection rackets and Organized Crime in Rio de Janeiro." pp. 139–57; Dintino, Justin J. and Frederick T. Martens. *Federal Probation*. 1981. "The Process of Elimination: Understanding Organized Crime Violence." vol. 45, no. 26.

91. Martens, Frederick T. *John Jay College of Criminal Justice*. 1973. *A Study of Organized Crime Homicides in New Jersey: 1960-1973*.

92. *The Morning Call* (Paterson, NJ). 1968. "Court Raps Bailey, Defers Decision." May 21st. *The Morning Call* (Paterson, NJ). 1968. "Bailey Isn't Popular Around the Courthouse." May 3rd. *The Morning Call* (Paterson, NJ). 1968. "Bailey Appeals Ouster from Murder Cases." May 4th. *Asbury Park Press*. 1969. "Newspaper Executive, Two Others Cleared of Slaying." February 7th. *The News* (Paterson, NJ). 1969. "Knew Defendants Says Counterfeiter." January 18th. Humphreys fired Muccio upon taking office, decades too late.

93. *The Home News*. 1969. "DeFranco Death a Gangland Execution." February 4th. p. 19. Both Vincent Hull and Burrell Ives Humphreys asked a similar question in the Carter-Artis triple murder prosecution, questioning why Eddie Rawls was not investigated by DeSimone?

As investigation after investigation has proven, the crime of prostitution does not occur in a vacuum. It is usually part of a panoply of other vice-related activities, murders and beatings, loan sharking, corruption, and the collateral crimes that involve criminal syndicates. [94]

Today there is a movement afoot to reinvent the term prostitution, transforming it into a form of legitimate labor that allows for all the protections afforded any other pariah industry.[95] In adopting the term "sex workers," there is a grudging recognition that a criminal justice approach has been counter-productive, allowing criminal syndicates to profit from the illegal trade of human smuggling and slavery.[96]

Naturally and understandably, there also is a significant backlash from women's rights groups. They argue that regardless of how the issue is packaged, it ultimately results in the exploitation of women.[97] "Prostitution is inherently violent . . . sex buying promotes sex trafficking, promotes pimping and organized crime, and sexual exploitation of children," argue the critics of legalization.[98]

Often cited is the *Nordic Model* as the answer to addressing the collateral consequences of criminalization. Again, the evidence is spotty.

---

94. Cameron, Lisa, Jennifer Seager, and Manisha Shah. *The Quarterly Journal of Economics.* 2020. "Crimes Against Morality: Unintended Consequences of Criminalizing Sex Work." September 26th.

95. The term "pariah industry" refers to those services rendered that may not be condoned by society but should not be criminalized. It was first introduced by Jerome Skolnick in his classic investigation of casino gambling. See Skolnick, Jerome H. 1980. *House of Cards: The Legalization and Control of Casino Gambling.* January 1st. Lister, Kate. *INews: The Essential Daily.* 2017. "Sex Workers or prostitutes? Why Words Matter." October 5th. *The Conversation.* 2018. "Who are we talking about when we talk about prostitution and sex work?" January 14th.

96. *Global Network of Sex Work Projects: Promoting Health and Human Rights.* Carol Leigh coins the term "sex work." See Nagle, Jill. 1997. *Whores and Other Feminists: Inventing Sex Work.* pp. 226-231. McKinley, Jesse. *The New York Times.* 2019. "Could Prostitution Be Next To Be Decriminalized?" May 31st.

97. Coulter, Saundra-Lynn. 2017. *Choosing the Nordic Model: Championing Women's Equality and Human Rights: Criminalize Johns and Pimps, not Women.* March. Powis, David. *Police Journal: Theory, Practices, and Principles.* 1964. "Males Living on the Earnings of Prostitution." October 1st. pp. 463–69.

98. McKinley, Jesse. *The New York Times.* 2019. "Could Prostitution Be Next To Be Decriminalized?" May 31st. Hughes, Donna M. *International Organization for Migration.* 2002. "Trafficking for Sexual Exploitation: The Case of the Russian Federal." June. Douthat, Ross. *The New York Times.* 2021. "Can the Left Regulate Sex?" July 24th.

Any number of caveats and conflicting interpretations permeates the research.[99]

New South Wales, Australia, recognized that corruption and control by organized criminal elements were endemic to this activity.[100] There, brothels are licensed and regulated, allowing for greater transparency. Nonetheless, even if regulated and controlled by the state, corruption is always a liability lurking in the background.

In the future, technology will play a central role in reshaping this industry. With a keystroke, liaisons between sex workers and their clients can be arranged. Ultimately the retail market will move from the streets to the suites. The residual effects this will have on police corruption will only be known over time.[101] Regardless, this industry, legal or illegal, will always be a viable intelligence source for law enforcement.

In the final analysis, legislators and policy-makers should answer the obvious question: Who should regulate sex work: the Mafia, vice czars, or the state?

While we endlessly debate how to civilly and responsibly address the "oldest profession in the world," a term rhetorically bandied about, let us not forget a simple lesson: laws can create black markets, and laws can eliminate black markets. As a society, the choice seems obvious. Getting there remains the struggle.

The Life-Blood of Organized Crime[102]

Gambling had been a steady money-maker for the Mafia. It has led to innumerable corruption scandals throughout our short history. It is studied incessantly, legalized incrementally, and now represents a sizable

99. Kingston, Sarah and Terry Thomas. *Crime, Law, and Social Change.* 2019. "No model in practice: a 'Nordic Model' to respond to prostitution?" May 15th. pp. 423–39. *The Conversation.* 2013. "The 'Nordic mode' of prostitution law is a myth." December 16th.

100. Sullivan, Barbara. *Journal of Law and Society.* 2010. "Regulating Sex/Work: From Crime Control to Neo-liberalism?" March. pp. 85–104. Queensland Police Service and Queensland Crime Commission. 1999. "Operation Krystal: A Strategic Assessment of Organized crime in Queensland." June. p. 51. It should be noted that Australia has 800 legal brothels, 350 illegal brothels that employ 16,000 sex workers, and generate industry earnings of $1.25 million.

101. *The Conversation.* 2017. "Technology drives the need to rethink sex work industry regulations." August 17th.

102. Ferentzy, Peter and Nigel Turner. *Journal of Gambling Issues.* 2009. "Gambling and Organized Crime—A Review of the Literature." June. pp. 111–55.

economic industry contributing to the national and regional gross national product.[103]

But that was not always the case. It took decades before we reacted to the apparent realization that illegal gambling would not disappear, regardless of how many bookmakers or policy operators are arrested, nor how many back-room casinos are raided.[104]

Gambling is a way of life in America, championed mainly by our frontier culture from our earliest days.[105] Once again, we resorted to an arrest and prosecution model to *defeat* this human inclination or, for some, uncontrollable frailty.

Undoubtedly, society's affinity toward criminalizing consensual (im)morality has often led to organized crime becoming its principal benefactor.[106] Anytime the law proscribes vaguely defined licentious behavior, the consequences will likely be an illicit market and an enterprise willing to take risks to meet the demand. Moral ambiguity in the promulgation of law *vis-a-vis* the public's prodigious appetite will result in systemic corruption over time. The socio-political and economic dynamics are that compelling and exacting.

Whether it was sports, numbers, policy, video poker, or casinos, gangsters and racketeers who have little to lose and much to gain saw an opportunity to make money and, in turn, accumulate political capital. And they took it. Often smaller gambling enterprises consolidated and became part of larger enterprises. In many instances, the small-time racketeer had little choice but to avail themselves of the financial resources and capital the Mafia had to offer.[107] They were often obligated to partner with the Mafia.

---

103. In New Jersey alone, four and one-half billion dollars were wagered just on sports in 2019, with 36 million deposited in the state's coffers. See *U.S. Sports Betting Revenue 2020.*

104. Rorie, Melissa. *UNLV Gaming Research and Review Journal.* 2017. "Regulating a Pariah Industry: The Need for a Responsive Approach in Gambling Markets." October 18th.

105. Hill, David. 2020. *The Vapors: A Southern Family, the New York Mob, and the Rise and Fall of Hot Springs, America's Forgotten Capital of Vice.*

106. von Lampe, Klaus. 2002. *Assessing organized crime: the case of Germany.* September. This is not limited to the United States. In Germany, von Lampe found that "the most common alliances between the underworld and the upperworld are the close relations between vice-entrepreneurs and public officials that have been found to exist in a number of cities throughout Germany." p. 22.

107. Anastasia, George. 2018. *Getting a Piece of the Mob's Action. Jersey Man.* August 9th. Goldstock, Ronald and Dan T. Coenen. *Cornell Law Review.* 1980. *Controlling the Contemporary Loanshark: The Law of Illicit Lending and the Problem of Witness Fear.* vol 65, p. 127.

Arresting bookmakers and policy operators usually was a game of metrics. They were easy targets, well-known to the community, and conducted their business relatively openly. If they were not connected, they were often the targets of a competitor who was.

Being connected meant that you had an "in" with the local police, the political elites controlling the police, or the Mafia. An independent gambling operation could not continue over a long period without police or political protection.

For decades, one of several gambling enterprises that proved invincible to law enforcement was Joseph "Newsboy" Moriarty, from Jersey City, New Jersey. "Newsboy" had partnered with John V. Kenny, the titular head of the Hudson County Democratic Party. Moriarty was immune from any enforcement by the law enforcement authorities in Hudson County until the late 1960s. Neither the Genovese nor Bonanno Mafia families, the reigning organized crime enterprises throughout Hudson County, New Jersey, could interfere with or crush Moriarty's lucrative gambling operation.[108]

For example, during Kenny's reign, Moriarty was invited to meet with the local Mafia bosses in Hudson County, New Jersey. The bosses had wanted to increase the odds on the numbers from 500-1 to 600-1. Moriarty politely entertained their proposal and caustically responded, "I'd never think of telling you how to run your business, don't tell me how to run mine." [109] Moriarty defied the Mafia's *request*.

This arrangement was also true in Scranton, Pennsylvania. There Elmo Baldassari, a local racketeer larger than life, controlled the illegal gambling that was part of the culture of Lackawanna County.[110] Baldassari's political connections were both notable and substantial.

Both Moriarty's and Baldassari's empires proved that political connections often trumped the Mafia's violent reputation.[111] Independent

108. Olszewski, Anthony. *Hudson County Facts.* 2009. "Jersey City's Master Numbers Banker, Joseph 'Newsboy' Moriarty." December 30th. *Farley v. $168,400. 97.* November 17, 1969.

109. Olszewski, Anthony. *Hudson County Facts.* 2009. "'*Newsboy' Moriarty at the Mob Meet.*" December 29th.

110. Potter, Gary W. 1994.*Criminal Organizations: Vice, Racketeering and Politics in an American City.*

111. Reuter, Peter. 1982. *The Value of a Bad Reputation: Cartels, Criminals, and Barriers to Entry.* December 1st. Massari, Monica. *Small Arms Survey* (Geneva). 2013. "Guns in the Family: Mafia Violence in Italy." pp. 74-101. Catino, Maurizio. 2019. *Mafia Organizations.*

gambling enterprises have continued to operate throughout the United States, utterly void of the Mafia's influence or control. Not only do "smart Mafia leaders cultivate friendly judges, sheriffs, and legislators for protection," so do local crime czars who recognize that alliances with political power-brokers usually spell the difference between success and failure. [112]

Baldassari operated an after-hours club frequented by the Bufalino Mafia Family members in one of the more legendary stories.[113] Having become rather rowdy, Baldassari instructed Bufalino to calm his henchmen down. Unresponsive, Baldassari ordered them out of his club. Here was a local racketeer dictating to a Mafia boss of Bufalino's infamous stature. Once again, it demonstrated the role of politics in organizing crime.[114]

Baldassari ultimately met his fate when the FBI arrested him for extortion.[115] Baldassari, unable to leverage his political and judicial connections, was held without bail, awaiting trial. While fuming in a 10 X 12 jail cell, Baldassari offered up a corrupt gambling/video poker payoff scheme. These were payoffs disguised as campaign contributions to the Attorney General of Pennsylvania.[116]

Paterson, New Jersey, on the other hand, was, as Ianni pointed out, controlled by the "mob."[117] The Genovese Mafia Family had infiltrated the police department's highest levels, the prosecutor's office, and the government.

112. Marshall, Jonathan. 2021. *Dark Quadrant: Organized Crime, Big Business, and The Corruption of American Democracy.* p. 80. Gardiner, John A. 1970. *The Politics of Corruption: Organized Crime in an American City.* Taylor Paul. *The Washington Post.* 1983. "Rizzo Says Police Acted Like 'KGB Agents' in Son-In-Laws Arrest."

113. Wikipedia: Russell Alfred Bufalino. *Patriot News* (Harrisburg, PA). 2019. "The Appalachian Meeting to Hoffa's disappearance: A Look back at the Bufalino crime family in Pa." May 22nd.

114. Ianni, Francis A.J. 1974. *Black Mafia.* pp. 107–99. Schulte-Bockholt, Alfredo. 2006. *The Politics of Organized Crime and the Organized Crime of Politics.* Vaaishnav, Milan. 2017. *When Crime Pays: Money and Muscle in Indian Politics.* January 24th.

115. Hambrose, John. *The Times-Tribune* (Scranton, PA). 1990. "Baldassari, Sons and Fourth Man Face Trial Dec. 3rd." November 3rd. Murray, L.A. *Sunday Sun.* 1991. "Baldassari Sentencing Due." June 2nd. Baldassari had afforded two federal judges and other public officials use of his Florida condominium on several occasions, resulting in their recusal and his case being transferred to another jurisdiction.

116. *The New York Times.* 1993. "Law Enforcer vs. Pennsylvania Crime Commission." May 14th. *The Christian Science Monitor.* 1994. "Pennsylvania Attorney General Accused of Ties to Poker Firms." April 13th. Martens, Frederick T. 2015. *We'll Make You An Offer You Can't Refuse: A Primer in the Investigation of Public Corruption.*

117. Ianni, Francis A.J. 1974. *Black Mafia: Ethnic Succession in Organized Crime.*

During my discussions with "Lil Hutch "involving the "Association"[118] and the LaPlaca Mafia organization, he obliquely mentioned the brutal torture and murder of Bobby Harris, the owner of the Blue Front Restaurant and Governor Bar and Grill—both known numbers venues.

Harris managed a significantly large policy/numbers enterprise in the Black community of Paterson. He butted heads with the Genovese Family. "Lil Hutch" chose not to elaborate on this murder, other than to say that there was no way the Blacks were ever going to be independent of Mafia control in Paterson. "They are just too strong . . . they own everybody . . ." referring to the Mafia and the politicians.

At the time, Tino Fiumara, a vicious up-and-coming *soldier* in the Genovese Mafia Family, asserted its dominance over its gambling interests in Paterson. Describing the macabre killing of Harris, federal authorities vividly drew a picture that was not pretty.

> His skull was crushed. His spine was broken. The ribs on his right side were caved in. Nine ribs on the left side were fractured, as was his right leg. For good measure, Harris was shot once in the chest. He was in the knelling position with his ankles tied to the back of his head with wire . . . He had [been driven around Paterson] trussed up . . . to make sure everyone knew that the Genovese family was very serious about its control of the bookmaking business in New Jersey.[119]

Not until I met with Ianni did I realize that he described Bobby Harris and this event in his book *Black Mafia*. Indeed, Ianni's description of the murder of Willie C. Squires (aka Bobby Harris), the fictitious name Ianni adopted, was virtually identical to what "Lil Hutch" had conveyed to me regarding the murder of Harris—mainly the part of Harris found tortured in the Meadowlands.[120]

---

118. The "Association" was a collage of Black vice entrepreneurs who organized in part, to resist Mafia control of the vice rackets.

119. Scarpo, Ed. 2014. *Decades of Mob Violence Behind Waterfront Case*. December 21st. *United States Senate. Hearings before the Committee on the Judiciary.* 1983. *Organized Crime in America.* February 16. pp. 219, 232. *The Morning Call* (Paterson, NJ). 1969. "Bullet Found in Body of Gambler." April 1st. p. 1. A similar murder of Alton Hughes, Newark's Black vice czar, occurred later in 1969. The killer was Mafia hit-man and Gambino soldier, Frank "Butch" Miceli.

120. Ianni, Francis A.J. 1974. pp. 72–106. Ianni refers to "Joe the Turk" in his chapter on Paterson. "Joe the Turk" or Joseph Hajar is in fact Emil "Bonesei" Esa.

In attempting to identify the body of a Black man found mangled in the Meadowlands, Ianni describes an open transmission over the police radio.

> I think it's that colored from down in Paterson who was muscling The Turk (Esa) . . . He used to work for The Turk (Esa) . . . Then . . . he split from The Turk(Esa) and tried to muscle The Turk (Esa) out . . . you push The Turk(Esa), you push Velia (Fuimara)) and when you push Velia (Fuimara), you push the organization . . . any [the N word] who's crazy enough to do that is going to get what Willie got.[121]

The Passaic County Prosecutor, John Thevos, refused to accept investigative jurisdiction over the murder of Harris, who was found dead in the adjoining county—Bergen County, New Jersey. Given Harris's significant role in Paterson's vice rackets, this refusal was a rather odd and astonishing public position to take by a prosecutor, given Harris's significant role in Paterson's vice rackets?[122] But one that made absolute sense when placed in the historical affinity of the Mafia's insinuation in the political culture of Passaic County and its' prosecutor's office.

Moreover, it sent a meaningful message to the underworld. Dispose of the bodies outside the jurisdiction of Passaic County, and we will look the other way. Thevos had a very cavalier approach to organized crime in a jurisdiction inundated with its' pernicious activities.

It was generally accepted that the Mafia had ensconced itself in the Prosecutor's Office and the Paterson Police Department. The County's chief investigator, Joseph Muccio, was connected to the Mafia.[123] He dismissed a gambling charge against Johnny Ventura, the maestro of vice in Paterson. But this was merely the tip of the iceberg.[124]

---

121. Ianni, Francis A.J. 1974. *Black Mafia*. p. 73.

122. *The News* (Paterson, NJ). 1969. "Husband's Secret Side Told by Harris Widow." April 1st. *The Morning Call* (Paterson, NJ). 1969. "Clifton Gambler Slips Away." December 17th.

123. Wren, Christopher and Margaret English. *Look Magazine*. 1970. "Murder—New Jersey Style: How gambling, incompetence and corruption led to the trials of five people for murders they did not commit." March 10th. *The News* (Paterson, NJ). 1970. "Thevos' 12 Year Tenure Ends." April 3rd. p. 4.

124. *The Herald News* (Passaic, NJ). 1969. "King Accuses Prosecutor's Aides." January 18th. p. 5.

One of the principal investigators in the Office was Raymond Kordja, the son of a state assemblywoman. Kordja was regarded as the Mafia's "go-to detective" in the Prosecutor's Office.[125]

Lt. Joseph Esposito, chief of Paterson's Vice Squad, and his deputy, Sgt. Donald Young, were on the payroll of Mafia member Peter LaPlaca, the Genovese Family's emissary to the rackets in North Jersey.

In a searing denunciation of the Passaic County Prosecutor's Office scandalous relationship with organized crime, a nationally-renowned magazine concluded, ". . . when Mafia rackets like gambling flourish in a climate of public fear and apathy and public officials do nothing, is there any reason to expect these officials to bring more honesty and competence to a murder investigation?" The article was referring to the murder of the bookmaker Gabriel DeFranco.[126]

It could have equally applied to the triple murder at the Lafayette Bar and Grill and the execution of Roy Holloway.

Once again, the Prosecutor's Office had become part of an ongoing pattern of incompetence, corruption, and official misconduct. It certainly portrayed New Jersey on the national stage in an unfavorable light.

With a mandate from the Superintendent of the State Police, David B. Kelly, to wreak havoc on the gambling syndicate that had gained control of both the Prosecutor's Office and Paterson's Vice Squad, raids were conducted of mob-controlled gambling operators.[127] This was a directive from the highest levels of State government, the governor's office.

Governor Byrne was the former Essex County Prosecutor, which was adjacent to Passaic County. He was well-aware of the ineptitude, dysfunction, and corruption that had infected the Passaic County Prosecutor's Office. It was not going to continue on his watch.[128] Byrne was committed to ensuring the integrity of the twenty-one prosecutor's offices

---

125. *The Record* (Hackensack, NJ). 2008. "Prostitution: Seven Arrested." p. A-1. Obituary of Raymond Paul Kordja. 2011. Festa Funeral Home. February 12th. *The News* (Paterson, NJ). 1973. "Esposito, Kordja Arraigned." June 29th.

126. Wren, Christopher and Margaret English. *Look Magazine*. 1970. "Murder New Jersey Style: How Murder, Gambling, and Incompetence Led to the trials of 5 People for Murders They Did Not Commit." March 10th.

127. *The News* (Paterson, NJ). 1973. "Esposito and Kordja Arraigned." June 29th.

128. Wice, Paul.

was first and foremost.[129]He was setting the stage to appoint an outsider as the prosecutor.

Following the State Police investigation, Burrell Ives Humphreys, an outlier not accountable to the political cronyism that permeated this office, was confirmed as prosecutor over the objection of the Democratic Party chairperson.[130]

Unfortunately, Humphreys had confronted an immutable culture. He, too, suffered the consequences that infected the body-politic of this office. The rest was history.

There is, of course, one common denominator that is criminalizing these vices have in common—corruption—both episodic and systemic. The historical record from New York to Chicago, St. Louis, Kansas City, Portland (Oregon), and Seattle is replete with stories that undermine the rule of law.[131]

Never-ending debates over criminalization, legalization, and decriminalization are waged among legislators, social scientists, and the public. Victims of these vices are arrested, prosecuted, and imprisoned. Cynicism, distrust of the police, and the debasement of our institutions of government are its dreadful consequences.[132]

Perhaps we should ask ourselves the obvious question. How many more police need to be arrested, prosecuted, and jailed before we realize these laws enable, encourage, and promote corruption on a grand scale?

---

129. Linky, Donald. 2014. *New Jersey Governor Brendan Byrne: The Man Who Couldn't Be Bought.* October 13th.

130. Pollak, Michael C. 1975. *Humphreys, a new kind of Prosecutor.* November 30th. p. A18.

131. Donnelly, Robert C. 2011. *Dark Rose: Organized Crime and Corruption in Portland.* Chambliss, William J. 2000. *Power, Politics, and Crime.* Hayde, Frank R. 2007. *The Mafia and the Machine: The Story of the Kansas City Mob;* Waugh, Daniel. 2010. *Gangs of St. Louis: Men of Respect.* Russo, Gus. 2002. *The Outfit: The Role of Chicago Underworld in the Shaping of Modern America;* Waugh, Daniel. 2010. *Gangs of St. Louis: Men of Respect. Wikipedia: Knapp Commission.*

132. It could be argued that the criminalization of the vices prevents the majority of the population from indulging in the behavior being criminalized. Laws reflect social condemnation of a particular behavior, usually what is believed to be an immoral act. Prevention is of course difficult to measure. Nonetheless, the argument is not necessarily one of criminalize or legalize, but rather one of regulation vs. incarceration. Even under the most rigorous form of regulation, corruption is inevitable but at least it is transparent.

Crack Cocaine Floods the Streets[133]

If there was ever a crime that demonstrated the systemic injustice in our criminal justice system, it is how crack cocaine was criminalized, prosecuted, and adjudicated.[134]

My initial foray into the world of crack cocaine was in 1985. Attending a conference in San Diego, California, a noted criminologist discussed the developing evolution of a substance referred to as "crack" that was inundating the streets of New York City.

This new method of cocaine refinement, which was essentially powder cocaine that was free-based and sold in rock form for three dollars a vial, had created a whole new niche market. Not only was this a highly lucrative reinvention for selling cocaine but believed to be quite addictive. Moreover, it could be secreted in ways that a traditional bag of cocaine could not.[135]

Returning to New Jersey, I queried the undercover agents who were then working with me about whether or not they had heard of "crack." No one had.

Several days later, Detective Roy Daniels, working undercover, came into my office. "It's all over the streets . . . crack cocaine is the new drug of choice," Daniels remarked.

Naturally, given the explosion of crack cocaine, we redirected our efforts to learning as much about "crack" as we could. Located primarily in the lower-socio-economic communities, vials of "crack" were selling for three dollars, making it easily affordable and accessible to the young.

---

133. Egan, Timothy. *The New York Times.* 1999. "CRACK'S LEGACY: A special report; A Drug Ran Its Course, Then Hid With Its Users." September 19th. Farber, David. 2019. *CRACK: Rock Cocaine, Street Capitalism, and the Decade of Greed.*

134. For a compelling documentary see Nelson, Stanley. Netflix. 2021. *Crack: Cocaine, Corruption & Conspiracy: A Brisk Look Back at a Crisis.*

135. *American Society of Criminology* (San Diego). 1985. "Directions in Cocaine Research." November, 15th. Johnson, Bruce D., Eloise Dunlap, Sylvie C. Tourigny. *Crack Distribution and Abuse in New York. National Development and Research Institutes, Inc. New York.* vol. 11, pp.19–57. Tierney, John. *The New York Times.* 2013. "The Rational Choices of Crack Addicts." September 16th. Chozick, Amy. *The New York Times Magazine.* 2014. "Carl Hart: 'Crack Wasn't The Real Problem.'" June 27th. Hart, Carl. 2013. *High Price: A Neuroscientists' Journey of Self Discovery That Challenges Everything You Know About Drugs and Society.* June 11th.

Dramatically described in the news media, babies being born to crack-addicted mothers. An instantaneous high was all but guaranteed, as was an addiction. Territorial wars between drug gangs were commonplace, adding to an immediacy to contain this scourge ravaging communities far and wide.[136]

Arrests of crack dealers, primarily minorities, were piling up. We were making more buys of crack than any other drug on the street. Its availability was pervasive. The criminal justice system could not contain it. Treatment facilities were overwhelmed. Another epidemic had foisted itself on the American public. Or that's what we were led to believe.

Naturally, the scourge of crack dens throughout American cities resulted in legislative action. A robust punitive approach was demanded before this newly-invented form of cocaine use and abuse could find its way into white upper and middle-class communities.

Federally, laws were passed distinguishing crack cocaine from powder cocaine—the latter the drug of choice among the intelligentsia, literati, and upper classes. States naturally followed.

Sentencing guidelines argued that 5 grams of rock cocaine should be subject to the same five-year minimum and mandatory sentence as a person selling 500 grams of powder cocaine. The logic was simple: crack was more addictive than powder cocaine; those involved in its distribution were more violent; the quality of life in communities where crack was sold suffered disproportionately from those communities where powder cocaine was distributed.[137]

This 100-1 quantity ratio resulted in a mass incarceration rate that has made the United States the largest penal institution employer in the

---

136. Blumstein, Alfred. *Journal of Criminal Law and Criminology.* 1995. "Youth Violence, Guns, and the Illicit Drug Industry." pp. 10–36. Fall. Ousey, Graham C. and Matthew R. Lee. *Journal of Research in Crime and Delinquency.* 2004. "Investigating the Connections Between Race, Illicit Drug Markets, and Lethal Violence, 1984-1997." November 1st.

137. *Stanford Law and Policy Review.* 2009. "Race, Drugs, and Law Enforcement in the United States." June 19th. *Missouri Law Review*, vol. 62, issue 4 (1997). "Criticism of Crack Cocaine Sentences Is Not What It Is Cracked Up To Be: A Case of First Impression Within the Ongoing Crack vs. Cocaine Debate." pp. 1–27.

world.[138] That this mainly affected the lower-socio economic classes of society was of little concern until 2005. Then the United States Supreme Court addressed in part this disparity.[139]

The Supreme Court found that the sentencing guidelines that mandated this apparent disparity were incompatible with the Sixth Amendment to the Constitution.[140] This disparity and a subsequent case ultimately addressed this inequity, contending that the sentencing guidelines were advisory and not binding.[141] However, it did not address the judiciary's broad discretionary power in sentencing crack cocaine defendants, who were eighty percent Black. A 2018 law, the *First Step Act*, authorized judges to reduce the sentences of those convicted of selling or possessing crack to ameliorate these blatant disparities.[142]

Today, the criminal justice system struggles with what is commonly referred to as mass incarceration and its attendant consequences.[143] The manifestations of systemic racism can be traced to the disparate manner in which we treat certain criminals and the crimes they commit.

It is characterized by a simple term: legislative, police, prosecutorial, and judicial discretion.[144] What is criminalized; who is arrested, prosecuted and incarcerated; and who is let go are at the heart of discriminatory and racially imbalanced enforcement.[145]

---

138. Alexander, Michelle. 2010. *The New Jim Crow: Mass Incarceration in the Age of Colorblindness*. Statistically, Russia incarcerates 334 inmates per 100,000 people versus the United States which incarcerates 639 per 100,000 people. See *Institute For Crime and Justice Research, World Prison Brief.*

139. Liptak, Adam. *The New York Times*. 2021. "Supreme Court Rejects Sentence Reductions For Minor Crack Offenses." June 14th.

140. *United States v. Booker, 543 U.S. 220* (2005).

141. *Kimbrough v. United States, 552 U.S. 85* (2007).

142. Federal Bureau of Prisons. *First Step Act (Public Law 115-39).*

143. Forman, James Jr. 2017. *Locking Up Our Own: Crime and Punishment in Black America*. Farrar, Straus and Giroux. April 18th. Alexander, Michelle. 2012. *The New Jim Crow: Mass Incarceration in the Age of Colorblindness*. *The New Press*. January 16th. Barkow, Rachel. 2019. *Prisoners of Politics: Breaking the Cycle of Mass Incarceration—(The Politics of Criminal Justice Reform).*

144. Vaidyanathan, Brandon. *The Public Discourse*. 2020. *Systemic Racial Bias in the Criminal Justice System is not a Myth*. June 29th. Gonclaves, Felipe and Steven Mello. *Princeton University: Working Paper #608*. 2017. "A Few Bad Apples? Racial Bias in Policing." March 6th. pp. 1–59. Jena, Anupam B., et. al. *The New York Times*. 2018. "The Benefit of Having the Same Name as A Police Officer." August 4th.

145. Barnett, Brittany K. 2020. *A Knock at Midnight: A Story of Hope, Justice, and Freedom*. Landau, Meryl Davids. *The New York Times*. 2021. "What Do Police Know About Teenagers? Not Enough." July 17th.

Until and unless we address both the explicit and the implicit bias that a culturally diverse society brings to the promulgation and enforcement of our laws, the reforms often promoted are nothing more than window dressing.

Waging Another Endless War with No Exit Strategy

Regardless of how one feels about applying the war metaphor to crimes of vice, the mental imagery is all-consuming. There are identifiable enemies, courageous and honorable soldiers, and collateral victims. The militarization of policing has created a mindset that often ignores a basic policing tenet: to serve and protect.

Most military strategists will tell you that an exit strategy must be contemplated when you begin a war. If not, you will be bogged down in perpetual violence that will only sap the morale of the soldiers waging war and the political will of the people paying for it.

Even the most die-hard proponents for continuing our prohibitionist policies can agree on one thing: the use and abuse of illicit and licit drugs have not declined.[146] If anything, the "war on drugs" has only exposed the depth and scope of corruption, systemic racism, decades of unnecessary deaths, unrelenting gang violence, and mounting overdoses. All are nurtured by a policy of prohibition that seems to ignore essential lessons from our not-so-distant past.[147]

More money, more resources, and more punitive laws are not the answer. The last fifty years have proven this to be a false and misguided narrative. The voters in the 2020 presidential election have demonstrated quite convincingly that the "war on drugs" is about to take an appreciable and well-deserved correction.[148]

---

146. Riley, jack and Mitch Weiss. 2019. *Drug Warrior: Inside the Hunt for El Chapo and the Rise of America's Opiod Crisis.* pp. 53, 148–50, 180.

147. McEnery, Thornton. *New York Post.* 2020. "Marijuana Stocks Surge as Investors Bet on a More Weed Friendly U.S." November 5th. Lopez, Oscar. *The New York Times.* 2021. "Mexico Set to Legalize Marijuana, Becoming World's Largest Market." March 10th.

148. Bromich, Jonah Engel. *The New York Times.* 2020. "This Election, A Divided America Stands United on One Topic: All Kinds of Americans have turned their backs on the destructive war on drugs." November 7th.

Pursuing a policy of an honorable, incremental disengagement seems to be a course that may address the concerns of the many interest groups that have a stake in this issue. Arguably, complete withdrawal of law enforcement resources would be impractical and unacceptable to a large swath of the general public.[149]

Mindful of the opioid crisis, any calls for decriminalization or legalization of drugs have been rightfully questioned by the appalling number of deaths—450,000-500,000 since 1996.[150] Nonetheless and certainly not trivializing these alarming numbers, a compelling case could and should be made for the complete legalization of all addictive and mind-altering drugs, if for no other reason than to ensure the chemical purity of the drug being ingested, thus mitigating fatal overdoses.

Legalization has demonstrated that drug makers and distributors' illegal and predatory practices can be severely sanctioned administratively, civilly, and criminally. Assets can be attached, and substantial fines levied.[151]

Enablers—doctors, marketing companies, pharmacists—can be held responsible for their egregious conduct. Exposure of the opioid crisis on the world stage, its greedy purveyors identified and ostracized, and its *philanthropic contributions* rebuked and banished from public glorification demonstrates the efficacy of regulation vis-à-vis prohibition.[152]

---

149. Templeton, Amelia. *OPB.* 2020. "Measure 110 would make Oregon 1st state to decriminalize drug use." October 14th. Fuller, Thomas. *The New York Times.* 2020. "Oregon Decriminalizes Small Amounts of Heroin and Cocaine; Four States Legalize Marijuana." November 4th. Jaquiss, Nigel. *Willamette Week.* 2020. "Former Gov. John Kitzhaber Urges 'No' Vote on Measure 110, Which Decriminalizes Drug Possession." October 19th. Roy, Eleanor. *The Guardian.* 2020. "New Zealand Votes to Legalize euthanasia . . . legalizing cannabis fails to find support." October 29th.

150. *GAO @ 100: Drug Misuse.* Barry, Colleen l., et. al. *International Journal of Drug Policy.* 2019. "Arguments supporting and opposing legalization of safe consumption sites in the U.S." pp. 18–22. Darke, Shane and Michael Farrell. *Society for the Study of Addiction: For Debate.* 2014. "Would legalizing illicit opioids reduce overdose fatalities? Implications from a natural experiment." pp. 1–6.

151. Hoffman, Jan. *The New York Times.* 2021. "Drug Distributors and J&J. Reach $26 Billion Deal to End Opioid Lawsuits." July 22nd.

152. *Forbes.* 2020. "#30 Sackler Family." December 16th. *Department of Justice.* 2020. "Opioid Manufacturer Purdue Pharma Pleads Guilty to Fraud and Kickback Conspiracies." November 24th. Coleman, Justine. *The Hill.* 2021. "OxyContin maker Purdue Pharma proposes $10B bankruptcy exit." Keefe, Patrick R. 2021. *Empire of Pain.* Macy, Beth. 2018. *Dopesick: Dealers, Doctors, and the Drug Company That Addicted America.* Quinones, Sam. 2015. *Dreamland: The True Tale of America's Opiate Epidemic.* Meier, Barry. 2003. *Pain Killer: A 'Wonder' Drug's Trial of Addiction and Death.*

Society will forever struggle with the misuse and abuse of drugs. Drug enforcement will never disappear.[153] The answer lies in how we have been mentally conditioned and culturally educated to address this inevitable reality.

There seems to be an awakening that the so-called "tried and proven" has accomplished just that—a proven failure.[154] Oregon, for example, has decriminalized the possession of heroin, cocaine, methamphetamine, and psychotropic drugs.[155] The marijuana market will become a thirty-four billion-dollar industry by 2025.

"Criminalization of drugs in the United States has failed by every metric," according to Alex Kral, an esteemed epidemiologist.[156] As the former Secretary of State George Schultz candidly and courageously stated, "This business of trying to curtail drugs by restricting supply has not worked . . . we've had forty years, it doesn't work."

Although the terms decriminalization and legalization tend to discredit and delegitimize efforts to mitigate the more harmful effects of prohibition, harm reduction modalities can have a similar impact.[157] They offer society yet another methodology to containing the disabling and often fatal consequences of drug abuse and addiction absent the draconian criminal sanctions that trail a person for a lifetime—however short that may be for some.[158]

---

153. It must be pointed out that even under the most stringent legal proscriptions, the law cannot address the vagaries inherent in the drug markets. See Keefe, Patrick Radden. *The New York Times*. 2021. "How Did the Sacklers Pull This Off?" July 14th.

154. Ostrowski, James. 1990. *The Moral and Practical Case for Drug Legalization*. BBC. 2020. "Plans for first US 'safe injection site' derailed again." February 28th. Hart, Carl. 2013. *High Price: A Neuroscientist's Journey of Self-Discovery That Challenges Everything You Know About Drugs and Society.* June 11th.

155. National Public Radio (NPR). 2021. "Oregon's Pioneering Drug Decriminalization Experiment is Now Facing The Hard Test." June 18th.

156. *Arnold Ventures.* 2020. "The Epidemic and the Pandemic: A Conversation with Epidemiologist Alex Kral on his Work Combatting Opioid Use Disorder." August 25th. Schultz, George P. *Issues on My Mind: Strategies for the Future.* 2013. "Drugs: The War with No Winner." Chapter 5. Sheff, David. 2013. *Clean: Overcoming Addiction and Ending America's Greatest Tragedy.*

157. Harm Reduction International. "What is Harm Reduction?" and the National Harm Reduction Coalition. "Principles of Harm Reduction." Vearrier, Laura. *Disease-A-Month.* 2019. "The Value of Harm Reduction for injection drug use: A clinical and public ethics analysis." May. pp. 115–42.

158. New Jersey is attempting this latest approach which is embodied in Senate Bill 3009 and Assembly Bill 4847. New Jersey Harm Reduction Coalition. 2020. "Harm Reduction Advocates, medical experts, and parents applaud introduction of harm reduction expansion bill." October 13th.

Diversion of drug (ab)users from the criminal justice system to harm reduction modalities that lessen the consequences of punitive sanctions twist the arc in the right direction.[159]

Unless we address the symbiotic relationship of law-making and law-breaking, our approach to drug control will be a return to the old normal at a time when a new normal is demanded.[160]

Perhaps the most enduring organized crime control strategy is one that recognizes this irrefutable albeit imperfect resolution.

159. Anderson, Steve. *The Eastern Illinois University Political Science Review.* 2012. "European Drug Policy: The Cases of Portugal, Germany and The Netherlands." vol. 1, no. 1. Article 2. It might also be pointed out that many drug users are also drug pushers, and many prostitutes are drug users. This complicates the diversion model, making it less amenable to public acceptance. Boyer-Dry, Margot. *The New York Times.* 2021. "What's The Best Way to Protect Sex Workers?" July 24th.

160. Johnson, Kirk. *The New York Times.* 2020. "In The Pandemic, a Shifting Ballot Debate on Legalizing Drugs." October 26th.

3

Terrorism Strikes Home

Pursuing a New Jersey State Police career in the sixties provided me with a birds-eye view of the radical social change enveloping America. The war in Viet Nam was attracting widespread anti-war protests. The civil rights movement was in its nascent stages. Violent crime was at an all-time high. Riots were consuming our major cities. Domestic terrorist groups were killing police, robbing banks, and creating social mayhem. In the demoralizing words of Barry McGuire, we were on "The Eve of Destruction." It was cultural kaleidoscope that invaded all our beliefs in "domestic tranquility."

The executions of Trooper Werner Foerster on the New Jersey Turnpike[1] and Trooper Philip Lamonaco in Hope, New Jersey,[2] were my initial foray into the worlds of intelligence and domestic terrorism.

Werner and Phil were the victims of an onslaught of terroristic violence directed at the police, financial institutions, and the business community. These groups, the Symbionese Liberation Army (SLA), the Black Liberation Army (BLA), the Black Panthers, the United Freedom Front (UFF), and others, were committed to radical and violent social change.[3]

---

1. *Officer Down Memorial Page. Trooper Werner Foerster.* May 2, 1973. *Asbury Park Press.* 1973. "Trooper's Killer Hunted by Police." May 3rd. Johnston, Richard J.H. *The New York Times.* 1974. "Trooper Recalls Shooting on Pike." February 14th.

2. *Officer Down Memorial Page, Trooper Philip Lamonaco.* December 21, 1981. Hanmley, Robert. *The New York Times.* 1981. "Highly Decorated State Trooper Slain on I-80." December 22nd.

3. Chepesiuk, Ron. 1995. *Sixties Radicals, Then and Now: Candid Conversations With Those That Shaped the Era.*

They believed selective violence was the only way to address the wrongs that state institutions had inflicted on the masses. Today, we politely and therapeutically refer to these miscreants as *victims* of the radicalization process.[4]

So it was when I was on a flight to San Francisco in 1972. A gentleman sitting next to me commented on a book I was reading. Written by the renowned criminologist Donald Cressey, *Theft of the Nation* was the fundamental architectural framework for what is now labeled "the war on organized crime."

He commented on the title, remarking, "That looks interesting . . . what's it about?" I responded, "a book on organized crime, the Mafia." "Interesting," . . . he replied . . . "do you think there is a Mafia?"

Unsure of where this conversation was going, I responded, "well, there seems to be an awful lot about it in the newspapers," to which he immediately retorted, "don't believe what you read in newspapers. "He then asked, "Why are you going to San Francisco?"

I referred to my time at Travis Air Force Base in Fairfield, California, and my affinity toward San Francisco—where I left my heart, mimicking Tony Bennett's iconic ballad. I was attending a conference on crime there.

He said that he, too, had served in the Air Force as a judge. He introduced himself—"my name is Leonard Weinglass."[5]

I immediately recognized the name. For the remainder of the flight, we discussed his career. Still sporting a beard and relatively long hair, I consciously avoided discussing my career, feeling my unkempt appearance would put him at ease. Anyway, I wanted to know more about him than I wanted him to know about me.

He told me that he was representing a client in San Francisco who was on trial for murder. Her name was Angela Davis.[6] Again, I recognized the name immediately.

---

4. Smith, Brent L., et. al. National Criminal Justice Reference Service. 2016. "Identity and Framing Theory, Precursor Activity, and the Radicalization Process." January.

5. Weber, Bruce. *The New York Times.* 2011. "Leonard Weinglass, Lawyer, Dies at 77; Defended Renegades and the Notorious." March 24th. Ironically, the son of Kathy Boudin, whom Weinglass unsuccessfully defended in the Brinks Armed Car Robbery in Nyack, N.Y., is now the District Attorney of San Francisco—Chesa Boudin.

6. Bradley, Kimberly. *The New York Times.* 2020. "East Germany's Love Affair With Angela Davis." October 26th.

Davis was on trial for killing four people in a shootout at the Marin County Courthouse. Davis allegedly supplied the guns used in the shootout. Represented by Weinglass and phalanx of attorneys, Davis was ultimately acquitted.[7]

As the attorney for Davis and other revolutionaries at the time, I queried him why he chose to defend those who wish to destroy the institutions that we, as military veterans, vowed to protect? His response was, "that's the reason we both joined the service . . . to protect the legal system and the rule of law . . . everyone has a right to effective counsel, even those who may want to destroy it . . ." or words to that effect.

When the plane landed at San Francisco International, Weinglass and I shook hands, wished each other well, and departed amicably. I never did tell him what I did for a living.

Shortly after that, I transferred to the Major Crime Unit. Several weeks later, Trooper Werner Foerster was executed on the New Jersey Turnpike. Arrested was Joanne Chesimard, a member of the Black Liberation Army (BLA).[8]

At the time, the State Police had scant information on the BLA.[9] I was dispatched to the New York City Police Department to gather as much intelligence as possible on the BLA. Driving through the Holland Tunnel, I would periodically reflect on that unexpected meeting with Weinglass. My world was now a mirror image of his. I was part of a legal system that allowed me to investigate the urban terrorists Weinglass saw as his obligation to defend.

The BLA was composed of members of the Black Panthers, a group of Black activists or militants from Oakland, California, who were intent on liberating Blacks from "the oppression and repression that the white, capitalist-imperialist society had imposed upon them."[10] The New York City Police, as had the FBI, developed dossiers on its leaders and members.

---

7. Stern, Sol. *The New York Times*. 1971. "The Campaign to Free Angela Davis and Ruchell Magee." June 27th.

8. It should be pointed out that Angela Davis visited Chesimard when she was incarcerated and started a gofundme account on her behalf.

9. Burrough, Bryan. 2016. *Days of Rage: America's Radical Underground, the FBI, and the Forgotten Age of Revolutionary Violence*. April 5th. *Maryland State Police: The Black Liberation Army*. October 1991. W-97-00384.

10. Wikipedia: Black Liberation Army.

The NYPD had infiltrated its ranks with several undercover agents I had the opportunity to speak with during my visits.

The NYPD was a leader in its approach to domestic terrorism. Their intelligence collection methods were perhaps the most advanced in the world. Undercover agents infiltrated these subversive groups, informant development techniques routinely honed to perfection, wiretaps used responsibly and prudently, and management dedicated to ensuring the effective use of their resources. They were certainly the *crème-dele-crème* of intelligence.

Joanne Chesimard, who later went by Assata Shakur, James Coston, and Clark Squire, was identified as a BLA member.[11] As its nominal leader, Chesimard was the only female who took up arms against the police as far as they knew.

At the time, the BLA was under surveillance, suspected of killing several New York City police officers.[12] One of the undercover detectives had infiltrated the group. He was a recent graduate of the police academy, having never worn a police uniform. His courage and street acumen were unmatched. He was a role model few in my career could come close to emulating.

There was, of course, a reluctance to share too much intelligence with me. The detectives were well aware of the probability that the defense attorneys representing the defendants in the execution of Werner would request all the reports, records, and documents that were part of this investigation. Intelligence reports could and likely would fall under this rubric. Sources of information, informants, wiretaps, and undercover agents could be exposed. Methods compromised. And lives placed in jeopardy.

As a consequence, written documents could only be read, not disseminated. While there were many conversations with the detectives who were intimately involved in the investigations of the BLA, they repeatedly cautioned me on taking information that would later be discoverable. Nonetheless, the intelligence verbally provided was nothing short of staggering.

---

11. *The Guardian*. 2014. "Assata Shakur: from civil rights activist to FBI's most wanted." July 13th.

12. Burrough, Bryan. 2015. *The Untold Story Behind New York's Most Brutal Cop Killings*. April 21st.

Murders and bombings, as many as seventy, across the country attributed to the BLA. Two New York City police officers were assassinated by the BLA one year before Werner's execution. Five more a year before that. The level of chaos and mayhem in the 1970s reflected an era of lawlessness that would make today's disturbances and riots look tame.[13]

Having collected as much intelligence as possible and permissible for consumption by another law enforcement agency, I returned to New Jersey bearing a comprehensive knowledge of the BLA. It dovetailed in many respects with the revolutionary rhetoric that I was accustomed to when I frequented the coffee houses and folk music venues in the San Francisco bay area. Marxist ideology, anti-government rants, and violence directed at the police were the themes that populated this domestic terrorist movement.

In the meantime, the MCU was assembling the case against Chesimard and Squire. Crime scene pictures and measurements memorialized the crime scene. Discarded weapons located, secured, and inventoried. Blood-stained clothing was preserved and processed. Witnesses were interviewed. Fingerprints were lifted from the vehicle and the weapons. Subliminal memories resurrected through hypnosis. No stone was left unturned.

Months later, I received a document from one of the detectives I met at the NYPD Intelligence Division. It was a letter written by Chesimard. In it, she writes,

> I am a black revolutionary, and by definition, that makes me part of the Black Liberation Army. The pigs [referring to the police] have used their newspapers and TV's to paint the Black Liberation Army to be vicious, brutal mad dog criminals . . . It should be clear . . . that we are victims . . . for every pig that is killed in the so-called line of duty, there are at least 50 black people murdered by the police . . . We must defend ourselves and let no one disrespect us. We must gain our liberation by any means necessary. We must fight on!!![14]

13. Burroughs, Bryan. 2015. *Days of Rage: America's Radical Underground, the FBI, and the Forgotten Age of Revolutionary Violence.* April 7th.
14. Chesimard, Joanne. *The Black Scholar.* 1973. "To My People." October. pp. 15–18.

This document was undoubtedly a welcomed piece of evidence, at least for the prosecution. I suspect it was of little consolation to Chesimard's defense attorneys. In her own words, it consciously demonstrated a predisposition to use whatever means necessary to resist arrest. Furthermore, it could impeach any testimony she might give if and when she took the witness stand, or so I thought.

Chesimard had a team of five attorneys, two of which were the most prolific and renowned defense attorneys in America. Raymond Brown, who had also represented Rubin Carter at his first trial, was considered the dean of the New Jersey defense bar. [15] William Kunstler, of course, defended many of the political activists charged with crimes during the sixties and seventies.[16] Claims of ineffective counsel were essentially moot. Chesimard and Squire had some of the best attorneys the defense bar had to offer.

Chesimard did take the witness stand. She claimed that she was wounded while attempting to surrender. She pinned the murder of Werner on Costan, who died in the shoot-out, and Squire, convicted in an earlier trial.[17] A classic defense. Her only defense.

Concerning her writings, Judge Theodore Appleby was adamant that the trial not be a political circus. The testimony was limited to the murders of Trooper Werner Foerster and Costan and the wounding and attempted murder of Trooper James Harper. This ruling by the judge recognized the danger of pursuing a line of questioning that would likely be prejudicial. [18] Belonging to a radical liberation organization would only inflame the juror's implicit bias. And a conviction likely would be reversed in the appellate courts.

However, the judge did agree that if the defense opened up this line of questioning, the writings and exhortations of Chesimard were fair game. The defense attorneys never did. There was no mention of the BLA. It was a brilliant judicial decision in retrospect.

---

15. Wikipedia: Raymond A. Brown.

16. Wikipedia: William M. Kunstler.

17. Kavanaugh, Reginald. *The Home News* (New Brunswick, NJ). 1977. "Chesimard Claims Innocence." March 16th. Kavanaugh, Reginald. *The Homes News* (New Brunswick, NJ). 1977. "Doctor Supports Testimony." March 17th.

18. *The Home News* (New Brunswick, NJ). 1977. "Tale that wasn't told at trial . . ." March 26th.

Chesimard was convicted of murdering Werner and her accomplice, James Costan. Both died in the shoot-out. Chesimard also was convicted of the attempted murder of Trooper Harper. While she maintained her innocence, the physical evidence was compelling and overwhelming.

Chesimard was sentenced to two consecutive life terms served in a high-security federal prison in West Virginia.

With the closing of this federal facility in 1978, Chesimard was transferred to the Clinton Correctional Facility for Women in New Jersey, which primarily housed medium to low-risk offenders. Less than two years later, Chesimard escaped from the Clinton facility, aided by armed members of the BLA. Smuggled to Cuba through a circuitous route, she remains there until this very day.

A two million dollar reward for her capture and return to the United States is still outstanding, encouraging any mercenary who has the courage and skills to effectuate her return.[19]

Clark Squire, her co-defendant, remains in federal prison in Cumberland, Maryland. He is not eligible for parole until 2032, although he has appealed his parole date to the New Jersey Supreme Court.[20]

The crime scene where Werner was brutally executed now reflects his name—The State Trooper Werner Foerster Memorial Exchange. It is and always will be a worthy tribute to a Trooper who served with dignity and humility.

Domestic Terrorists Strike Again[21]

It was December 21, 1981, my oldest son's twelfth birthday. I had left Division Headquarters in West Trenton, New Jersey, early that day to celebrate. As I was pulling into my driveway, over the radio came that dreaded call, "Trooper Down."

Philip Lamonaco, whom I had known personally, stopped a vehicle on Interstate 80 in Hope, New Jersey. Unbeknownst to him at the time,

---

19. Wikipedia: Assata Skakur aka Joanne Chesimard.

20. Wikipedia: Sundiata Acoli aka Clark Squire. Chesler, Caren. *The Washington Post*. 2021. "A Former Member of the Black Panther Party seeks parole nearly 50 years after he was convicted of murder." March 13th.

21. Stark, John. 1993. *TROOPERS: Behind the Badge*. pp. 203–50. Devlin, Ron. *The Morning Call* (Allentown, PA). 1987. "Shooting Was Turning Point For Radicals." January 4th.

the car's occupants were members of the Sam Melville-Jonathan Jackson Unit, a domestic terrorist group responsible for bank robberies and bombings on the east coast. This group shared allegiances with the BLA both philosophically and through physical and telephonic contact. Ultimately it had changed its name to the United Freedom Front (UFF).

At the time, I was in the Intelligence Bureau, dedicated to investigating organized crime and public corruption. We had very little information about this group. Through our sources in the Central Security Unit, we learned pretty quickly who they were, what they represented, where they resided, and how they operated.

Richard Williams and Thomas Manning were the occupants in the vehicle that Phil had pulled over.[22] After a brawl on the highway, which on-coming motorists witnessed, Phil was executed. The killers had escaped to Pennsylvania and subsequently separated and dispersed to other locales.[23]

Again, the MCU was tasked with the investigation, protecting the crime scene, gathering all the physical evidence, and ensuring that it was inventoried correctly and secured. Once again, a remarkable demonstration of the State Police's professional investigative skills.[24]

Investigating terrorist organizations was and is indeed one of the most challenging assignments. Usually, these criminal organizations comprise persons who have long-standing, personal, one-on-one relationships. Seldom are you able to recruit informants? Their ideological commitment to a cause usually outweighs any financial incentives.[25] Infiltrating their ranks is nearly impossible. Nonetheless, lacking real-time information, Pagano and Dintino agreed that an undercover operation might elicit leads to determine where Phil's assassins were hiding.

Colonel Pagano made it a dedicated mission to avenge the murder of Phil. In addition, Pagano's brother Lester died in an unfortunate

---

22. Thompson, AK. *Selected Essays on the Culture of Revolt.* 2006. "They Never Crushed His Spirit: A Tribute to Richard Williams." January 10th.

23. *State of New Jersey v. Richard A. Williams, 377 N.J. Super. 130, 871 A.2d. 744* (2005).

24. The New Jersey State Police hosts an Advanced Homicide Seminar at Princeton University annually.

25. Smith, Brent L., et. al. 2006. *National Institute of Justice. Pre-Incident Indicators of Terrorist Incidents: The Identification of Behavioral, Geographic, and Temporal Patterns of Preparatory Conduct.* March.

vehicular accident during this investigation. Pagano committed endless resources to catch those who assassinated Phil.

Capt. Charles Coe was in charge of the overall investigation. As many as fifty-plus detectives were assigned to this investigation over time.

Dintino, recognizing the lack of real-time information on the where-abouts of Manning and Williams, had asked me who I thought might be used to infiltrate this insular terrorist organization. Dintino knew that absent developing informants willing to cooperate, the most likely inves-tigative approach would be developing probable cause to effectuate elec-tronic surveillances of Manning's and Williams' immediate associates, friends, and family members. Sally Stoddard, the mother of Williams' children, would be a likely person of interest.[26]

Immediately I thought of a colleague whom I had worked with in the Narcotics Bureau. At the time, there were few undercover agents that I had more respect for than Detective Sergeant Jack Cole.[27]

Cole was an exceptionally experienced undercover agent. He was well-respected for his investigative acumen. Cole was methodical, ob-sessive, and tenacious. Give him a goal, and there was no wall that he couldn't climb, go around, or go through. And Jack was well thought of by Pagano, whom he had worked for in the Narcotics Bureau.

Insofar as this would not be your typical undercover assignment, Cole would be asked [as opposed to ordered] if he was amenable to un-dertaking a project that would upend his life?

Now we were talking about *deep undercover.* It would require months, presumably and optimistically only six, away from Cole's family. No nights nor weekends home. At best, there could only be telephonic com-munication with members of his family. Visits would seldom be. He would physically relocate to the Boston, Massachusetts area. He would attempt to make contact with members of the UFF and their associates. It was dangerous and had all the earmarks of placing Cole in physically challenging, emotionally wrenching, and legally precarious situations.[28]

---

26. *Sallyann Stoddard v. United States of America, 710 F.2d 21* (2nd Cir. 1983). Janson, Don-ald. *The New York Times.* 1986. "Prosecution Rests Case in Slaying of Trooper." December 21st.

27. Both Cole and former State Police Detective David Leonardis afforded me their time and knowledge in addressing the investigative anomalies that permeated this massive investigative undertaking.

28. Interviews conducted on May 23, 30, 2021 of Jack Cole in New York City.

Cole would not have a cover agent to respond to his requests twenty-four seven. He was essentially on his own, left to his own devices, and constrained only by his wits. Classic protections and restrictions were no longer relevant.

Needless to say, when Jack discussed this with his wife, Barbara, she was less than enthusiastic or understanding. It turned out to be the end of Jack's marriage.

While working undercover in Boston, Jack insinuated himself in the world that Williams and Manning had once occupied. He traveled throughout New England, respited in Canada, and even attended meetings with their former colleagues. He had insinuated himself in their world, just as we expected. Unfortunately, Williams and Manning had wholly divorced themselves from their former associates, family, and friends.[29] They remained incommunicado, denying their former UFF colleagues and sympathizers any insight into their whereabouts.[30]

Dintino instructed me to maintain regular contact with Cole, a virtually impossible task given Jack's propensity to disappear for days and weeks at a time. I would receive sketchy updates, but Jack was Jack. He was not one to follow routines. Cole was his own man. It's what made him who he was—an exceptional undercover detective yet challenging to manage.

Weeks, months, and years had passed. Information on the whereabouts of Manning and Williams was rare and often inaccurate. Many false alarms, all pursued. Ignoring any lead could be a missed opportunity. After two years in deep undercover, and with no credible leads developed, Jack surfaced and returned to New Jersey. Assigned to work with the detectives that comprised this unprecedented investigative undertaking, Cole became their intelligence officer.

Then in 1984, there was a significant break in the case. A U-Haul storage facility manager in Binghamton, New York, had discovered a tranche of weapons and documents in one of the pods. The FBI quickly

---

29. They did stay in contact with one former associate, Raymond Luc Lavasseur, who was wanted by the FBI for a number of bank robberies. Lavasseur was also a fugitive from justice. Lavasseur was the original leader of the UFF.

30. *The Boston Globe.* 1982. "The Old Melville-Jackson Gang Continues to Elude the Law and The Woman in the Midst of the Hunt." September 12th. *The Boston Globe.* 1984. "To Vermont Friends, Man They Knew Was No Criminal." February 26th.

determined that the guns and papers had been stored there by Raymond Luc Levasseur, a close associate and confidante of Williams and Manning.

Stumbling on a magazine addressed to Jack Horning, at 122 Mount Pleasant Street, Derby, Connecticut, Troopers Richard Touw of the New Jersey State Police and Michael Nockunas of the Connecticut State Police initiated a classic "shoe-leather" investigation. Through a series of neighborhood interviews in Derby, Touw and Nockunas ultimately struck the proverbial "mother lode."

Jennifer Browne, a babysitter for Horning's children, had in her possession a family picture. Upon seeing the picture, Touw and Nockunas immediately identified the male and female as Raymond Levasseur and Pat Gros, his wife. Browne told Touw and Nockunas that Paula Horning was involved in a motor vehicle accident while Jennifer was in the car driven by Horning.

Searching through the accident reports maintained by the local police department, Touw and Nockunas uncovered a six-year-old accident report that involved a vehicle driven by one Judy Hymes, an alias that Gros was using. Jennifer Browne was a passenger in the car.

The report in hand, Patricia Glabb, a New Jersey State Police communications dispatcher, began tenaciously researching the name "Judy Hymes" through the national motor vehicle indices. Glabb found a "Judy Hymes" in Columbus, Ohio. Hymes recently had purchased a vehicle. This discovery ultimately led the FBI in Ohio and a contingent of State Police from Connecticut, Rhode Island, and New Jersey to a post office address in Columbus, Ohio.[31]

After almost three weeks of exhausting round-the-clock surveillances at a post office drop-box, FBI agents and State Troopers observed Gros retrieve mail from the post office.[32] Following her over one hundred

---

31. Burroughs, Bryan. 2015. *Days of Rage: America's Radical Underground, the FBI, and the Forgotten Age of Revolutionary Violence.* pp. 531–36. Typically, the investigative scenario related by Burroughs differ substantially from that reported in Wren's description of events as they unfolded (Wren, George J. Jr. 2009. *Jersey Troopers II: The Next 35 Years (1971-2006).* pp. 479–82.

32. It should be pointed out that the relationship between the FBI and the Troopers assigned to this investigation left much to be desired. There were unfortunately, inter-agency rivalries that resulted in leads not being pursued immediately, surveillances going astray, and the typical personality conflicts.

miles to the house of Raymond Luc Lavasseur and his family in Deer-field, Ohio, the FBI and troopers struck gold.

Lavasseur was on the FBI's most-wanted list for a series of bank rob-beries.[33] With the arrest of Lavasseur and Gros, the investigation was re-energized. They located Richard Williams through telephone calls made to a house in Cleveland, Ohio. Williams and family members were surrounded and surrendered to the FBI, Cleveland Police, and the State Police.[34]

Coincidentally, Manning was en route to Lavasseur's house to cel-ebrate Williams' birthday. Forewarned by Williams' wife, Manning and his family avoided capture just as the police were closing in.

Six months later, in April of 1985, Thomas Manning was arrested by the FBI in Virginia Beach, Virginia.[35]

Extradited to New Jersey to stand trial for the murder of Phil, both Manning and Williams were convicted. Their convictions were upheld on appeal, again attesting to the State Police's professionalism and skill.[36]

In 2005, Williams died in prison. Fourteen years later, Manning met a similar fate.

Phil's son, Michael, now dons the uniform that once was worn by his courageous father—a living legacy of which Phil would surely be proud.[37]

By the way, Jack met his current wife while working undercover in Boston. He has been happily cohabitating and married for twenty-nine years.

---

33. Burroughs, Bryan. 2015. *Days of Rage: America's Radical Underground, the FBI, and the Forgotten Age of Revolutionary Violence.* pp. 514–29.

34. *The New York Times.* 1984. "F.B.I. Arrests 4 Fugitives in Ohio in 1981 Slaying of New Jersey Trooper." November 5. Wren, George J. Jr. 2009. *Jersey Trooper II: The Next 35 Years (1971-2006).* pp. 478–82.

35. McNair, Jean. 1985. *Associated Press. 10 Most Wanted Fugitive Lived Quietly Before Arrest, Neighbor Says.* April 25th.

36. *State v. Manning, 234 N.J. Super 147* (1989).

37. Miglis, John. 1995. *In the Line of Duty: Hunt for Justice* is a movie that describes the investigation which led to the arrest and convictions of Manning and Williams for the murder of Trooper Lamonaco.

The Act of International Terrorism That Changed the World

Life, as does death, has a cruel way of visiting the unforeseen on the unsuspecting. One of the analysts, Joelle, came into my office, sitting at my desk on the 23rd floor of the iconic art-deco McGraw-Hill building in what was once known as Hell's Kitchen. "Fred, did you hear a plane struck the World Trade Center?" "No, I responded, who told you?" "My mother just called . . . said it was a small aircraft."

In less than several minutes, we heard sirens wailing throughout the city. Unable to witness the smoke pouring out of the WTC, we turned on the television in an adjacent office. It indeed appeared to be more than a small aircraft that had struck the tower of the trade center. A gaping hole could be seen through the billows of smoke.

As we watched what was later determined as an act of international terrorism unfold, a second aircraft struck the remaining tower. At this point, we realized that this was more than an accident—it was an attack on one of the most recognized structures in one of the most famous cities in the world. We were about to confront an enemy that dared challenge America on its' soil.[38]

With the 9-11 attack on the WTC, a new era in addressing terrorism was about to unfold. Security of buildings, aircraft, critical infrastructures, airports and seaports, electrical grids, and computer technologies were about to undergo radical proctology.

Passed were laws to address electronic surveillance missteps. A prison to house international terrorists off mainland USA, presumably to constrain the reach of United States jurisprudence, was transformed. And a beefed-up international and domestic intelligence effort was about to be initiated, transforming the FBI into a domestic intelligence-gathering entity.

Having begun my position as Director of Corporate Investigations at Thacher Associates, located in the heart of mid-town Manhattan, we

---

38. Eight years earlier, the WTC had been bombed by international terrorists. Targets were hardened, never expecting an attack from the skies. Greenspan, Jesse. *HISTORY: Remembering the 1993 World Trade Center Bombing.* September 1, 2018.

were summoned to the offices of Thomas "Toby" Thacher and Joseph "Joe" DeLuca, its' principals.

We discussed the role of the Mafia and corruption in addressing the devastation that consumed the site of the WTC.[39]

Known for the systemic corruption of the construction trades in New York, it was only a matter of time that the Mafia would find a way to profit from the chaos and disarray that this vile act of international terrorism wreaked on the city and the country.

In meetings with the Mayor's office, the Port Authority, and the City's Department of Investigations, a plan of action was promulgated. Four zones or quadrants within the site of the WTC were designated. Four integrity monitoring firms were selected. Each quadrant was assigned to a general contractor responsible for searching and recovering persons who may have been killed or maimed in this attack. The general contractor would be obligated to retain an integrity monitoring team accountable for preventing Mafia infiltration. An outside accounting would audit the costs. This arrangement was an experiment never before undertaken on such a grand scale.

As this process was unfolding, DeLuca asked me, "Did you hear they haven't been able to find Fred Morrone?" I hadn't. I reached out to several colleagues in the State Police. They knew Morrone was at the site but were unaware of his status. Days later, I learned that Fred had died entering the North Tower, courageously directing its occupants out through the emergency stair-wells. He died as the building collapsed.[40]

Fred and I served together in the State Police, both in the Intelligence Bureau. Responsible for investigating the solid waste industry in New Jersey—an industry that was ripe for criminal exploitation by organized crime—we had developed credible sources and criminal informants who educated us on the evolving role of the Mafia in this industry. During

---

39. "The more things change, the more they stay the same," see Rosenberg, Rebecca. *The New York Post*. 2020. "Ex-Construction exec pleads guilty for role in $15M Bloomberg bribery scheme." October 6th.

40. Goldstein, Richard. *The New York Times*. 2001. "Fred V. Morrone, 63, Is Dead. Lead Port Authority Police." September 27th. *The Desert Sun*. "Fred V. Morrone."

these investigations, Fred and I lectured throughout the United States. We testified before Congress on the subject matter.[41]

Our relationship was more than that of mere colleagues. We traveled together throughout Europe. We both worked in the casino industry and would often meet for dinner in Atlantic City. Our families would converge at the Jersey Shore.

When Fred was appointed the Superintendent of the Port Authority of New York and New Jersey Police, we routinely shared information regarding the Mafia's role in the construction trades. The "Port" had several construction projects at the airports that Thacher Associates was selected as their monitor to investigate. I was an instructor at his police academy. It proved to be a 30-plus year personal relationship culminating in our last dinner with his wife Linda on an evening in late August 2001 in Saddle Brook, New Jersey.

As I stumbled around and over the rubble that was at one time, two 110-story skyscrapers, I would often reflect on the "last supper" we shared just weeks earlier. Linda, concerned about her health should it falter, was more troubled about Fred and how he would survive? They indeed were "joined at the hip."

Often, I would sit on a piece of twisted steel and say a prayer on Fred's behalf. Or attend the Sunday morning mass conducted by Father Brian, thinking of Fred's last terrifying minutes on this earth.[42]

Fred's remains were finally found. He was interred at the Memorial cemetery at State Police headquarters in West Trenton. In his honor, the Fred Morrone Memorial Award is presented annually to "those who have displayed outstanding leadership and contributions in strengthening the security of the nation's airport, seaport, cargo, and transportation industries."[43]

It was a horrific ending to a brilliant career. But knowing of Fred's commitment to his religion, his faith in the Lord, and his trust that

---

41. *United States Congress: Committee on Energy and Commerce.* 1981. "Organized Crime Links to the Waste Disposal Industry: Testimony of Lt. Col. Justin Dintino, Sgt. Fred Morrone, Sgt. Fred Martens, and Deputy Attorney General Steven J. Madonna." May 28th. vol. 4, pp. 6–39.

42. *Irish America.* 2002. "Father Brian Jordan: Comfort at Ground Zero." April/May.

43. *Bulk Transporter.* 2007. "Guliani to receive Morrone Memorial Award." June 4th.

Linda and his family are well, there is no doubt in my mind that Fred is resting in peace.

Assigned to oversee the activities of an Australian construction company, Bovis Lend-Lease, Bill Rogers, Rod Leith, several other colleagues, and I were tasked with mitigating both Mafia influence and infiltration as well as the corruption that plagued the construction trades. It was a challenging assignment, but given our knowledge of organized crime and construction-related corruption, Thacher Associates was well-prepared and equipped for what was about to come our way.[44]

As with any national emergency, fraud, abuse, and corruption are endemic to the chaos that reigns. No-show jobs, inflated invoices, double-billing, inoperable equipment moved to the site. They billed, ghost-trucking of debris from the site, sabotaging equipment, and of course, threats of violence mainly directed toward non-union labor were likely to occur.

Given the rigorous oversight of the WTC, there was little doubt our presence and the protocols established had prevented or mitigated Mafia infiltration.[45] Why risk engaging in fraud at the WTC when the costs of being sanctioned elsewhere were now negligible? With the enormous investigative resources devoted to the WTC, it was doubtful that other construction sites in the city would be closely monitored and investigated. Rationality and logic dictated. The Mafia adjusts to changing market conditions seamlessly and swiftly. There's a reason its' called *organized crime.*

I would often engage Vito, the Teamsters steward, in conversations. Vito secured the vehicular entrance to the site directly outside the Thacher-manned trailer. Vito, 6-2 with shoulders as broad as a commercial refrigerator, ensured that a Teamster drove any trucks entering the site. New York was a labor union city, and Vito ensured that the Teamsters received their share of the federal government's allocation. No one knew or understood the going-on at the site better than Vito.

Naturally, Vito was quite cautious and selective in what he conveyed to me. His only interest was the welfare of his union members. Vito had

---

44. Thacher Associates, LLC. Company Profile. Also see K2 Integrity "Construction and Real Estate Risk Management."

45. Short, Martin. 1996. *Crime Inc.: The Story of Organized Crime.* pp. 269–75.

his eyes and ears positioned throughout the site. Nothing would escape his sphere of influence.

While working on reports in our office trailer, out of the blue, in bursts Vito.

"All roads lead to Texas," Vito excitedly announces! "What are you talking about, Vito?" I asked. "Just watch the news tonight . . . not one fucking truck will enter or leave this site if what is about to happen happens . . . ," Vito bellowed.

Days would pass, and nothing on the evening news regarding "all roads lead to Texas." Then one evening, the broadcaster announced that the Giuliani administration had solicited the Bechtel Corporation from San Francisco to oversee the clean-up of the WTC. Vito, of course, was livid.

Bechtel was a non-union international general contractor. Many of its Board members were steeped in classic Republican politics. If Bechtel was contracted to oversee the recovery process, Vito anticipated non-union companies permitted to work on the site. In Vito's world, that was a non-starter.[46]

Bursting into the trailer days later, Vito asked, "Did you see the news last night?" "I did. They are bringing in a company from San Francisco to oversee the clean-up," I responded. "Not if we have anything to do with it, "Vito retorted. "We told Giuliani if Bechtel comes in, not one fucking truck will enter or leave this site . . . we will shut the site down . . . Tell Bush this is our city, not his."

Bechtel quickly and quietly disappeared. The price tag for their anticipated engagement was never publicized.

And Mafia influence? Never found anything substantial that would have imperiled the cleanup—which finished two months early and $250,000 under budget.

I guess you could say, between Thacher and Vito, we were a success.

We prevented organized crime from profiteering.

46. SFGATE.com. 2001. "N.Y. rejects Bechtel / City Had Considered using S.F. firm to manage cleanup." December 11th. McCartney, Laton. 1989. *Friends in High Places: The Bechtel Story: The Most Secret Corporation and How It Engineered the World.*

Louis Auricchio Mafia "capo"

Major William J. Baum, Dr. Francis Ianni, and Det. Fred Martens,
New Jersey State Police Headquarters, West Trenton, New Jersey

Bergen County Mafia round-up

Gov. Florio swearing in Justin Dintino, wife Doris

Changing of the guard—Col. Dintino and Col Pagano.

Meritorious Service Award, 1971, Col. David B. Kelly

Organized Crime Seminar, Sea Girt, New Jersey, 1983

Col. Justin J. Dintino

Maj. Joseph A. Rogalski,
author of *Rogalski's Rules*

Special Agent Rockey, Director Martens, Special Agent Ditmore,
William D'Elia Contempt Hearing in Harrisburg, 1988

G. Robert Blakey, Fred Martens, Charles Rogovin, Ralph Salerno

Executive Director Martens and
Vice Chairman Rogovin

Dsgt. Cliff Colye, Det/Lt. F. Martens, Dsgt. Al Taggert

Det. L. Churm, Dsgt. C. Coyle, Det/Lt. F. Martens, Det. V. Modarelli

Willie Rinaldi and Martens undercover, 1971

World Trade Center, 2001

Det. Patrick Aramini, N.J.S.P., Gen. Victor Kovalev, Col. Sergi Roukhlyadev,
Capt. Valdimir Knyazev, Martens, Regional Dept. of the Struggle Against
Organized Crime, Belarus, May 1991

Martens, U.S. Air Force, 1962

Martens, Travis AFB, 1962

Martens, N.J. State Trooper, 1967

Gen. V. Kovalev, Capt. V. Knyazev, Exec. Dir. Fred Martens,
Col. S. Roukhlyadev, Belarus

Knyazev, Roukhlyadev, Kovalev, Ronald Goldstock, Director, NY OCTF

Maria Coppola, Reception for Belarus Dignitaries, Wantage House

Martin Aronchick a/k/a Robert DeNiro a/k/a Al Pacino

Knyazev, Dintino, Kovalev, Roukhlyadev, Morrone

N. J. State Police: Ground, Sea, and Air.

4

The Organization of Crime

With New Jersey rocked by one political scandal after another, Col. David B. Kelly engineered one of the country's boldest organized crime control initiatives.[1] Establishing an Organized Crime Bureau and an Intelligence Bureau, complemented by a Special Prosecutions Unit staffed with deputy attorneys general, the New Jersey State Police was quite serious about containing the political damage caused by organized crime.

The cherished informal courtesy of "home rule"—the sacred cow of New Jersey politics—gave way to unfettered state intervention without acquiescing to the whims of political party bosses. Political machines that governed local and even state politics were ignored. We were told to go wherever the crimes and crime bosses were plying their trade. The more urban counties of Passaic, Hudson, Essex, Bergen, Camden, and Atlantic, were no longer "off-limits." Simply do your job!

In the course of patrolling in rural Millstone Township, New Jersey, on July 13, 1968, unremarkably, I cited Salvatore Profaci Jr., the nephew

---

1. Sackett, Russell, Sandy Smith and William Lampert. *Life Magazine.* 1968. "The Congressman and the Hoodlum." August 9th. *The Record* (Hackensack, NJ). 1967. "Sills Disagrees on Probe Call." December 6th. Robinson, Donald. *The New York Times.* 1970. "Jersey Leaders Deny Mafia Ties Implied on Tapes." January 8th. Hoffman, Paul. Newjerseymafia.getnj.com. "The Tale of Two Tapes: DeCarlo's illegal operations required protections—and bought it, all over the state." Dubill, Bob. *The Daily Register* (Red Bank, NJ). 1970. "Prominent Figures Are Tied to Mob." January 7th. Stern, Herbert J. 2012. *Diary of a DA: The True Story of the Prosecutor who Took on the Mob, Fought Corruption, and Won.* Wren, George J. Jr. 2009. *Jersey Trooper II: The Next 35 Years (1971-2006).* p. 76. *Asbury Park Press.* 1970. "Mob, Top N.J. Officials, Tied Again in FBI Logs." January 7th.

of the late Mafia boss, Joe Profaci, for a traffic violation.[2] As I requested his driver's license and registration, he belligerently asked, "What the fuck are you bothering me for?" At that point, I advised him that he was under arrest for using "loud and profane language," a disorderly person's charge under New Jersey's criminal code. It was at that point, after handcuffing Profaci and placing him in my vehicle, that he stated, "I'll take care of you."

Conducted in a one-room courthouse in Millstone Township, New Jersey, Profaci retained Michael Querques, one of the most prominent criminal defense attorneys in New Jersey. As the principal witness against Profaci and represented by Clinton Cronin of the Office of Attorney General, I testified to Profaci's tirade. Profaci, of course, denied it under direct testimony.[3]

Testifying as character witnesses for Profaci were Middlesex County Assemblyman John Selecky and East Windsor Police Chief Joseph Michinsky.[4] Cronin essentially eviscerated their testimony when he questioned them about their knowledge regarding Profaci being "caught" digging a grave in a remote part of Millstone Township months earlier.[5] Both sheepishly admitted to knowing about this incident.

Profaci was found guilty and assessed a nominal fine. He appealed the conviction to the Appellate Court, which affirmed his conviction. The court gratuitously pointed out that threatening a law enforcement officer is a crime and could have been levied.[6] Seeking relief from the State Supreme Court, Profaci finally was vindicated. The law, loud and profane language, was ruled unconstitutional.

---

2. *Asbury Park Press.* 1969. "Profaci: A Land Empire." August 13th. It is appropriate to make a distinction between Salvatore Profaci, Jr. and Salvatore J. Profaci, the latter who lived in Holmdel, N.J. and was the son of Mafia boss Giuseppe "Joe" Profaci. On August 15, 1969, I observed Anthony Zerilli at the home of Salvatore J. Profaci. Zerrilli was the son of the Mafia boss that ruled Detroit, Joseph Zerilli. Salvatore J. Profaci was married to a Zerilli. Anthony Zerilli was in business with the mayor of Jersey City, N.J., Thomas Gangemi. Salvatore J. Profaci was picked up on a now infamous recording, saying, "Good fellows don't sue good fellows. Good fellows kill good fellows." Reference: Button Guys of the New York Mafia, Salvatore J. Profaci—"The Prodigal Son."

3. *State v. Profaci, 56 N.J. 346* (1970). June 26th.

4. *The Daily Home News* (New Brunswick, NJ). 1969. "Crime Prober: Lot of Trouble Ahead." January 8th.

5. *The Home News* (New Brunswick, NJ). 1968. "Brennan Names His Names." December 31st. Baud, Chris. *The Trentonian.* 1970. "Entirely Too Comfortable with the Jersey Mafia." January 17th.

6. *Asbury Park Press.* 1969. "Conviction of Profaci Upheld." September 6th.

Unbeknownst to me at the time, but two other cases were winding their way through the courts. One involved the arrest of a Genovese Mafia soldier, John DiGilio, for loansharking. Intervening on DiGilio's behalf was a state Assemblyman, David Friedland.[7]

The other case involved State Senator Sido Ridolfi, who was involved in a business arrangement with a member of the Bruno Crime Family of Philadelphia.[8]

On December 11, 1969, Deputy Attorney General William J. Brennan III made an imprudent and intemperate comment before the Sigma Delta Chi newspaper fraternity.[9]

Alleging that certain legislators were "too comfortable with organized crime," the State was rocked by scandal. The Legislative leaders demanded that Brennan "put up or shut up," Kelly came to Brennan's defense.

Summoned to Troop "C" Headquarters in Princeton, N.J., I met with Lt. Lacey of the State Police Intelligence Bureau and Brennan. Queried as to the circumstances regarding the testimony of Selecky and Michinski, I reiterated my testimony and the testimony of Profaci's character witnesses. Driving back to the Tennent Barracks, all I could ponder was how this might affect my continued employment in the State Police? I never anticipated a routine traffic stop would evolve into a state scandal involving some of the most politically powerful politicians in New Jersey.

Brennan courageously withstood a withering examination by the Legislature. He provided them with the intelligence the State Police had collected on Selecky, Ridolfi, and Friedland and their relationships with these respective organized crime figures. Not forgiven for his perceived political indiscretion, Brennan ultimately was forced to resign his position.[10]

The Legislature censored Selecky, Ridolfi, and Friedland.

---

7. *The Home News* (New Brunswick, NJ). 1970. "Prosecutor Denies Perira Charge He Knew of Pay Off." April 8th.

8. Soda, Ralph. *The Home News* (New Brunswick, NJ). 1969. "Senator's Partner Linked to Mafia." January 11th.

9. *United Press International. 1968.* "Brennan Names 3 New Jersey Solons Tied to Mafia." December 31st. Saxon, Wolfgang. 2004. *William Brennan 3rd, 71, Leader of New Jersey Bar Association.* May 21st.

10. Sullivan, Ronald. *The New York Times.*1969. "BRENNAN RELIEVED IN CRIME INQUIRY; Accuser of Six Legislators in Jersey is reassigned by Attorney General Brennan Is Relieved as Prosecutor in Jersey Inquiry." January 7th.

Confronting the body-politic proved to be impolitic—a lesson that proved decades later to be the ruling ethos regardless of the jurisdiction or who the political party in power is.

As is often said, "no good deed goes unpunished."

The Campisi's: A Renegade Clan[11]

My initial introduction into the world of organized crime came about quite fortuitously. While working at the Little Falls State Police Barracks, which housed the Narcotics Bureau and the Organized Crime Bureau, I became acquainted with Lt. Walter King. Division Headquarters had dispatched him to oversee the investigations into the rackets in Paterson, New Jersey.

Often I would meet with King to discuss the information that I had gleaned from my sources. King was well-aware of the shenanigans orchestrated by the Paterson Vice Squad. He recognized that some detectives in the Organized Crime Bureau had become too familiar with the Vice Squad detectives and were compromised, either wittingly or unwittingly.[12]Over time King and I had developed a personal relationship that opened up doors for me at Division Headquarters in West Trenton, New Jersey.

One day, Major Howard Graff, who was in charge of the Criminal Investigation Section, called me into his office. Naturally, as a young detective with no rank, meeting with a State Police major was quite an honor and privilege, especially in those days.

"Detective," he said, "how would you feel about establishing an organized crime homicide analysis unit within the Major Crime Unit?" I had no idea what Graff meant. Graff then told me that there were many mob-related murders throughout the state that remained unsolved. He believed that they were likely inter-related. Graff felt that if someone would be willing to gather and analyze all the information collected in these investigations, cases could be re-investigated. If prosecuted, it

---

11. Hoffman, Paul, and Ira Pecznick. 1976. *To Drop A Dime: The Mafia's Hit Man's Uncensored Story.*

12. Rudolph, Robert. *The Star-Ledger*. 1991. "Former Wayne administrator admits bribe guilt." November 27th.

would put a crimp in organized crime. The opportunity sounded great, but I had no idea where to begin.

Nonetheless, I agreed to do it. Passing up an opportunity when presented in this manner would have not only been impolitic but career suicide.

I was transferred to the Major Crime Unit, which DSFC Herbert Ulbrich commanded. When Ulbrich was told by Graff what he expected of me, Ulbrich was as much in the dark as was I. Nonetheless, Ulbrich gave me free rein to develop the concept known as "organized crime homicide analysis." He encouraged me to visit other police agencies that were employing this relatively new concept.

New York City Police Department's Intelligence Bureau was, of course, my first choice. There I met with several detectives who were assigned to investigate mob-related murders. As they would often say, "we may not solve the murder, but the intelligence we would gather is indispensable. A mob-related murder tells you about the internal operations of a Mafia Family and can lead you to other sources and informants."

It was a lesson that served me well as I embarked on this relatively new adventure. The more I read, the more I realized that Graff might have been on to something. Mob-murders were seldom solved. The classic saying was, "so long as they kill themselves, who cares?"

But with the passage of the Racketeering Corrupt Organizations Act (RICO) in 1970, if a murder or a kidnapping, among other enumerated crimes, was committed in furtherance of a criminal organization, this constituted a pattern of racketeering. In other words, a murder without convicting anyone of the actual murder was sufficient to include in a racketeering prosecution.[13] RICO was now the nuclear weapon in the "war against organized crime."

Graff, either knowingly or simply intuitively, recognized the implications of RICO long before federal and state prosecutors had implemented it?[14]

---

13. *HG.org. Legal Resources. Legal Articles. What is RICO? The United States Department of Justice: Criminal Resource Manual #109.*

14. Taplin, R. Clinton. *The Bergen Record* (Hackensack, NJ). 1980. "How The State Police Put The Mob on Trial." June 1st.

While leaving the NYPD's Intelligence Bureau, one of the detectives called me to the side. He gave me the phone number of a former NYPD detective who was now a consultant for the newly-proposed Off-Track Betting (OTB) consortium. His name was Ralph Salerno.

Salerno was a former detective sergeant in its intelligence division. He had decided to take early retirement at twenty years.[15] Proffered as a walking encyclopedia on organized crime, I contacted Salerno and arranged to meet with him in his office at OTB. I advised him what I was attempting to accomplish. He could not have been more supportive. Reaching into his desk, he pulled out a paper he had written. The title was "The Conspiracy of the Gangland Murder." It was just what I needed to invigorate and focus my inquiries into mob-murders in New Jersey.[16]

As I became more familiar with the concept, I began visiting law enforcement agencies throughout the state and along the east coast that collected information on mob-related homicides, most of which remained unsolved. Meeting with John Sweeney of the New England Organized Crime Intelligence System, I was educated on collecting and analyzing mob-related murders.[17] Sweeney also pointed out that undertaking intelligence investigations into mob-related homicides opened up witnesses and sources that would never be interviewed when conducting a formal homicide investigation. He only reaffirmed Graff's belief that there was a pattern to many of these homicides. This pattern would envelop the higher echelons of these organized crime enterprises and networks.

Collecting and reading through the voluminous reports that I had gathered, it was apparent that I would need to interface with the State Police Intelligence Bureau. Of course, territorial boundaries, even in the State Police, were often difficult to break down. Nonetheless, I was not poaching arrests. Hence I was not threatening. Cooperation was grudgingly given and generously received.

---

15. *The New York Times*. 2003. "Ralph Salerno, a Police Expert on the Mafia, Dies at 78." October 21st. Salerno, Ralph F. and John F. Thompkins. 1969. *The Crime Confederation*.

16. Marks, Peter. *The Star-Ledger*. 1981. "State Police intensify mob 'hit' probes." *The Record* (Hackensack, NJ). 1980. "State to Put the Mob on Trial." June 1st.

17. Letter dated December 14, 1972 from Major Howard Graff to John Sweeney citing the New England Organized Crime Intelligence System as "one of the most progressive on the east coast."

After several months, Major Graff had asked me to address the Organized Crime and the Intelligence Bureaus on what I had learned. Standing before hundreds of years of experience sitting in the audience was an intimidating experience. Surprisingly, the lecture went over quite well. Or at least I thought it had. Ultimately, I was assigned to work with the Organized Crime Bureau on an investigation that they had just initiated.

The Campisi's had developed a reputation for engaging in deliberate and unprovoked violence that not only included those involved in the rackets but innocent witnesses and bystanders. They had no regard for the unspoken rules that governed the traditional Mafia Families. They were essentially a renegade family comprised of blood relationships but not truly part of the Mafia. Fathers, sons, cousins, and in-laws constituted the family's criminal hierarchy.[18]

Instructed to partake in several meetings at the Hightstown State Police Barracks, I listened intently as Lt. Walter Decker, who headed up the investigation, outlined the investigative strategy.[19] I was mesmerized by the talent, taking copious notes that I would later translate into flow charts and timelines.

Detectives Ray Castellano, Tony DeMasi, Dominick Trocchia, Joseph Yachimack, Charlie Kuyl, and several others whose names escape me were the crème of the crop. Again, it was an unforgettable experience that would fully bode well in my understanding of organized crime.

This investigation was not the so-called low-hanging fruit—the bookmakers, prostitutes, or retail level drug dealers that law enforcement routinely arrested. These were not the usual suspects arrested to justify and validate vice statistics.

These were the gangsters who *ordered* murders, maimings, and shootings. These were the racketeers who arranged payoffs to the police, to the politicians. They were featured in books, magazines, splashed across movie screens, and the subject of congressional hearings. As a young

---

18. Sullivan, Joseph F. *The New York Times.* 1973. "10 in Gang in Jersey Indicted in 5 Killings. Short," Martin. 1996.
19. *The News* (Paterson, NJ). 1968. "State Cop, Pair Deny New Counts in Bribe Case." May 4th. James, George. *The Morning Call* (Paterson, NJ). 1968. "Satz Deflates Bet Probe Import." January 5th.

detective in my late 20's, this was undoubtedly an exciting and eye-opening experience.

One of the members of the Campisi clan was an outlier. Ira Pecznick had developed a reputation as a cold-blooded, hardened killer who had no remorse, savored every ounce of pain he could inflict on his victims, and had not an iota of respect for the law. Socio-path, psychopath, he represented the personification of evil.[20] Pecznick had agreed to become a government witness and provide us with the evidence necessary to convict the Campisi's in a wide-ranging criminal conspiracy.

Every word Pecznick uttered had to be corroborated. Cold-case murders revisited. Evidence collected during the initial investigations was secured and inventoried. Witnesses, if any, re-interviewed. Graves and bodies disinterred. Polygraph examinations were administered. All the while, Pecznick was under a 24/7 security blanket manned by the State Police. This investigation was no small endeavor. Nor was there a blueprint of how to proceed.

Besides the investigative logistics, complicated legal issues compelled the state to assign both trial attorneys and appellate lawyers to the case. Conspiracy laws were critical in assembling the evidence and packaging the case. Briefs and oral arguments were endless. Edwin Stier, Peter Richards, and Barry Goas, all deputy attorneys general, addressed the myriad of legal issues that complicated these prosecutions.

Reinforced security at the courthouse. Thousands upon thousands of hours of investigative and legal time expended. An enormous commitment of personnel and resources was required. And the principal witness was Pecznick, this ruthless, heartless killer.

Here we were, contemplating immunity from prosecution if Pecznick would testify against those who were still eviler, more dangerous, and more dismissive of the rule of law.[21] It was the classic Faustian bargain. It was my introduction into the nasty and sleazy world that we were

20. Sullivan, Joseph F. *The New York Times*. 1975. "5 Murders Are Admitted By Accomplice to Campisi." January 8th. Anderson, Jack and Les Whitten. *The News* (Paterson, NJ). 1975. "Life Perilous For Former Hitman." September 10th.

21. Sullivan, Joseph F. *The New York Times*. 1973. "Seven Held in Murder of State Witness." October 5th.

obligated to enter if law enforcement was to mitigate the pernicious activities of organized crime.[22]

Ultimately and only after several years of legal gymnastics, the Campisi's entered into plea bargains. Finally forcing their hand and clinching the deal was another hired killer, John Patrick Tully, who also agreed to testify as a state witness. His bargain was not quite as generous as that given to Pecznick.

Entering into an unprecedented plea arrangement, Tully was permitted to serve his time in prison while in the federal witness protection program. The plea bargain he agreed to would require him to do twelve years in prison for committing four murders, an armed robbery, and drug trafficking. Tully's cooperation and corroboration were enough to encourage the Campisi's to enter into a series of plea bargains.[23]

Ironically, Tully received a more severe sentence than several of the Campisi's. Others were sentenced to years in state prison, followed by consecutive federal prison terms.

Attorney General William Hyland savored victory. He pointed out, "For the first time, law enforcement officials have been able to penetrate the inner workings of an organized crime group and, in a single indictment, present in detail the objectives of such a conspiracy together with the means to carry out its objectives."[24] He was clearly describing a RICO case—exactly as Graff had earlier envisioned.

And to a large extent, Hyland was correct. Arresting and prosecuting the upper-echelons of organized crime was unheard of until now. Often the minions and mules bore the brunt of prosecutions. Finally, the organizers of syndicate crime were arrested and prosecuted. The costs were enormous, but doing nothing was out of the question. I learned pretty quickly, black and white often takes a back-seat to shades of gray when addressing the vagaries of organized crime control policies, strategies, and tactics.

---

22. Genovese, Peter. *The Home News.* 1979. "Police Defend Role of Informers." February 6th.

23. *Asbury Park Press.* 1975. "Campisis' Plea Bargain." January 15th. DeSantis, Susan. *Asbury Park Press.* 1983. "Federal Program Protects witnesses." January 5th.

24. Eastmond, William. *Asbury Park Press.* 1976. "Short Campisi Jail Terms Deplored." August 11th. McNulty, Sheila. *Associated Press.* 1991. "New Jersey Attorneys Remember Austin Mayoral Candidate as a Mobster." April 4th.

Pecznick, a maniacal, unrepentant killer, was set free, pardoned by the governor of New Jersey. He was allowed to roam the streets with a new identity—one shielded from his unsuspecting neighbors and newly-made friends.[25] A few years later, Pecznick passed away in Tucson, Arizona. He died in police custody, although they attempted to save the life of this stone-cold killer who viciously took the lives of others.[26]

Tully, on the other hand, remained in prison. He was outraged over the relatively lenient sentences meted out to the Campisi's—the bosses of organized crime. "In the eyes of the underworld, the Campisi's can't even get put away for murder . . . I've seen guys get more than ten years for narcotics which some of the Campisi's got for murder," Tully lamented.[27]

He had served more time in prison than many of the Campisi's. Tully's corroboration was essential to convicting the Campisi's.[28]But his bitterness toward what he believed was a raw deal by the State of New Jersey remained a sore point with him throughout his confinement and years after that. "They [the Campisi's] got away with murder, and I'm the last guy out. I'm the one who got burned," Tully shamelessly whined.

Upon being released from prison in 1982, Tully remained in the witness protection program. Relocated to Austin, Texas, Tully lived under the assumed name of John Johnson. His prior life and criminal past were shielded from the public. Austin's police intelligence unit was well aware of his true identity and gruesome history.[29] As members of the Law Enforcement Intelligence Unit (LEIU), of which Dintino was its chairman, it was only appropriate that they would have access to Tully's criminal exploits.

In 1991, Tully filed a petition to run for mayor of Austin, Texas. No longer comfortable living under an assumed identity, Tully publicly announced, "My legal name is John Johnson . . . I would like to reintroduce

---

25. *New York Magazine.*1975. "A Murderer Informs—And Walks." March 24th. p. 34.

26. *Asbury Park Press.* 1979. "Campisi Informer Dies. 'Freaks Out' in Service Station." August 19th.

27. Eastmond, William. 1976. *Short Campisi Jail Terms Deplored.* August 11th.

28. *The Record* (Hackensack, NJ). 1982. "Plea Bargain was no deal, mob killer says." February 1st.

29. Ward, Pamela. *Austin American-Statesman.* 1991. "Mobsters to Mayor?" April 4th.

myself to you. My original name, and the name I will always consider my real name is John Patrick Tully." [30]

Endorsing Tully's bid for mayor was none other than the legendary Frank Serpico of Knapp Commission and Hollywood stardom.[31]

"Johnson knows the workings of the system from both within and without, but unlike some politicians, John Johnson doesn't claim to have never erred. John Johnson is a symbol of hope for the true American process. For without men like John Johnson, our system of justice and reform would be an illusion," Serpico unabashedly proclaimed. [32]

Perhaps in Tully, Serpico saw a man who was no worse than the politicians that sold him out twenty years earlier.

It's the only explanation that makes any sense.

By the way, Tully never did win the election.

A Senate President, A Mob Killer, and a Short-Circuited Investigation

New Jersey's affinity for public corruption has been the topic of history and political science buffs for decades. Cataloging the endless scandals that engulfed the Garden State would be a *magnum opus* if one had the tenacity to undertake such a massive endeavor.[33] The stories, the legends, the characters, and the outcomes tragically have sullied the state's reputation as being one of, if not the most corrupt state in the nation.

Edwin Stier, a former Director of New Jersey's Division of Criminal Justice, recently commented, "What we failed to recognize was the extent to which county machine politics had become captive to organized crime . . . racketeers had so infested governmental institutions [in the

30. *Austin American Statesman* (Austin, TX). 1991. "Ex-hitman comes clean in mayoral race." April 4th. Maraniss, David. *The Charlotte Observer.* 1991. "From Mob to Hot Dogs to Mayor?" April 8th. McNulty, Sheila. *Associated Press.* 1991. "New Jersey Attorney Remembers Austin Mayoral Candidate as Mobster." April 4th.

31. Maas, Peter. 2005. *Serpico.* January 4th.

32. *Austin American-Statesman.* 1991. "Frank Serpico Endorses Johnson in Mayor's Race." April 26th.

33. Deitch, Scott M. 2017. *Garden State Gangland: The Rise of the Mob in New Jersey.* December 8th.

50s and 60s] that they were able to name a State Police Superintendent to whom they paid a regular salary alongside his government check."[34]

As did the legions of crime busters that undertook some of the most delicate investigations in the state's history during the 60s and 70s, Stier understood that arresting and prosecuting corruption was a necessary, nonetheless partial goal. Without a change in its political culture, New Jersey would revert to its natural form, embracing bribery as a way of life.

New Jersey was and is a rich environment for all sorts of financial schemes. Being one of the wealthiest states in the nation, organized crime, fraudsters, grifters, and hustlers all have their sights on the bounties that the state had to offer.

The fact that New Jersey had the most organized crime families—7 in all—operating within its borders, more than any other state, tells still another part of its sordid history. It was and is ripe for unrestrained plunder by a cadre of professional, well-connected gangsters and racketeers.[35] It also provided the most complicated and intriguing milieu to study and understand the dynamics of organized crime.

Certainly, the Gambino and Genovese Mafia families were considered the dominant organized crime families in New Jersey. While the DeCalvalcante was the only home-grown Mafia family, the Bruno, Bonanno, Lucchese, and Columbo all had a stake in various aspects of the illicit economy that thrived in New Jersey.

The Genovese Family maintained an influential position among the organized crime hierarchy in the State. Its leader, Vito Genovese, lived in Atlantic Highlands, New Jersey, one of the wealthier enclaves along the Jersey Shore. His Family's influence reached into the inner sanctums

---

34. Stier, Edwin H. 2019. *Col. Justin Dintino: Duty, Honor, Fidelity. Dedication of the Justin J. Dintino Repository on Organized Crime Literature.* Sea Girt, New Jersey. October 30th.

35. Sackett, Russell, Sandy Smith and William Lambert. *Life Magazine.* 1968. "The Congressman and the Hoodlum." August 9th. *University of California, Berkeley Campus Library.* 1970. *DeCarlo Wiretap Transcripts.* Duke, Harry. 1977. *Neutral Territory: The True Story of the Rackets in Atlantic City.* Ingle, Bob and Sandy McClure. 2008. *The Soprano State: New Jersey's Culture of Corruption.* Blackwell, Jon. 2008. *Notorious New Jersey: 100 True Tales of Murders, Mobsters, Scandals and Scoundrels.* Johnson, Nelson. 2002. *Boardwalk Empire: The Birth, High Times and Corruption of Atlantic City.* Deitch, Scott M. 2017. *Garden State Gangland: The Rise of the Mob in New Jersey.* Gavzer, Bernard, Michael J. Sniffen and Don Battle. *Internet Archives. Sam The Plumber Lets the Worms out of the Can.*

of local and even state government. Whether it was New Jersey's largest city of Newark or its smallest hamlet of Old Tappan, the tentacles of this family were and are vast and deep.[36]

In Newark, Geraldo Catena was the *capo* in the Genovese Family who commanded a crew that ran a significant portion of the illegal gambling, loansharking, and waterfront rackets. Catena owned Runyon Sales, a vending machine company that had forged relationships with prominent political figures throughout New Jersey.[37]

With the passing of Catena in 2000, his likely successor was a *soldier* in the family, Tino Fiumara.[38] Known for his propensity for violence, friend and foe alike feared him. He had killed his best friend and underling, Richie Santos, to whom Fiumara was the godfather literally to his son. Lawrence Ricci, a Genovese *capo* who was his eyes and ears on the New Jersey waterfront and on-trial for waterfront racketeering, was found in the trunk of his car, a bullet in his head. Fiumara had ordered his execution. Bobby Harris, the Paterson numbers czar, was tortured and murdered by Fiumara. Without question, Fiumara ran the most disciplined and efficient Mafia crew in New Jersey.[39]

With the death of Anthony Salerno, the boss of the Genovese Family, Fiumara was promoted. He emerged as one of a triumvirate to lead the Genovese Family.[40]

Answering to Fiumara was an up-and-comer, Louis Auricchio. A soldier and ultimately a *capo* in the Genovese Family, Auricchio was viewed

---

36. *The New York Times*. 1970. "SUBURB'S 5 POLICE INDICTED IN BRIBE." March 18th.

37. Mintz, John. *The Washington Post*. 1980. "Shadow of the Mob Over Casino Hearings." December 14th. *The New York Times*. 1978. "The Big Players on the Boardwalk." February 5th.

38. Revealed during a background investigation of the then United States Attorney Chris Christie was the fact that he visited Fiumara while he was incarcerated at the behest of his aunt, who was married to Fiumara's brother. Halpfinger, David M. *The New York Times*. 2009. "For Christie, Family Tie No Candidate Can Relish." September 23rd.

39. Delaney, Eileen. *The Herald News* (Passaic, NJ). 1979. "Disturbing Parallels." March 18th. Sowers, Prudy. *The News* (Paterson, NJ). 1979. "Clifton Police Keep Santos Murder Under Wraps." March 16th. *The News* (Paterson, NJ). 1980. "Unruffled suspect portrayed as tough ranking mobster." January 8th. *Asbury Park Press*. 2005. "Lawyer: Body Found outside Union diner is reputed mobster." December 2nd. Rashbaum, William K. *The New York Times*. 2005. "Three Longshoremen Not Guilty of Fraud and Other Charges." Nov. 9th.

40. *The New York Times*. 2011. "Tino Fuimara Escapes the Law One Final Time." February 1st.

within the law enforcement community as the successor to Fiumara, both in the traditional rackets and on the lucrative New Jersey waterfront.

Unaware of Auricchio's political relationships, an investigation of his sprawling criminal operations by the Narcotics Bureau-North, was initiated in 1986. We had acquired sufficient probable cause to initiate wiretaps on his telephone and place bugs in his office located in North Arlington, New Jersey.

Before installing the bugs and wiretaps, surveillances on these premises witnessed the comings-and-goings of drug dealers, bookies, and "mob enforcers" meeting with Auricchio. Of course, some were our informants, who provided us with the probable cause to initiate electronic surveillance.

With a court order in hand and under the guise of darkness, our electronic surveillance experts entered the building where Auricchio held court daily. We were prepared to record incriminating conversations by planting five bugs in the ceiling and tapping all the phones in his office. Hopefully, these recordings would define his criminal network, who it comprised, the roles they played, and of course, criminally implicating Auricchio as its leader.

Days monitoring the bugs and taps would pass and nothing. Weeks would pass, and still, nothing. Auricchio's pattern of arriving at the office in the early afternoon had changed. He was seldom there. Something was wrong.

Thirty days was the limit that we could electronically monitor. We were running out of time. To extend the electronic surveillance, we would have to "freshen up" the probable cause. Another thirty days proved unproductive. The investigation legally had to be terminated.

Months later, in what reflected our failure to understand the political dynamics that encapsulated this investigation, we learned of Auricchio's political affiliation.

John Lynch, the most powerful politician in New Jersey and President of the Senate, was married to Deborah Auricchio, the sister of Louis.[41]To

---

41. Kocieniewski, David. *The New York Times*. 2006. "In New Jersey, Political Bosses Meld Politics and Business." January 1st. Petersen, Melody. *The New York Times*. 1997. "Whitman Makes Issue of 911 Call By Critic's Wife." September 27th.

some of the more astute or perhaps cynical detectives, we were sold out in Trenton. To others, Auricchio discovered the bugs and phone taps. But of course, knowing the sordid history of New Jersey, the answer to this nagging question will and has remained an unanswered mystery.

In 1993, six years after our aborted effort, New Jersey's Division of Criminal Justice, in cooperation with the F.B.I. and U.S. Attorney's Office, charged Auricchio with racketeering and the murder of John Di-Gilio [a racketeer who was prominent on the N.J. waterfront]. Auricchio was convicted and sentenced to 30 years in state prison.[42] He was paroled in 2010.

John Lynch was charged with and convicted of tax evasion, mail fraud, and official misconduct eleven years later. At his sentencing, the then U.S. Attorney Chris Christie stated, "No one, absolutely no one in New Jersey is above the law. A few years ago, he was the most powerful figure in the state. I don't think John Lynch ever expected to go to jail."[43]

As we would often say, the invisible hand appears innocuous for a reason. It usually lurks somewhere below the surface, unseen but lethal; inconspicuous but malevolent.

And it leaves no fingerprints.

Political Aspirations, Mafia Intrigue, and Dashed Dreams

In 1974 I was assigned to work with Joseph Delaney, the Bergen County Narcotics Task Force chief. Not knowing Delaney personally but aware of his ambitious reputation for self-promotion and higher aspirations, I

---

42. Sterling, Guy. *The Star-Ledger.* 1992. "Investigators feel they'll soon crack killing of reputed Jersey mob boss." June 14th. Sterling, Guy. *The Star-Ledger.* 1989. "Jury Finds Holmdel Mob figure guilty on three counts of tax evasion." May 27th. Sterling, Guy. *The Star-Ledger.* 1989. "Mob Suspect accused of muscling witnesses." Sterling, Guy. *The Star-Ledger.* 1989. "Successor to DiGilio is sentenced to 12 years for tax evasion." Heine, William K. *Asbury Park Press.* 1994. "Mobster admits killing his boss." March 31st. 1994. "'Cold Blooded' crime cited at sentencing." June 11th. O'Dea. Colleen. NJSpotlightnews.org. 2018. "Murphy Socked by Lawsuit over Christie's Decision to End Harbor Compact." January 17th.

43. Kocienewski, David. *The New York Times.* 2006. "Ex-Leader of the New Jersey Senate is Guilty of Corruption." September 16th. It should be noted that Christie's aunt was married to Fuimara's brother. *The New York Times,* 2009, "For Christie, Family Tie No Candidate Can Relish." September 23rd.

realized early on this would not be an easy task. Egos had to be checked at the door if we were to successfully investigate the Gambino Crime Family's influence in the most populous and wealthiest county in the state.

Front and center in this investigation was Frank "Butch" Miceli, a soldier in the Gambino Family. I had, over the years, developed an extensive dossier on Miceli.

Miceli reported to Gambino Mafia *capo* Joseph Paterno, headquartered in Newark. Miceli's mother was a respected Democratic Party operative in Massachusetts politics. Miceli was indicted with Gambino Mafia boss Carlo Gambino for conspiracy to rob an armored car.[44] Boston-based Mafia informer Vincent Teresa referred to him as the hit squad leader who answered to Joe Paterno, a *capo* in the Gambino Mafia Family.[45] And Miceli was married to a former beauty contestant who Ronald Donatell, a well-regarded philanthropist, employed.

My intelligence sources told me that Miceli was involved in the murder of Alton Hughes, a Black policy operator, whose body was found in Howell, New Jersey.[46] Like other Black policy operators, Hughes attempted to break away from the Mafia-dominated gambling rackets that were part of the underworld landscape in the major cities throughout the country.[47]

Ironically, several years earlier, I cited Miceli for speeding on the Garden State Parkway. In his vehicle was a bag containing copper slugs that passed for coins.[48] These slugs were used to defraud the Parkway of revenue in the automatic toll lanes—a relatively amateurish and rank act

---

44. *Paterson News.* 1970. "Gambino, East Paterson Confederate Indicted. April 30th. *Paterson News.* 1970. "Raid Nets a .38 and a Blush." April 30th.

45. Teresa, Vincent C. 1973. *My Life in the Mafia.* January 1st. *Paterson News.* 1970. "E. Paterson Man Held for Having Fake Securities. Raid Nets a .38 and a Blush." June 29th. *Paterson News.* 1970. "Gambino, E. Paterson Confederate Indicted." April 30th.

46. *Asbury Park Press.* 1969. "Freda in Custody To Be Questioned." July 31st. p. 22.

47. Vaz, Matthew. *The Journal of American History.* 2014. "'We Intend to Run It': Racial Politics, Illegal Gambling, and the Rise of Government Lotteries in the United States, 1960-1985." pp. 71–96. See the murder of Robert "Bobby" Harris in Paterson, N.J. by Genovese member Tino Fuimara. Scarpo, Ed. 2014. "Decades of Mob Violence Behind Waterfront Case." December 21st.

48. *Paterson News.* 1970. "Miceli Fined on Speeding Charge." May 14th.

for a Mafia hit-man. Miceli, of course, denied knowing they were in his vehicle.

When I learned that Delaney had insinuated himself in Miceli's orbit, there was no doubt that this investigation would lead to Gambino's extensive criminal holdings in which Miceli played a leadership role.[49]

While the investigation was in its earlier stages, we learned that Miceli had nothing but disdain for Anthony Carminati, a *capo* in the Gambino Family who had "made his bones" across the river in New York City.

Carminati had replaced Paterno, who had relocated to Florida to avoid a New Jersey State Commission of Investigation subpoena. Miceli considered Carmanati ill-suited for the position of *capo*. He felt that Carminati was unfamiliar with the political terrain of Bergen County and New Jersey, which was essential to effectively navigate the myriad of competing Mafia interests that spanned seven Mafia families.

As Delaney began gaining the confidence of Miceli, we developed information on several attorneys and political bosses who were financially indebted to both Miceli and Carmanati.[50] This investigation was now taking on a dimension that we knew would make the prosecutor, Joseph Woodcock, to whom Delaney reported, quite uncomfortable.

Woodcock, a former State Senator, was appointed by Governor William Cahill to head the prosecutor's office in Bergen County.[51] Larry McClure was the operational brain running the office. Woodcock envisioned the investigation into organized crime as a stepping stone to the governorship or higher office. On the contrary, the investigation opened up Pandora's Box, creating several political firestorms that were difficult to extinguish.

The first revelation involved Republican Party Chairman Herb Blayer. From conversations with Miceli, Delaney learned that Blayer had borrowed $20,000 from Carminati. According to Delaney, Blayer could not repay the loan and was obligated to take a mortgage out on his home or suffer the nasty consequences if he reneged.

49. Short, Martin. 1996. *Crime Inc.: The Story of Organized Crime.* pp. 313–16.
50. Sullivan, Joseph F. *The New York Times.* 1975. "2-State Roundup Nets 17 Linked to Loan-sharking." May 7th.
51. *The New York Times.* 1973. "Woodcock in Line for Prosecutor's Post." November 12th.

Of course, at this point, Carminati, for all practical purposes, owned Blayer. Consorting with a Mafia *capo* was not likely to endear Blayer to Woodcock, who relied upon the Republican Party for political support. Woodcock was undoubtedly in an awkward situation.

Delaney later learned that two loansharks were awaiting sentencing after pleading guilty. Scheduled to appear before Superior Court Judge James Madden, Carminati boasted that he had gained entre' to Madden through a county freeholder, Gerald Calabrese. Neither loan shark would receive a sentence over 365 days. They could serve their time in the Bergen County Jail. They would enter a very flexible work-release program.

Upon learning the "fix was in," Woodcock met with Madden, unbeknownst to Delaney or me. The case was summarily postponed. This meeting essentially forestalled the sentencing and bungled further investigative avenues.

Naturally, this conversation placed Woodcock, Calabrese, and Madden in a very delicate and legally precarious position. All who were part of the investigation knew about this attempt to obstruct justice. We also were aware of Woodcock's earlier, surprising, and unannounced intervention with Madden. It was necessary to present this to a grand jury—a local instead of a state grand jury.[52]

After taking testimony from Blayer, Madden, Calabrese, and twenty other interested parties, the Grand Jury concluded, "Although this grand jury is satisfied that every witness who had relevant knowledge and information had been called to testify . . . not one single piece of evidence was produced that would support the allegation that Judge Madden had been approached or influenced." Case closed.

Aware of the political implications that were evolving if this investigation continued, it was becoming increasingly evident that additional politicians and public officials within the sphere of Carminati's and Miceli's web of influence might be implicated in wrong-doing.

Woodcock decided to terminate the investigation and surface Delaney as an honest cop who had exposed corruption and organized crime.

---

52. For a robust discussion on the power of prosecutors over grand juries, see Dewan, Shaila, Will Wright and John Eligon. *The New York Times*. 2020. "In Breona Taylor Case, a Battle of Blame Over the Grand Jury." September 29th.

Of course, Woodcock would derive the ultimate credit for courageously pursuing organized crime—a bell-weather issue in the State's political circles.

Shortly after that, Woodcock resigned as a prosecutor and announced his intention to run for governor. Failing to receive the backing of his own Republican Party, he ultimately withdrew. He endorsed Thomas Kean, who went on to win the governorship.[53]

Ultimately, Miceli was indicted for racketeering, gambling, and bribery. Suffering from multiple sclerosis, Miceli pled guilty to nine counts of bribery.[54] He received a two to a six-year suspended sentence, five years' probation, and a $9,000 fine.

Carminati, to whom Miceli reported, did not fare as well. He received a 3 ½ to 5-year sentence in state prison. He was not quite as adept at negotiating New Jersey's political terrain as Miceli earlier predicted.

Like so many organized crime investigations that take unexpected detours, Miceli's criminal exploits resulted in many twists and turns that illustrate the power of the "invisible hand."

Before this investigation into the Carminati-Miceli network began, I had developed very high-placed sources that implicated Miceli in the murder of a Black rackets czar, hijackings, and many burglaries, one which involved the United States Post Office in Paramus, New Jersey in 1969.[55] Although these burglaries and the murder were never solved, my sources were adamant that Miceli was involved.

Months later, a situation developed which involved a "friend of a friend." Arrested for receiving stolen property, Ronald Donatell [who employed Miceli's estranged wife], Genaro Calendrillo, and Frank Schneider were caught red-handed with a truckload of fabric that was earlier reported stolen from a warehouse in Fairfield, New Jersey.[56]

---

53. Sullivan, Joseph F. *The New York Times*. 1977. "Woodcock Leaves Governor Race and Support Kean in the Primary." August 15th.

54. Hanley, Robert. *The New York Times*. 1977. "A Top Mobster Pleads Guilty to 9 Bribery Charges." June 14th. Locklin, Bruce. *The Alicia Patterson Foundation*. 2011. "My Favorite Mobster." April 4th.

55. *The Record* (Hackensack, NJ). 1975. "Police List Bi-State Mafia Leaders." May 7th.

56. *The Herald News* (Passaic, NJ). 1972. "Three indicted on Stolen Goods Rap." December 22nd. In order to comply with the family's wishes, certain names were changed. The events and facts surrounding the events are true and accurate.

Donatell was a well-regarded philanthropist, sports advocate, devoted father, and multi-millionaire entrepreneur. He had all the accouterments that success could deliver and then some. His arrest made no sense at all. Taking possession of a truck-load of stolen fabric was not something that Ronnie likely would consider, nonetheless chance. Schneider, of course, was another matter. His criminal arrest record had demonstrated a propensity toward property crimes, such as stealing and receiving stolen property.

As I began to inquire of my sources, it became increasingly evident that there may have been an organized crime element involving his arrest? How was it that the police were present when Donatell arrived at the scene of the crime? They had been alerted to the delivery of the stolen goods by someone, but who?

There were rumblings among my underworld sources that the arrest had to do with settling an old score.

Apparently, Ronnie was courting Miceli's estranged wife. When Miceli learned about this arrangement, he was outraged. Miceli put a "contract" (i.e., an order to kill or maim) out on Donatell. Scared for her beau's life, Miceli's wife sought the counsel and intervention of Gambino Mafia Family *capo* Joseph Paterno. Paterno ordered Miceli to "back off"—no harm was to come to Donatell.[57] This relationship was a personal matter. It did not involve "our business," Paterno cautioned.

Miceli, still seething from this romantic betrayal, apparently was not satisfied. Revenge was still in the cards. But Miceli's fingerprints had to be invisible. Any harm to Donatell could not be attributed to Miceli.

Indicted by a Passaic County Grand Jury, Donatell, Schneider, and Calendrillo all pled not guilty.

Donatell and Calendrillo testified at their trial that they were unaware the fabric was stolen property. Schneider decided against testifying, knowing that his prior criminal record would not bode well for an acquittal. The jury returned verdicts of guilty for all three.

Now the events surrounding this investigation and prosecution had taken on some Machiavellian-like schemes. It reinforced my belief that Donatell had been framed or set up.

---

57. *The Courier-News* (Bridgewater, NJ). 1972. "Paterno Rising in Underworld." August 3rd. *The Miami Herald*. 1983. "Reputed Mobsters Settle in South Florida." September 5th.

When I learned that Judge William J. Woods would be the sentencing judge, I was confident that Donatell would be treated quite leniently, given my previous experience before this particular judge.

Two years earlier, I appeared before Judge Woods and gave testimony regarding the arrest of Michael Astarita, a well-connected bookmaker who was part of the Genovese Mafia Family's extensive gambling network in North Jersey. Astarita was arrested for gambling paraphernalia, namely eighty-two football betting slips that amounted to twenty-five thousand dollars in bets. He had in his possession approximately thirteen hundred dollars in cash.

After presenting testimony at a preliminary hearing, Astarita's defense attorney motioned to dismiss the charges. Judge Woods granted the motion, contending that the possession of sports bookmaking paraphernalia was insufficient to prove Astarita was a bookmaker.

The prosecutor Frank Donato vehemently objected to the dismissal, arguing that it was up to a jury to decide whether or not Astarita was a bookmaker. Donato argued that the state was only required under the statute to prove that Astarita possessed gambling paraphernalia. Never before, Donato argued, did the state need to prove that a bookmaker took bets. Donato said he would appeal what he believed was the judge's legally flawed decision. He never did.

While I certainly was not happy with Judge Woods dismissing the case against Astarita, it was certainly within his judicial discretion.

Consequently, I was dumbfounded when I learned that Donatell was sentenced to one to two years in state prison by Judge Woods. Incarcerating Donatell in state prison for any time was inconceivable, given his unblemished record and generous philanthropic history.[58] Imprisonment of any sort by a judge who appeared to be quite charitable in his approach to organized crime seemed like a remote possibility.[59]

---

58. *The News* (Paterson, NJ). 1973. "Sportsman, 2 Others Guilty." September 21st. *The News* (Paterson, NJ). 1973. "Two Imprisoned, Third Fined As Receivers of Stolen Goods." October 18th.

59. Astarita was part of a Genovese Mafia Family gambling network that extended throughout North Jersey and New York, which involved acquiring information on the various New York Giant's football players from the team physician. *Paterson News.* 1971. Amdur, Neil. *The New York Times.* 1974. "Giants' Ex-Doctor Tied to Bookies in a Conspiracy." August 21st. *Man Cleared of Bookmaking; Appeal Promised.* October 10th. *Paterson News.* 1974. "Area bookmakers charged in a 40 count indictment." August 21st. Zimroth, Peter L. 2011. *Thomas Musto and Michael Astarita, Petitioners v. New York. U.S. Supreme Court Transcript of Record with Supporting Pleadings.* October.

In another unexpected detour, two Passaic Police Department police officers, Stefano Mazzola and Dennis Sieper, made an unsolicited appeal to Judge Woods, requesting leniency for Schneider. Schneider had been sentenced to three to five years in state prison by Woods. Mazzola and Sieper claimed that Schnieder saved their lives in a gunfight by ramming his vehicle into the shooter's car. They testified that they likely would be dead if it had not been for Schneider's courage and heroics.

"I accepted the fact that I was going to die . . . I knew I was trapped . . . A guy can't be all bad if he risks his life for a cop . . . I even recommended him for the highest award given by the State PBA." Mazzola testified. "If it wasn't for this gentleman, I might be dead," Sieper echoed.[60]

A rather chilling story. It placed Judge Woods in a rather uncomfortable situation. As the judge pointed out, if he was to suspend or reduce Schneider's prison term, *how would he address Donatell's prison sentence of 1-2 years?* Ultimately Judge Woods disregarded Mazzola's and Seipers' plea for a reduction in Schneider's sentence.[61]

Both Donatell and Schneider, with their appeals exhausted, were remanded to prison.

While at Yardville Correctional Facility, DSFC Charles Coe and I visited Donatell. Dressed in typical prison garb, Donatell welcomed us, and we began discussing the event that landed him a prison sentence. He, of course, was embarrassed and reflected on how it affected his children and his parents. "I hope you know, Fred, I had nothing to do with this . . . I have my suspicions, but what does it matter . . . I'll be out of here soon."

Donatell was resigned to his fate and only looked forward to his release. I was able to arrange for an earlier release than he had anticipated.

But time and distance have a funny way of clarifying history.

Three years later, Astarita was indicted on 40 counts of bookmaking. He was part of the *Genovese* Mafia Family's twenty-six million-dollar sports gambling network that spanned northern New Jersey and involved the New York Giants football team physician.

---

60. *The News* (Paterson, NJ). 1973. "2 Cops Testify For Their 'Hero'." November 27th.
61. The State PBA never did give Schneider that award.

Ten years later, Mazzola and Sieper were involved in an armed robbery for which they were prosecuted and convicted.[62] Mazzola also was charged with extortion on behalf of the *Genovese* Mafia Family. He was convicted of stabbing Nicholas D'Aloisio in the arm while collecting an $80,000 loan.[63] Years later, Mazzola again was charged and convicted with extorting and strong-arming a local businessman.[64] And as recently as 2014, Mazzola was charged with and convicted of loan fraud.[65]

Although Mazzola's ongoing relationship with the *Genovese* Mafia Family illustrates the lengths the mob would go to "spring" Schneider from prison, Peter Polidori's history with the *Genovese* Mafia Family tells an equally compelling story.

For those unfamiliar with Mafia's inter-family politics, disputes are resolved peacefully and honorably in most instances. Violence is viewed as a liability, usually provoking unnecessary law enforcement scrutiny. Cooperation vis-à-vis confrontation tends to be the governing norm. Reciprocal relationships rationalize what could be a somewhat unruly and violent criminal environment, especially in New Jersey—the only state with seven Mafia families.[66] Navigating this underworld landscape can be rather tricky.

---

62. *The Herald News* (Passaic, NJ). 1982. "Passaic Cop's reproof recalled." April 23rd. *The Record* (Hackensack, NJ). 1982. "Former Passaic Cop Found Guilty of Robbery." January 21st. *The Herald News* (Passaic, NJ). 1983. "Court Upholds retrial of cop: Officer faces new court date." July 8th. *The Record* (Hackensack, NJ). 2014. "Ex-Passaic Cop Admits Loan Fraud." August 21st.

63. Pristin, Terry. *The New York Times*. 1996. "Extortion Charge For Officer." November 21st.

64. DeMarco, Jerry. *Daily Voice*. 2013. "FBI Arrests ex-Passaic Cop turned mobster, 68, for threats." February 8th.

65. *The Record* (Hackensack, NJ). 2014. "Ex-Passaic Cop Admits Loan Fraud." August 21st.

66. Simone DeCalvalcante, the boss of the only home-grown New Jersey Mafia Family, discussed why he refused to testify before the New Jersey State Commission of Investigation. He reflected on the current efforts of the State to coerce his testimony and that of other Mafia leaders in New Jersey. He was especially chagrined over the State's efforts to sow discord among and between the various Mafia families that were part of New Jersey's political landscape for decades; interview by author October 21, 1970, Hackensack, N.J. The made for television series, *The Sopranos*, represents a caricature of the real DeCalvalcante Family. Grutzener, Charles. *The New York Times*. 1970. "New Tapes by F.B.I. Link Politicians to Jersey Mafia." January 7th. Martens, Frederick T. *Organized Crime Digest*. 1997. "Sam the Plumber: Fred Martens Reflects on an Era." February 19th. Tuohy, John William. Mobstudy@aol.com. 2001. "Vinnie Ocean, Sam the Plumber and the Manhattan Excursion." April.

The Polidori's have been a fixture in Passaic County's gambling rackets for decades.[67] The elder Daniel Polidori was part of the Genovese Family combine that controlled gambling in Paterson and throughout Passaic County during its hey-days in the 50s and beyond.[68] His boss was the late Gerardo Catena, a *capo* in the Genovese Mafia Family. Catena's influence extended into the upper echelons of Passaic County politics.[69]

Upon the passing of Catena, the vice rackets were inherited by Tino Fiumara.[70] His underlings, Peter LaPlaca and Louis "Streaky" Gatto, exercised absolute control over the rackets in Paterson and Passaic County, N.J.[71] Peter Polidori, Daniel's son, answered to LaPlaca and Gatto, serving as their policy comptroller in Passaic County.

Peter, a *Genovese*, was arrested with Miceli, a *Gambino*, in 1975. Peter Polidori was charged with bribery, offering our undercover operative, Joseph Delaney, a $15,000 bribe to dispose of several gambling arrests in Passaic and Bergen counties.[72] Miceli was charged with nine counts of bribery also involving Delaney.[73]The symbiotic arrangement between these two Mafia Families should put to rest any doubts about reciprocity and its reach into the inner sanctums of the criminal justice system. Simply connecting the dots tells a compelling story—or as the Greek philosopher Phaedrus said, "things are not always what they seem; the first appearance deceives many; the intelligence of a few perceives that which is hidden."

---

67. *The News* (Paterson, NJ). 1970. "Vice Squad Arrests Bares Big Operation." October 9th. *The News.* 1974. "Pair Arraigned on Lottery Rap." July 29th. *The News* (Paterson, NJ). 1975. "Mob Indictments Continue." May 23rd.

68. *The Herald News* (Passaic, NJ). 1963. "Judge Fines 3 in Gambling Raid $4,000." February 2nd.

69. Runyon Sales was a vending machine company owned by Catena. It had insinuated itself throughout Passaic County, partnering with politically-connected vending machine owners and operators.

70. *The Herald News* (Passaic, NJ). 1989. "Boss Eludes the Law." July 24th.

71. Scarpo, Ed. 2014. "Decades of Violence Behind the Waterfront Case: Grisly Murder Credited to Fiumara." December 21st.

72. *The News* (Paterson, NJ). 1975. "Officer's Informant Led to Mob Arrests. Raids Net 17 Reputed Mobsters." May 7th. *The Herald News* (Passaic, NJ). 1975. "Organized Crime Figures Indicted." May 9th. *The Herald News* (Passaic, NJ). 1978. "Man Gets Jail, Fine in Bribery Case." January 30th. *The Record* (Hackensack, NJ). 1975. "Bergen Calling 80 Witnesses in Mafia Probe."

73. *The Record* (Hackensack, NJ). 1975. "Police List Top Racketeers." May 7th. *The Record* (Hackensack, NJ). 1978. "Can't Avoid Grand Jury, Miceli Told." February 28th. *The Record* (Hackensack, NJ). 1977. "Leniency Plea Denied in Bribe Case." September 18th.

That's why we call it *organized* crime.

Political Parties Aside, Politics Rules

Pennsylvania politics, much like Pagano and Dintino had warned me, was unforgiving and lethal. While I had seen the collateral damage inflicted on the son of a prominent United States Supreme Court Justice, nothing could prepare me for entering the belly of the beast.[74]

Indeed, the bi-partisan investigation by the New Jersey legislature into Deputy Attorney General William Brennan's proven allegations against three legislators made me appreciate the wrath that could and would be brought to bear on the Pennsylvania Crime Commission (PCC).[75] But like most who engage in these high-profile investigations, it can "never happen to me."

When the PCC embarked on its investigation of Pennsylvania's Republican Attorney General, Ernest Preate, it was with the belief that having bi-partisan representation on the Commission would buffer us from any partisan political sniping or retaliation.[76] Naively believing the rule of law applied to the Attorney General just as it had to the drug dealers he regaled in arresting and prosecuting, the PCC cautiously and methodically executed our investigative strategy. We collected, analyzed, and amassed volumes of documentary evidence to corroborate what we had learned through our primary source, Elmo Baldassari, a convicted racketeer.[77]

"I made Ernie the Attorney General," were the words Baldassari angrily uttered to Special Agents James Kanavy and Paul Spear. They had

---

74. *Observer.* 2007. "Entirely too comfortable with organized crime." April 25th.

75. The Pennsylvania Crime Commission was established in 1968, a direct outgrowth of the 1967 *Task Force Report: Organized Crime.* The *Task Force Report* called for states to establish independent crime commissions to ferret out organized crime and public corruption. Initially it was located in the Office of Attorney General but was later made an arm of the legislative branch of government. It was given full law enforcement authority.

76. When the Pennsylvania Crime Commission investigated the Philadelphia Police Department in 1974, it subsequently was re-organized as an independent agency *unanswerable* to the Attorney General. This arrangement never was accepted by successive attorney's general who were intimidated by the Commission's independence. Burnham, David. *The New York Times.* 1974. "Police in Philadelphia Called Corrupt; Panel Says Rizzo Tried to Bar Inquiry." March 11th.

77. Pennsylvania Crime Commission. *Organized Crime in Pennsylvania: A Decade of Change.* 1991. pp. 73, 85.

interviewed him as part of the Commission's focus on public corruption. He then described the scheme, providing detailed information of who "contributed" to Preate's campaign and how the monies were structured. It was an allegation that had substance. The information could not be ignored. It involved the highest law enforcement officer in the State.[78]

Much like a grand jury conducting an investigation, persons that possessed knowledge of the scheme to extort campaign contributions from video poker vendors in return for the non-enforcement of the state's gambling laws were *subpoenaed* and sworn in under penalty of perjury.[79] They were advised of their rights. They were questioned, and their testimony formally recorded. Counsel could represent them.

The process was far from what some politicians had described it—a kangaroo court.[80]The Commission strictly followed all the rights afforded under Miranda. A witness could request immunity from prosecution, which could or could not be granted depending upon whether another law enforcement organization had an objection. The Commission would share exculpatory evidence with a witness's counsel if it were material to the investigation.

Nothing in the rules of the Commission compelled the Commission to hold public hearings or bring the witnesses before a public forum. That was a decision made by the five Commissioners, appointed by both political parties. Many were former prosecutors or attorneys who were well-versed in legal procedure and the law.

The five Commissioners voted on the Chairman. During my tenure, Michael Reilly, a Pittsburgh labor attorney, former assistant district attorney, and a Democrat, was appointed to the Commission by then-Gov. Richard Thornburgh, a Republican. Reilly served as the chairperson.

---

78. Bumsted, Brad. 2013. *Keystone Corruption: A Pennsylvania Insider's View of a State Gone Wrong*. pp. 38–45.

79. The Commission was legally permitted to issue subpoenas and had full law enforcement authority. No other state law enforcement agency had this authority, other than the Attorney General and local district attorneys. The political clamor over a lack of prosecutorial powers was a red herring. The Pennsylvania State Police, the F.B.I., D.E.A. and a myriad of other law enforcement agencies lack the authority to prosecute. They are solely investigative agencies that lacked subpoena powers.

80. Kelly, Robert J., Ko-Lin Chin and Rufus Schatzberg. *Handbook of Organized Crime: United States*. 1994. Rogovin, Charles H. and Frederick T. Martens. *The Role of Crime Commissions in Organized Crime Control*. pp. 389–400.

The vice-chairperson was Charles Rogovin, a Democrat turned Republican and appointed by the President of the Senate, Robert Jubelirer, a Republican. Rogovin's credentials were unparalleled—LEAA Administrator, deputy district attorney, assistant attorney general, a member of Reagan's Commission on Organized Crime, and law professor.[81]

The remaining members, Arthur Coccodrilli, was a Democrat and appointed by Senator Mellow, the ranking Democrat in the State Senate. James Manning, a former Assistant United States Attorney, was appointed by Matthew Ryan, the Republican Speaker of the House of Representatives. Rounding out the Commissioners was Allen Hornblum, a Democrat appointed by Dwight Evans, the ranking minority member of the House of Representatives.

Given that sort of political firepower, anyone would think that the Commission had all its political bases covered—both Democrats and Republicans.

With the investigation of Preate instigated by Baldassari stating, "I made Ernie Preate the attorney general," we knew that we were about to encounter a political free-for-all.[82]

Corroborating an allegation made by a convicted racketeer against an incumbent and highly respected attorney general would require a precise investigative strategy.[83] The politics of the investigation were equally as relevant and foreboding.

Meeting with several legislators to apprise them of the substance of our investigation without addressing the details, we were met with a barrage of skeptical statements.

One Republican senator, Stewart Greenleaf, suggested that we step down and have the federal government pursue the investigation? "Under what authority is the Commission investigating the Attorney General," Greenleaf asked? When the Commission's Chief Counsel John Ryan responded by citing the legislative mandate authorizing the Commission's investigation, Greenleaf countered, "Isn't that [investigating an attorney general] better left to the Federal government?" Perhaps in retrospect, Greenleaf was warning us what lay ahead.

81. Harvard Kennedy School: Institute of Politics. 1972-1973. *Charles H. Rogovin.*
82. Short, Martin. 1996. *Crime Inc.: The Story of Organized Crime.* pp. 368–72.
83. Murray, L.A. *Sunday Sun.* 1991. "Baldassari Sentencing Due." June 2nd.

A Democratic senator, Vincent Fumo, claimed that the investigation was predicated on an anti-Italian agenda.[84] "Isn't it true that the only reason you are investigating Preate is that he is an Italian-American," Senator Fumo postured? Fumo met with an American-Italian fraternal association the previous weekend at their annual retreat in New York City. They voiced their uninformed objections to the investigation of Preate.

In a scathing retort, Commissioner Coccodrilli responded, "This may surprise you, but we do not start our meeting with an order of business dedicated to what American of Italian heritage we can pick on next . . . it's about time we stop using the worn-out excuse of Italian American bias . . . There are those of us who don't need to hide behind it."[85]

State Representative John Lawless, who ignored the volumes of corroboration accumulated during the investigation, publicly criticized the Commission, claiming that all it had uncovered was "unsworn allegations . . . from unsavory characters . . . people that the Crime Commission itself had called 'corrupt sources.'" [86]

Representative Michael Veon voiced such disdain for the PCC that he drew up a petition circulated among House members calling for defunding the Commission—long before the term defunding became a commonly-used phrase.[87]

It was evident that political party affiliations were less critical than generic, down and dirty politics.[88] If Preate, an attorney general, could be investigated, no one is safe. The message resonated among the political elites.[89]

Led by Fumo and Veon, both Democrats, the Commission underwent withering harassment and strategically disruptive intrusions for two years. They were intent on eliminating the Commission, and in the

84. Lynch, Sharon L. 1993. *The Morning Call* (Allentown, PA). "Senate Split Over Crime Commission." December 14th.

85. Letter dated December 15, 1993 from Commissioner Coccodrilli to Fumo.

86. For a rather colorful career biography of Lawless, see Wikipedia: John A. Lawless.

87. Connolly, Sean. *The Morning Call* (Allentown, PA). 1993. "Crime Panel Targeted." May 13th.

88. Hinds, Michael deCourcy. *The New York Times*. 1993. "Law Enforcer vs. Pennsylvania Crime Commission." May 13th.

89. Martens, Frederick T. 2015. *We'll Make You An Offer You Can't Refuse: A Primer on the Investigation of Public Corruption.* pp. 59–95.

process, politically wounding Preate, their Republican nemesis. A classic two for the price of one strategy.

The Commission was at a disadvantage as to what it could release publicly. The investigation was enveloping both Preate and members of his immediate staff in a "pay to play" scheme. Testimony of witnesses and the attendant documentary corroboration was compelling; in fact, overwhelmingly convincing.

The skeleton of a racketeering case emerged, with numerous financial documents subpoenaed and analyzed, providing the glue to bind the disparate pieces of evidence together. Notwithstanding the self-aggrandizing grandstanding and bloviating by Fumo and Veon, there was no doubt that Preate had engaged in a statewide effort to protect video poker vendors from enforcement of the state's gambling laws.[90]

What proved more perplexing is where Governor Casey, a Democrat, weighed in on this investigation. Insofar as Reilly had been re-appointed by Casey, he never sought Reilly's counsel or attempted to ascertain the investigation's legitimacy—perhaps for good reasons.

While Fumo and Veon were effectively undermining and maligning the investigation, Casey removed himself from opining on the future of the Commission.

However, he took the unprecedented step of appointing the Pennsylvania State Police Commissioner Glenn Walp as the Chairman of the Commission and solicited the learned legal counsel of the Honorable Arlin Adams to serve as a special counsel to the Commission.[91]

To the uninformed, Adams was a devout Republican who was a former Third Circuit Court Appellate Judge. He was appointed as a special prosecutor to investigate corruption in the U.S. Department of Housing and Urban Development. As Casey's eyes and ears at the Commission, initially, we believed that a clever but subtle effort to make the investigation disappear was being orchestrated.

---

90. *United States District Court, Middle District of Pennsylvania. United States of America v. Ernest D. Preate, Jr. 1:CR-95-153. Plea Agreement.*

91. *The Morning Call* (Allentown, PA). 1994. "Ex-Judge to help abolish crime panel." February 3rd. *The Morning Call* (Allentown, PA). 1994. "Crime Panel Praised for Preate Probe." April 18th. Walp, Glenn. 2011. *Implosion at Los Almos: How Crime, Corruption and Cover-Ups Jeopardize America's Nuclear Weapons Secrets.*

Nothing was further from the truth. Politics aside, Adams, who had worked with Preate's father in the Shapp Administration, bought into what he had personally discerned from the volumes of sworn testimony and corroborating documentation the Commission presented to him. His oratory skills were on full display at one of our Saturday morning meetings, where he waxed an opening statement profusely to an imaginary jury. It was a brilliant and articulate distillation of the facts and evidence.

With Adams now on board, the Commission believed it had the ammunition to thwart Fumo and Veon's effort to defund the Commission.[92] We also were more at ease. We felt that the Commission's longevity was assured. Based upon what Adams and Walp were telling him, Casey would veto any bill that would defund the Commission—or so we thought?

Preate was in the fight of his political life. He was running in the primary Republican gubernational election against Tom Ridge, a Congressman from the western part of the State. Ridge had the endorsement of the Republican Party, which was in effect the Republican titan, Bob Asher.[93]

After meeting with Fred Cusick, a tenacious and skilled reporter for the *Philadelphia Inquirer,* Asher dispatched Senator Richard Tilghman to obtain a copy of our investigation. Tilghman demanded the findings of our investigation be publicly released before the primary election. And they were.

Ridge wound up winning the Republican primary election. Ridge went on to win the gubernatorial race, succeeding Casey as governor. He ultimately was appointed by President George Bush as the country's first Homeland Security Director following 9-11.

With the longest-serving member of the state Assembly, Democrat Thomas Caltagirone calling for public hearings, the Commission was legally obliged to report its findings to the Legislature. Adams and

---

92. In a Memorandum dated August 6, 1993, Veon argued ". . . the Crime Commission's recent attacks on Attorney General Preate . . . I am again calling on the House to consider and pass House Bill 1711 to officially terminate the Commission . . ." Of course the U.S. Attorney who assumed jurisdiction after the Commission was defunded, sustained all the evidence the Commission uncovered and then some. *York Dispatch* (York, PA). 1993. "Report: FBI Eyes Preate." July 29th.

93. Asher was a codefendant with Budd Dwyer, who committed suicide at a press conference on January 22, 1987. Wikipedia: Robert B. Asher. Wikipedia: Robert Budd Dwyer.

Rogovin laid out a convincing and compelling narrative that implicated Preate in a corrupt arrangement with video poker vendors throughout the Commonwealth.

Appearing on behalf of Preate was a former justice of the Pennsylvania Supreme Court, Bruce Kauffman.[94] In a raucous hearing, Caltagirone ordered Kauffman physically removed from the hearing room.[95] Just another outlandish stunt in this twisted journey to undermine the legitimacy of the Commission's investigative findings.[96]

Despite being presented with overwhelming evidence implicating Preate in this campaign money-laundering scheme, Casey signed the legislation defunding the Commission. Apparently, the future of the Commission was not worth the political capital required to ensure its continued existence.

Fortunately, the United States' Attorney for the Middle District took jurisdiction of the investigation. The Commission's staff were reassigned to several different agencies in the state. I decided to enter the private sector. Investigating public corruption had taken its toll.

Ultimately Preate, after entering negotiations with Federal authorities to avoid a racketeering indictment, pled guilty to a charge of mail fraud.[97] Defending Preate at his sentencing hearing was none other than New Jersey's legendary corruption-buster Herbert Stern.[98]

Prosecuting Preate was a former assistant attorney general who had worked for Preate, William Barasch. Capturing in words the essence of

---

94. Kauffman was later appointed to the Federal District Court by President William Clinton. After retiring from the federal bench, Kauffman became a partner in the law firm of Pennsylvania State Senator Stewart Greenleaf—the Senator who earlier questioned the Commission's authority to investigate Preate.

95. *Philadelphia Daily News.* 1994. "Don't Let the door hit ya . . . Preate's lawyer is booted from House panel hearing." May 21st. Blumenthal, Jeff. *Philadelphia Business Journal.* 2009. "Federal Judge Kauffman joins Elliot Greenleaf." July 14th. George, Hunter T. *Associated Press.* 1995. "Caltigirone Declares Vindication." September 28th.

96. Connolly, Sean. *The Morning Call* (Allentown, PA). 1994. "Officials Urge Special Prosecutor." May 21st.

97. Mallowe, Michael. *Business Philadelphia.* 1994. "How The Bad Guys Won: The Untimely Death of the Pennsylvania Crime Commission." vol. 5, no. 6.

98. Moran, Robert. *The Philadelphia Inquirer.* 1995. "Preate Gets 14 months, $25,000 fine." December 15th. Hoffman, Paul. 1973. *Tiger in the Court.* Stern, Herbert J. 2012. *Diary of a D.A.: The True Story of the Prosecutor who took on Mob, Fought Corruption, and Won. Los Angeles Times.* 1995. "Ex-Atty. General of Pennsylvania Gets Prison Time." December 15th.

Preate's corruption, Barasch, the U.S. Attorney for the Middle District of Pennsylvania, argued,

"Preate's reliance upon the Crime Commission as part of this belated effort to trivialize the illegality of video poker is in itself cruelly ironic since Preate . . . vigorously and successfully lobbied to destroy this independent agency when it had the courage to investigate his own ties to illegal gambling . . . Sadly, the successful prosecution of this corrupt high-ranking law enforcement official has now fulfilled that prophecy . . ."—that being the growth of video poker and corruption.

Preate served 14 months in prison. Upon his release, the Pennsylvania Supreme Court reinstated his license to practice law. Today, Preate takes on pro-bono work on behalf of prisoner rights organizations.[99]

Decades later, Mellow, Fumo, DeWeese, and Veon, all who voted to defund the Commission, met their waterloo as well.[100] They ended up serving time in prison for several corruption-related offenses.[101]

Simply put, "when you swim with the sharks, it's only a matter of time before you're bitten."

Theft of a City[102]

Newark can serve as the picture-perfect template for those who refuse to appreciate the damage organized crime does to a city.[103] After the 1967 riots that stripped the city of its economic base, businesses and many

99. *The New York Times*. 1995. "Pennsylvania's No. 3 Official Agrees to Plea On Mail Fraud." June 10th. *Philly Magazine*. 2008. "Power: The Importance of Being Ernie." January 30th. Wikipedia: Ernest D. Preate Jr.

100. Bumsted, Brad.2013. *Keystone Corruption: A Pennsylvania Insider's View of a State Gone Wrong*. pp. 79–96, 120–41.

101. Wikipedia. Bob Mellow; Wikipedia, Vince Fumo; Wikipedia, Mike Veon; Wikipedia, Bill DeWeese.

102. Mele, Christopher. 2017. *Race and the Politics of Deception: The Making of An American City*. NYU Press. Kelly, Morgan. 1998. *SPEEC: A History of Chester*. February. Florio, Gwen. *The Philadelphia Inquirer*. 1991. "Nacrelli Runs Chester, Crime Commission Says." April 24th. Anastasia, George. *The Philadelphia Inquirer*. 1988. "Probe Finds Chester in grip pf organized crime, drugs." December 18th. Hart, Joe. *The Delaware County Daily Times*. 1988. "Nacrelli Admits Job Role."

103. Herman, Max Arthur. 2017. *Summer of Rage: An Oral History of the 1967 Newark and Detroit Riots*. July 31st. Short, Martin. 1996. *Crime Inc.: The Story of Organized Crime*. pp. 309–12.

of its residents relocated to the suburbs.[104] Today, Newark is a work in progress, attempting to regain its cultural luster and economic relevance.

Ninety miles southwest of Newark lies another city that has also declined, mainly due to organized crime and public corruption.[105]

Chester, Pennsylvania, a blue-collar, working-class city that once housed an economically vibrant naval shipyard, has seen an exponential decline in population over the last five decades. Suffering from decades of neglect by local, county, and state governments, Chester is a classic study in the theft of a city.[106]

When the Commission initially investigated Chester's government in the 1970s, it came away with a picture of abject social decay and systemic political dysfunction. Routinely investigated by federal authorities, the local district attorney essentially ignored for political reasons the corrupt machinations that contributed to the rapid decline of this once prosperous city.[107] It's elected, and later, de-facto mayor John "Jack" Nacrelli was charged with racketeering by the federal government in the 1970s.[108]He was convicted, given six years in prison, and five years' probation.

Upon his release from prison and precluded from officially holding public office, Nacrelli worked for a mob-owned vending machine company. As its salesman, Nacrelli placed video poker machines throughout

——————————

104. Shields, Krisoffer. 2018. *Rutgers University: Governor Richard Hughes' Select Commission for the Study of Civil Disorder in New Jersey: Looking Back 50 Years.* Curvin, Robert. 2014. *Inside Newark: Decline, Rebellion, and the Search for Transformation.* Martens, Frederick T. *Delaware Valley Citizens Crime Commission.* 1987. *Theft of A City: When Business, Organized Crime, and Government are in Bed Together.* October 26th.

105. Pennsylvania Crime Commission. 1991. *Organized Crime in Pennsylvania: A Decade of Change.* pp. 74, 76–78, 91, 162, 196, 198, 212–13, 121, 225–27, 309, 311–21, 326.

106. Ladet, Janae and Joseph Schilling. Urban Institute. 2018. "Chester, Pennsylvania." May.

107. When the Commission exposed the rampant corruption that encapsulated the city, the local district attorney demanded proofs. Of course, he had access to a grand jury that would have uncovered all that the Commission had as well as that unearthed by the federal government. Not surprisingly, his career blossomed, serving later on as the chairman of the state's gaming commission and for a time as acting attorney general. Hart, Joseph. *The Delaware Valley Daily Times.* 1989. "DA: No Mob Probe: I Need Concrete Evidence, Ryan Says." January 29th. Hinds, deCourcey Michael. *The New York Times.* 1992. "Pennsylvania City Hopes Its Bouncing Back from the Bottom." January 5th. Also see Mele, Christopher. 2017. *Race and the Politics of Deception,* pp. 119–20.

108. *United States v. Nacrelli, 468 F. Supp. 241* (1979). Leagle.com.

the city. This was a task that Nacrelli was well-suited for, particularly given his former position as mayor of Chester.

The vending machine business was one of the more lucrative and cash-rich businesses that the Mafia routinely invested in for those unfamiliar with this industry.[109] It provided both unreported cash to its owners, served as a method to insinuate itself in the bar and cocktail lounge business, and was a viable avenue to launder money. And it provided the racketeer with the moniker of a legitimate businessman.[110]

This industry in most cities is exclusively controlled by either the Mafia or local racketeers. A property-rights system endures. The bar businesses are often beholden to the vending machine company's owners. Through loans extended to the bar owners, most of whom are risk-challenged business entrepreneurs, the vending machine owners become de-facto or hidden partners with the on-paper licensee of the bar or cocktail lounge.[111]

This scheme was undoubtedly the case in Chester, where the Bruno Crime Family maintained exclusive control of the vending property-rights system. If an outlier attempted to gain a slice of this lucrative market, he paid tribute to the Bruno Family, or the foreign vending company would have to partner with an existing mob-controlled company.[112]

In the mid-1980s, Alphonso Sanbe began placing his video poker machine in cocktail lounges and bars "owned" by the Bruno Mafia Family.[113] Sanbe had partnered with Freddy Lupi, an associate of New York's Gambino Family. Santo Idone, the *capo* in the Bruno Family who controlled the video poker rackets in Chester, retaliated. Sanbe's machines

---

109. In 1984, the Permanent Subcommittee on Investigations, United States Senate, concluded, "Police officers and other officials are bribed by distributors and operators to look the other way instead of cracking down . . . on this $15 billion dollar tax free industry rife with corruption."

110. Woodall, Candy. *USA TODAY.* 2021. "Fight over skill games, "illegal gambling" prompts Pa. lawmakers to return campaign cash." June 14th.

111. Martens, Frederick T. *Federal Probation.* 1984. "The Illusion of Success: A Case Study in the Infiltration of Legitimate Business." p. 40.

112. *New Jersey State Commission of Investigation: Video Poker.* 1991. p. 23.

113. "Owned" refers to an exclusive arrangement by a bar to partner with a video-poker vendor.

were sabotaged. Sanbe was physically assaulted and warned to remove his video poker machines from Idone's locations.[114]

With Idone's financial interests in the video poker industry challenged by Sanbe, Idone met with Nicodemo Scarfo, the boss of the Bruno Family. Throughout the years, there was collegiality between the Bruno and Gambino Families. This relationship became solidified with the advent of casino gaming in Atlantic City, New Jersey.

John Gotti, at this point, was firmly in charge of the Gambino Family. Scarfo met with Gotti, seeking to resolve the situation. While both shared a mutual affinity for violently settling disputes, they agreed that Sanbe would quietly and voluntarily relinquish his gambling interests in Chester. Idone would retain exclusive control over the gambling rackets. It was, after all, the Bruno Family's territory.[115]

In January of 1989, one year after the Commission conducted its exhaustive investigation patently ignored by the district attorney, Idone and his video poker associates were indicted by the Federal government for racketeering, illegal gambling, and extortion. Convicted in 1990, Idone received a twenty-year prison sentence, of which he only served eight years. He died in 2005.

As for Nacrelli, he served as the de facto mayor of Chester, exercising his influence over various government agencies. Whether it be appointments to the school board, promotions in the police department, or engineering the bureaucratic process to locate a trash incinerator inside the boundaries of this economically distressed and politically disenfranchised community, Nacrelli's invisible hand guided the decision-making.[116] Life

114. In Paterson, New Jersey, a similar situation arose. When its vice-czar, Johnny Ventura did not get his cut from the video poker rackets, ". . . Johnny Ventura went out and . . . robbed a lot of machines from another vendor. They busted them up and all they said," See if you're not with us, this is what could happen."(NJ SCI: Video Poker. 1991. p. 23). Similarly, in Allentown, Pennsylvania, a dispute over the placement of video-poker machines distributed by M&J Vending and Bethlehem Music was mediated by Joseph Scalleat, a member of the Bufalino Mafia Family. *The Scranton Times*. 1988. "Scalleat Is Directed: Go Before Crime Unit." August 11th.

115. Hart, Joe. *The Delaware Valley Daily Times*. 1989. "Dispute Used 'Family' Ties." January 25th.

116. Hart, Joe. *The Delaware Valley Daily Times*. 1989. "Panel Links ex-mayor to trash plant." February 17th. Lieber, Dave. *The Philadelphia Inquirer*. 1989. "Ex-mayor denies using a heavy hand in Chester." February 25th. *The Delaware Valley Sunday Times*. 1989. "Nacrelli Admits Patronage Role." February 26th.

with Nacrelli in Chester, Pennsylvania, was a never-ending saga of urban decay, political dysfunction, and deep-rooted racial animus.

Unfortunately, the beat goes on!

The Mob Protects the Philadelphia Industrial Correctional Center

Investigating organized crime and public corruption often leaves you with the feeling that if I didn't know better, I would think it was all a dream. How and why events evolve in ways that, on the surface, make little sense, but when further investigated, make complete sense, is what makes the investigation of complex crimes so intriguing and yet so misunderstood.

Initially, in 1988, when the Crime Commission first learned that William D'Elia was a night watchman at the construction site of the newly-designed Philadelphia Industrial Correctional Center, it made little sense. Why would the successor to the renowned mob boss Russell Bufalino have a job 90 miles from home in a city where his Mafia Family had no noticeable presence?[117]

Indeed it was below him to perform such a menial task? Moreover, retaining a mob boss to secure the construction site that would ultimately house mobsters and racketeers would not fare well publicly had it been exposed. It must be some kind of joke.

Several sources in the Scranton area informed the Commission to "look specifically at the company installing the windows and doors at the construction site." The Commission initiated an inquiry.

As we rummaged through the volumes of construction documents filed on behalf of the general contractor with the City of Philadelphia, we uncovered a bid submitted by a Scranton-based window and door company. Superior Fireproof Door was awarded the contract to install doors and windows at the correctional facility.[118]

---

117. Russell Bufalino was featured in the 2019 movie, *The Irishman*. He was played by Joe Pesci. Bufalino was also an attendee at the now infamous Appalachia Mafia Conference in New York in 1957.

118. Coveleskie, Vince. *The Tribune* (Scranton). 1990. "Superior Door selling building to pay creditors." August 31st.

Philadelphia was the epicenter or base of operations for the Bruno Crime Family. Construction projects in the city that involved union and even non-union labor often had to make accommodations with the Bruno Mafia Family to avoid labor unrest, slow-downs, or strikes. It was the cost of doing business in Philadelphia as well as other cities in the Northeast. It was starting to make perfect sense.

Superior Doors and Windows, located in Bufalino's territory, required an emissary to work in an area controlled by the Bruno Family. D'Elia was from Pittston and had an ongoing and comfortable relationship with the Bruno Family. Superior was buying labor peace by putting D'Elia on their payroll, mainly since Superior was a non-union company. D'Elia could ensure that no harm would come to Superior or its workers.

Our investigation began to focus on D'Elia's role. It became apparent it was essentially a no-show job. Interviews of workers, as well as surveillances, could not place D'Elia at the job site. Although the management of Superior claimed he was working the graveyard shift, 11-7, surveillances never put him at the site. D'Elia's role was to ensure labor peace.[119]

Armed with incontrovertible evidence, subpoenas were issued to the CEO and CFO of the company and the foreman on the job site. Nothing draws out the heavy artillery—the political surrogates—like a subpoena.

Contacted by the Chairman of the Commission, Michael Reilly, requested a complete debriefing on what we had uncovered and where we intended to go with this investigation. Reilly was reacting to an inquiry from the minority leader of the state Senate, Robert Mellow.

Mellow was a Scranton-based politician who was well-respected among his constituents and peers. Affable and charismatic, he had proven to be a supporter of the Commission.

Reilly decided to fly to Scranton and wrap his head around the investigation and its political implications. As a former Pittsburgh police detective and assistant district attorney in Allegheny County, Reilly was completely comfortable discerning the facts from the innuendo and political fall-out that this investigation had generated.

---

119. See *D'Elia v. Pennsylvania Crime Commission, 521 Pa. 225* (1989).

Being thoroughly briefed and meeting with Mellow, Reilly decided that the Commission would privately take the CEO and project superintendent's testimony.

Under oath, the construction project superintendent testified that he was experiencing labor strife, stolen tools, sabotaged equipment, and received threatening phone calls. After retaining D'Elia, and paying him approximately $5,000, the labor problems disappeared. The superintendent did not know of D'Elia ever being on the site.

With this incriminating testimony, coupled with what the Commission uncovered, we issued a subpoena to D'Elia. The subpoena commanded D'Elia to appear before the Commission and provide testimony regarding his role as a security guard at the Philadelphia Detention Center.

His attorney contacted the Commission and informed us that D'Elia would take "the fifth" and refuse to testify. Confronted with the decision to accept D'Elia's refusal to testify or extend him a grant of use immunity that would compel his testimony, the Commission opted for the latter.

By extending use immunity to D'Elia, the Commission was limiting his testimony strictly to his role at the Philadelphia Industrial Correctional Center and nothing more. It would also allow the Commission to obtain the necessary waivers from federal, state, and local agencies interested in pursuing an investigation of D'Elia on other matters. With releases in hand, the Commission now upped the stakes: testify or be imprisoned for contempt of court.

Appearing before Judge Bernard McGinley of the Commonwealth Court in Harrisburg, I was qualified as an expert witness. I testified to D'Elia's mob stature and how the Mafia resolves territorial incursions and disputes. I painstakingly addressed D'Elias's role, or lack thereof, at the construction site.

Commission counsel Alan Bailey testified regarding the legal protocols that were adhered to regarding extending use immunity to D'Elia. Based upon the refusal of D'Elia to testify after being afforded immunity, McGinley held D'Elia in contempt of court, which required him to serve time in jail until he was willing to testify.[120]

---

120. Taylor, Wendy. *The Scranton Times.* 1988. "Contempt Motion Filed as D'Elia Fails To Honor Subpoena." June 3rd.

Immediately, the court stayed D'Elias' sentence at the request of his attorney. He could appeal McGinley's contempt order directly to the Pennsylvania Supreme Court, which he did.

In deciding the case, the Pennsylvania Supreme Court relied upon a rare provision found perhaps only in its Constitution:

"We have in our Constitution a fitting expression of the great importance of our founders attached to a person's good name . . . all men are born equally free . . . and have certain inherent and indefeasible rights . . . among which are those enjoying and defending . . . *reputation* . . ." the Court opined. Absent the "fires of due process," the Court concluded, "exposure and the magnitude of the infamy that might follow . . . is enormous."

Simply said, the Supreme Court stripped the Commission's legislative right to grant immunity to a *recalcitrant* witness. It did not, however, preclude a witness from requesting immunity from prosecution.

The investigation of the Philadelphia Industrial Correctional Center was thus, concluded. D'Elia was spared from testifying before the Commission. No criminal charges were lodged. Nor did the City of Philadelphia or its emissaries take any affirmative legal action.

However, in 2006, D'Elia was charged by the federal government with laundering $600,000 in drug proceeds and plotting to kill a government witness. He served five years in federal prison, earning an early release for testifying against the owner of a Pennsylvania casino, Louis DeNaples.

Six years later, Mellow, who had served as President of the Senate and was an ally of DeNaples, was charged and pled guilty to conspiracy to commit mail fraud and tax evasion.

Denied his state pension of $138,958 under a provision in the state law for those convicted of corruption charges, Mellow appealed. In a narrowly decided decision (i.e., 6-5), the State Employee's Retirement System reinstated his pension, the only time in 11 years that it had done so.[121]

As the state's motto reflected, "You've Got a Friend in Pennsylvania."

---

121. *The Philadelphia Inquirer.* 2017. "Pa. Officials restore six-figure pension for former state senator convicted of corruption." December 5th. See also, *Used, Abused & Forgotten—Bob Mellow: A Targeted Senator.* 2016. Infinity Publishing. June 20th.

The Misery Merchants Strike It Rich

During a national emergency, one thing is sure. It is only a matter of time that those looking to capitalize on the chaos that ensues will invent any variety of schemes to extract revenue from the misery of others. A case in point was the once-in-a-hundred-year hurricane that ripped through New Orleans in 2005.

Given the history of Thacher Associates investigating Mafia-dominated companies and monitoring the World Trade Center post 9-11, the inspector general of New Orleans requested that we examine the procurement of closed-circuit cameras following the devastation caused by Hurricane Katrina.

Dispatched to New Orleans, my colleagues and I met with many government officials. Repeatedly contractors testified that the contracts to install closed-circuit monitors throughout the French Quarter district were rigged and resulted in an inferior product that did not perform as required.

Completing nearly thirty hours of interviews and reviewing volumes of documents, it was increasingly evident that "there was something rotten in New Orleans."

As we began to decipher and analyze the information we had collected, our investigation focused on several principals responsible for awarding the contracts for the closed-circuit monitors.

First and foremost was Mark St. Pierre. Those interviewed repeatedly suggested that after leaving government service, St. Pierre started his own technology company. He had, they believed, an "inside track" on bids for newly-developed technology systems that would improve the surveillance capabilities of the police in the tourist-rich district known as the French Quarter.

Hurricane Katrina had essentially wiped out the old surveillance cameras installed in the French Quarter. An entirely new and state-of-the-art closed-circuit monitoring system was required. Awarded no-bid contracts valued at several million dollars by Gregory Meffert were St. Pierre's companies. Meffert was the chief technology officer for the City and a close political ally of its mayor, Ray Nagin.

Alluded to repeatedly in interviews of the police and those involved in the bidding process was Meffert's unusually close *personal* relationship with Nagin. If our experiences in New York taught us anything, interviews of competitor businesses were often fountains of helpful information.

Our interviews of several disgruntled competitor companies attempting to cash in on the federal largess that Katrina brought to the City revealed many shady practices, none of which could have been a secret. There seemed to be no shame or guile involved in the audacious behavior of St. Pierre, or for that matter, Meffert.

One of the most egregious findings of our inquiry was the poor quality of the photographic images from the closed-circuit monitors in the French Quarter. When queried about their inability to rely on the closed-circuit technology in identifying suspects and certifying the photographic imagery in court, the police were exorcised about their inability to rely on the closed-circuit technology.

Claiming what the city bought was a "pig in a poke," these competitors were adamant that there was an *unusual* if not a corrupt relationship between St. Pierre and Meffert. They were unaware of the payoffs made to Meffert by St. Pierre, as were we. Nonetheless, they were undoubtedly in an uproar about the less-than-transparent bidding process.

As is often the case, the most obvious and annoying usually begets the lion's share of attention. In this case, it was "the yacht." With few exceptions, those interviewed would incessantly raise the issue of "the yacht" and how certain city employees, including Meffert and the mayor, were routinely entertained on the yacht.

St. Pierre owned the yacht. Neither St. Pierre nor Meffert was held in high regard by those we interviewed. Referred to in bevy of pejorative terms, those interviewed were not reticent in articulating their bitterness and resentment towards Meffert and St. Pierre.

They probably questioned why two investigators from New York were in New Orleans uncovering what seemed to be common knowledge among the local gentry? At times, so did we?

Naturally, we were at a disadvantage in tackling many of these issues. We lacked the investigative tools available to a traditional law enforcement agency. While afforded the bidding documents, the executed contracts, and access to the government employees responsible for approving the various expenditures, we could not access Meffert's or St. Pierre's tax returns, financial records, or bank accounts.

Political corruption investigations usually rely on the proverbial phrase, "follow the money." Inevitably money laundering, tax evasion, and mail and wire fraud are the predicate acts that result in an indictment and conviction.

Before we departed from New Orleans, we were "wined and dined" in the French Quarter. Naturally, the food was exquisite, the ambiance pleasant and exuberant, the wine and spirits plentiful, and southern charm and beauty enticing. Were we naturally suspicious? Was this an attempt to discern what we had learned and whether or not there was any information uncovered that implicated Nagin? They, of course, had nothing to fear. There was a lot of smoke but no fire. Which led us to question what was this assignment was about?

Indeed the Inspector General was well-aware that the city awarded several no-bid contracts? They knew of the competitor's squawking about being frozen out of the bidding process. They knew the cameras were under-performing, and most were inoperative. And more than likely, they were aware of the notorious parties occurring on St. Pierre's yacht. Many included the mayor and a bevy of scantily-clad women or referred to us as "strippers."

The red flags were everywhere. It was classic Louisiana corruption. What had occurred was the worst-kept secret in New Orleans. Even the federal government was aware of it.

Shortly after we departed and filed our findings, the FBI and the United States Attorney's Office pursued Meffert and St. Pierre with a vengeance. Uncovered were bribes amounting to $860,000 paid to Meffert by St. Pierre. Publically exposed were city officials being entertained by strippers. Vacations in the Caribbean, paid for by St. Pierre, were revealed. The evidence was overwhelming.

Meffert ultimately became a government witness. As a result, St. Pierre was indicted. Convicted of 53 felony counts in less than six hours of jury deliberations, St. Pierre faced 53 years in prison. He ultimately was sentenced to ten years in prison. [122]

---

122. Hammer, David. *The Times-Picayune.* 2011. "Jurors convict former City Hall vendor Mark St. Pierre after only 6 hours of deliberations." May 27th.

It was a resounding victory for the people of New Orleans. But the stain that had soiled the city's government still had not been erased. Ray Nagin, the reform-driven mayor, had escaped indictment.

Five years later, on January 18, 2013, Nagin was indicted on charges related to receiving more than $200,000 in kickbacks from contractors doing business with the City of New Orleans. Meffert again was a key witness, testifying that Nagin was well-aware of St. Pierre's involvement in the kickback schemes that he, Meffert, had engineered. Several other businessmen implicated Nagin in various kickback schemes, one involving a significant amount of free granite given to him in the form of a bribe. Again, the evidence was formidable.

Nagin was convicted on 20 of 21 counts of bribery and sentenced to ten years in prison.

Once again, the perennial adage "he that lieth down with dogs shall rise up with fleas" raised its ugly head.

5

A Con-Man, A Mystery-Writer, and the FBI

Never would I have contemplated that one of the world's most prolific mystery writers, Mary Higgins-Clark, would be duped by an FBI informant. Thomas "Tommy" Giacomaro proved to be one of the most audacious con-men I encountered during my career investigating organized and white-collar crime.[1]

Giacomaro was by far the "best of the best" when transferring your assets to his bank account. He certainly knew how to insinuate himself in financial arrangements that would disgorge the unsuspecting of their assets.

Known for his ability to entice and convince even the most ardent skeptic, Giacomaro was charismatic and engaging. His penchant for the grandiose and inflated hyperbole was certainly humorous if it were not so tragic and destructive.[2] Simply put, "Tommy G" was the reincarnation of Frank Abagnale, Jr. (played by Leonardo DiCaprio in *Catch Me if You Can)* only with a much more flair and Chutzpah.

Our initial engagement to investigate Giacomaro focused on his involvement with what were "roll-ups" or consolidations. This involved nationally-known waste management companies, trucking companies,

---

1. United States Attorney, District of New Jersey (Newark). 2003. "Convicted Con-Artist Pleads Guilty to $73 Million Fraud." June 6th.

2. Giacomaro, Thomas. 2018. *The King of Con: How a Smooth-Talking Jersey Boy Made and Lost Billions, Baffled the FBI, Eluded the Mob, and Lived to Tell the Crooked Tale.* Ben Bella Books. September 25th.

and recycling enterprises. Acquiring the assets and liabilities of smaller companies to squeeze profits by reducing overhead and increasing the company's purchasing power was a relatively simple formula. Giacomaro was a master at selling this concept. As the de-facto owner and president of Wellesley Services and Windham Associates, Giacomaro was considered the guru of "roll-ups."

Serving as legitimate fronts for Giacomaro were two respected businessmen, Keith Moody and Anthony Bianco. This corporate arrangement allowed Giacomaro to "fraudulently obtain funds to finance his lavish lifestyle." Among his assets was a $6.2 million home. He had spent $5.9 million on renovations. Millions more spent on buying luxury goods and services and paying legal bills. This was just the tip of an iceberg.

What, of course, remains an utterly perplexing mystery is how "Tommy G" accomplished all this while working as an informant for the FBI?[3]

In just one of several examples of Giacomaro's skills and stealth, my colleague Rod Leith and I met with an "investor" in Giacomaro's business venture. The "investor" had reflected on his relationship with Giacomaro. It was symbolic of how adept "Tommy G" was in relieving him of his "investment."

Interviewed in Wilmington, Delaware, this "investor" described how he became entangled in Giacomaro's web of deceit. Having invested $30,000 with Giacomaro and promised a hefty return of anywhere from 15%-20%, he had grown suspicious when Giacomaro refused his telephone calls.

He was insistent on the return of his initial investment or would report "Tommy G" to the police. Traveling from Wilmington, Delaware, to a restaurant in New Jersey, IL Villagio, the investor was "wined and dined" by Giacomaro. Informed and cultivated on how well his investment was performing and more significant returns were imminent, Giacomaro did what a good con-man often does: he doubled-down. With

---

3. Markmuellerjournalism.com. 2002. "The Man who stole $80 million while working for the FBI." May 5th. Hanley, Robert. *The New York Times*. 2003. "Ex-Informer Admits to Fraud As He Helped F.B.I. on a Case." June 7th.

an additional $20,000, the "investor" would likely see a more respectable return, sooner rather than later.

What Giacomaro instinctively knew, "greed is good," and will always clinch the deal. Giacomaro wrangled another $20,000 from this "investor." Arguably, Giacomaro's cunning and clever ability to convince even the most suspicious is what propelled him into the upper tiers of twentieth-century con-artists.

Naturally, the investment that made headlines was that which enveloped the renowned mystery writer, Mary Higgins-Clark. Her involvement simply demonstrates the age-old adage, "you rob banks because that's where the money is."

In the course of our investigation of Giacomaro, Rod and I learned of Mary Higgins-Clark's entanglements with this charismatic, narcissistic, and unremorseful grifter.

Higgins-Clark was renowned for her classic mystery novels that populated virtually every airport and library in the world. She was the president of the Mystery Writers Association of America. She was an inductee in New Jersey's Hall of Fame. It seemed unfathomable that Higgins-Clark would become victim to this slick-talking, morally-depraved, and culturally challenged con-artist? It made no sense then, nor does it make any sense now.

Only today, after having spent 14 years in prison, can we begin to appreciate how this FBI informant hood-winked Higgins-Clark, the FBI, the U.S. Attorney's Office, and a slew of investors.[4]

With the publication of his autobiographical book in 2018, a psychological portrait of Giacomaro emerges, which is in large part, a continuation of his skills at duping even the most sophisticated and savvy "investor."

Those who have not had the opportunity to indulge in Giacomaro's creative tales, "Tommy G" claims at the age of 19 that he transported briefcases filled with cash on behalf of a mob-owned trucking company

---

4. Certainly not in the same league as Giacomaro, George Salemo of Allentown, Pennsylvania was another con-man who crossed my path. He too exhibited all the narcissistic traits that made Giacomaro so successful. See the 3-part series by Mary Ellen Alu, *The Morning Call* (Allentown, PA). 1993. "Ex-Agent Says scams only work for so long." April 27th; "He Has Style, brass and a silver tongue; Informant's Role Isn't A License to Steal."

to the late Teamster's boss, Jimmy Hoffa. That Hoffa would accept cash from a 19-year-old untested "gopher" (his term) speaks again to Giacomaro's controlling need to remain relevant.[5]

Not content with purportedly meeting and carrying money to Hoffa, Giacomaro regales in his ability to arrange a peace agreement between the Genovese Crime Family and James "Whitey" Bulger of Boston.[6] The mere thought of the Mafia using the services of Giacomaro to negotiate a "pay-to-play" arrangement with a person of Bulger's underworld stature is simply ludicrous.[7]

While serving time in prison, Giacomaro insists that he had the protection of the Bonanno Mafia Family, *"even though I was a Genovese."*[8]

Giacomaro was never a member of any Mafia family.

Like most successful con-men, the underlying and common trait of Giacomaro is his unflinching ability to "gild the lily." Preying upon both the greed of his prospective clients and accentuating his relationships with influential, prominent, well-connected, and even unsavory characters, Giacomaro was and did create a fictional narrative and persona. Seen as a financially- successful, clever, and savvy businessman and surrounded by all the material accouterments of success, the optics were convincing.[9]

Essentially this narrative made him an incredibly successful and proficient con-man, a charismatic character straight out of central casting. Fourteen years in prison had little effect on Giacomaro's penchant for grandiose and gratuitous exhortations.

After dissecting Giacomaro's ruminations, what remains a mystery is how he could deceive the FBI with all its "checks and balances" that

---

5. Giacomaro, Thomas. 2019. *King of Con.* pp. 54-58. Short, Martin. 1996. *Crime Inc.: The Story of Organized Crime.* pp. 246–68.

6. Giacomaro, Thomas. 2019. *King of Con.* pp. 52–54. Third Report by the Committee on Government Reform. 2004. "Everything Secret Degenerates: The FBI'S Use of Murderers as Informants." February 3rd.

7. Lehr, Dick and Gerard O'Neill. 2001. *Black Mass: Whitey Bulger, the FBI, and The Devil's Deal.*

8. Giacomaro, Thomas. 2019. *King of Con.* p. 246.

9. Markmuellerjournalism.com. 2002. *The Man who stole $80 million while working for the FBI.* May 5th.

were promulgated following the debacles of the sixties and seventies and ABSCAM.[10]

We all know that the informant procurement business is a dirty business. It requires close and intimate interactions between criminals and law enforcers. These relationships can often lead to overlooking sure telltale signs of criminality, deception, and ethical misdeeds. It can result in the handler becoming enamored with the informant's ability to persuade, deceive, and misrepresent. It represents a distorted form of the Stockholm Syndrome. Time and again, handlers get caught up in the criminal exploits of those they are obligated to police and control. The case of FBI agent John Connolly, "Whitey" Bulger's handler, is just one of several egregious examples.[11]

Giacomaro certainly was no wall-flower when it came to embarrassing the FBI. Able to organize and execute multi-million frauds that disgorged investors of their monies under the wandering eyes of his FBI handler Harry Mount certainly proved to be one of his bolder schemes.[12]

Mount was ultimately hired by Giacomaro as head of security at Wellesley, providing another veil of legitimacy to a corrupted organization.[13] Mount was also on the adjunct faculty at a local university, teaching a course on organized crime. This relationship brought added value to Giacomaro's stature and prestige.

Attracting the services of former or current law enforcement officials was a trait that Giacomaro used quite effectively. It provided, as he proudly acknowledged, legitimacy to his criminal enterprises.

Reflecting on his *alleged* cozy relationship with the Chief of Detectives in the Passaic County Prosecutor's Office, Giacomaro was well-aware of the sleazy reputation that had infected the Passaic County Prosecutor's Office. *Alleging* that he purchased a travel agency from the wife of its chief of detectives, Giacomaro retained the name "Reiser Travel Agency."

---

10. Wikipedia: ABSCAM. Aronson, Trevor. *The Intercept.* 2017. "The FBI Gives Itself Plenty of Rope To Pull In Informants." January 31st. Charles, Douglas M. *The Conversation.* 2017. "The FBI's History of scandals: From Bielaski to Hoover, Sessions, and Comey." May 17th.

11. Klein, Christopher. *History.* 2019. "How Whitey Bulger Manipulated the FBI Into Locking Up His Enemies." July 25th. Fitzpatrick, Robert and John Land. 2012. *Betrayal: Whitey Bulger and the FBI Agent Who Fought to Bring Him Down.* January 3rd.

12. Sujo, Aly. *New York Post.* 2003. "Scammer made FBI Suckers." June 7th.

13. Giacomaro, Thomas. 2019. *King of Con.* pp. 164–66, 173–76, 182, 191–92, 202, 236.

"It was a connection that we knew would come in handy for our new line of work [drug trafficking] . . . [The Chief] was good friends with all New Jersey politicians and cops . . . we kept the name . . . so that everyone could see we had the law on our side . . . We donated generously to the [Oatsie Reiser Social] club, to their election campaigns, and to the [Police] Benevolent Association. Sometimes, we donated directly to Oatsie, if you know what I mean," Giacomaro gleefully volunteers.[14]

It was yet another trophy for Giacomaro to enhance his cachet among those with whom he would target for future "investments."

Which led us to Giacomaro's financial entanglements with Higgins-Clark.

So it was when Rod Leith and I approached Higgins-Clark to alert her to Giacomaro's frauds and her apparent victimization, her husband promptly rebuffed us. He essentially told us that she chose not to speak with us.

Knowing Larry McClure, who was her attorney, I arranged a meeting with him. After doing away with all the usual niceties and formalities, Rod and I attempted to alert McClure to Giacomaro's exploits and his unsavory relationship with his client, Higgins-Clark. McClure was quite abrupt in his response. "We are aware and have it all under control." It was a quick ending to a relatively unproductive meeting.

Years later, we learned that Higgins-Clark had clawed back $20 million or more of the monies she invested with Giacomaro.[15] Moody and Bianco were arrested by the F.B.I., convicted, and sentenced to prison. McClure was disbarred for misappropriating clients' funds. Giacomaro was sentenced to 14 years in prison.

If made into a movie, the travails, exploits, and trials of Tommy Giacomaro would rank among the more audacious con-schemes that found their way to the big screen.

Indeed, his induction into New Jersey's Hall of Shame would be a fitting tribute for the King of Con.

---

14. Giacomaro. Thomas. 2018. *The King of Con.* pp. 80–81.
15. *The Record* (Hackensack, NJ). 2006. "Bergen con artist ordered to repay investors $69M." August 10th.

6

"The Russians Are Coming!"

In 1990, at the behest of the Dick Ward of the University of Illinois, I traveled to Barcelona, Spain, to lecture on organized crime and public corruption.[16] I realized that every trip was another learning experience that would only advance and enhance my knowledge of organized crime.

Developing a global perspective, understanding the nuances of the respective cultures, and trading war stories on the investigation of organized crime and public corruption only reinforced what my parents had told me time and again. Travel is the best education you will ever receive. You will learn that the issues, problems, wants, and desires are usually the same the world over: a better life for your children and grandchildren.

While attending this seminar, two Russian police officers befriended me.[17] Vladimir Knyazev and Sergei Roukhlyadev were from Minsk, Belarus. Vladimir was a captain, and Sergei, his superior, was a colonel in its internal security and law enforcement apparatus. Vladimir served as Sergei's translator.

Needless to say, when you are at a disadvantage speaking the language, the conversation can become quite cumbersome and taxing. Sentences took twice as long. The inflection of your voice may have conveyed something other than that which was intended. Vladimir was naturally

16. University of Illinois, Chicago Circle. 1990. PICK Fifth Annual International Symposium on Criminal Justice Issues. Illicit Drugs and Organized Crime. July 16-20th.

17. Office of International Criminal Justice, University of Illinois at Chicago Circle. 1990. Illicit Drugs and Organized Crime. July 16-20th.

quite patient with Sergei and me. A smile or a hearty laugh would often convey the sincerity of the thought.

The seminar lasted a week, and I found myself dining with Vladimir and Sergei every evening. I could not discern whether they saw me as a potential human asset for their security services or merely as a friendly American. But it didn't matter all that much, for there would likely be no further contact after the conference.

As we were approaching the end of the seminar, Vladimir pulled me aside. He began discussing America and what it was like living here. He then sprung the question on me, a question for which I was unprepared. "Do you think you could sponsor my family and me to America?" Thinking he was looking to defect, I inquired why he would want to come to America? His answer was quite simple and reinforced the universal desire: to provide my children with a better way of life.

I said I would look into it but made no promises. Sponsoring an entire family was not only costly but would require diplomatic and bureaucratic gymnastics. It would not be easy. We exchanged phone numbers—email was not an option.

Upon my return to the United States, his response continued to nag at me. "To provide a better life for his children" seemed so patronizing yet equally as sincere.

Russian organized crime was becoming more and more prevalent in the United States. I began thinking that perhaps we could use Vladimir's skills. Understanding its scope in Pennsylvania was worth considering. Or possibly in New York or New Jersey, too. A tri-state project might work. It was more a dream than a reality, particularly given the hurdles we would have to overcome.

I contacted Ron Goldstock, who was in charge of the New York State Organized Crime Task Force, and Jim Morley, the Executive Director of the New Jersey State Commission of Investigation. We discussed the logistics of a cooperative arrangement. Goldstock agreed to take the lead and arrange for the funding to be administered through his agency. Morley and I would financially contribute one-third each toward a salary for Vladimir. The more we discussed the project, its reality became increasingly doable.

We agreed to initiate the project on May 1, 1992. Vladimir would be obligated to pay for the family's airfare. He would arrive at Newark International Airport in New Jersey. I would collect him and his family. They would temporarily reside in New Jersey. Vladimir, his wife Natasha, his two daughters, Nina and Tonya, would remain there until they could find appropriate housing. It was a done deal.

Upon their arrival at the airport, I remember these two little children, Nina, nine, and Tonya, five, looking up at me as I rambled on with Vladimir and his wife, who spoke fluent English as well. The two children said not a word of English.

Proceeding to my home in New Jersey, we stopped off at an ice-cream parlor on Rte. 23 in Riverdale, New Jersey. I bought Nina and Tonya two huge soft ice cream cones. Their eyes lit up. They had seen nothing like this in Belarus.

Upon arriving at my home, I had previously re-arranged the bedrooms for Vladimir, Natasha, Nina, and Tanya. Everybody was exhausted, so we retired.

The following day, I was discussing with Vladimir and Natasha the plan for the next week. Enrolling the children in school was at the top of the list. Without any knowledge of English, I wondered how they would fare. "We're Russians," Vladimir would say. "We can suffer through anything." The television proved to be their language and cultural tutor.

As we discussed various issues, Natasha abruptly said, "Fred, I must tell you something. I am sick." I thought that perhaps she didn't feel well and she just needed aspirin or an Advil. "No, she said, I had a mastectomy before we came here. If I didn't go to America, the doctor said the drugs needed to treat the cancer were not available in Belarus . . . I brought all my medical records with me."

She then left me with one heartbreaking message. "Fred, I only want is to live long enough to see Nina and Tonya graduate school."

Of course, all I could contemplate was her lack of health insurance would preclude any medical care in the United States. I immediately started to reflect on the many issues that I would confront. Who would pay the doctor bills, the hospital costs, and the drug prescriptions that would be required? What if Natasha passed away here? Who would pay for her return to Belarus? Funeral arrangements? All these thoughts raced through my head.

The following morning I contacted a good friend, Maria Coppola, to discuss my dilemma. She calmly said, "Only you could get yourself into this predicament." Maria reached out to her friend, Dr. Joseph De-Luca, a local physician. Not one to shy away from a problematic situation, he told her to bring Natasha and her medical records to his office. Upon reading the diagnosis, DeLuca commented to Maria, "she is quite sick . . . I have a doctor in Goshen, New York, who is Russian . . . let me see if he will see her."

DeLuca contacted Dr. Mark Tuckfelt, a specialist in hematology and oncology. Fortunately, he was willing to treat Natasha simply for the cost of the therapeutics. Indeed, Natasha was blessed by a choir of angels. Her cancer was in remission when she and her family returned to Belarus two years later.

Natasha lived for another fifteen years. Her cancer returned with a vengeance in 2009. Speaking to her the day she passed away, her last words were, "Fred, I saw my children graduate college . . . that was more than I asked for."

Natasha was never one to lament about the cards she was dealt. She cherished all she had, never envious of those who had more. Neither she nor her family was the devils portrayed during my years growing up under the looming images of that enormous mushroom cloud. They were no different than the average American—wanting to see their children do better than them.

Our investigation into the incursion of Russian racketeers continued throughout 1992 and 1993. The topic was, without question, one that both federal and state law enforcement were struggling to understand. Language barriers, as well as the lack of informants, hindered our investigations.

Retaining the services of Vladimir was the first step, but one that only allowed us to collect the most basic information. We were not in a position to infiltrate the many networks that existed in such Russian enclaves as New York's Brighton Beach, Philadelphia's Bustleton section, or New Jersey's "Gold Coast."

Aiding us in our endeavor was the United States Department of Justice. They solicited proposals to study Russian organized crime. Partnering with two university professors, James Finckenauer and Elin Waring, the *Tri-State Project on Russian Organized Crime* was integrated with our investigative efforts.[18] Its findings advanced to some degree our knowledge of Russian organized crime.[19]

Addressing the nomenclature (or lack thereof) of Russian organized crime, the Tri-State Project found that "these structures [referring to the intricate network structures] do not resemble those commonly associated with conventional organized crime, but they apparently are responsive to the particular criminal opportunities in which Russians have engaged . . . there is no Russian organized criminal enterprise that mirrors Cosa Nostra families and that the most that can be said about the criminal activities of Russian emigres in the United States are that they tend to be "organized."

With the return of Vladimir, Natasha, Andrew, their son, Nina, and Tonya, to their home in Minsk, Belarus, our friendship remained solid.[20] The cultural exchanges between their children and mine have created lasting memories and periodic visits.

They will always have a special place in our hearts.

---

18. Finckenauer, James O. and Elin J. Waring. 1998. *Russian Mafia in America: Immigration, Culture and Crime*. NIJ. Martens, Frederick T. *Crime & Justice International*. 1999. "Is There Russian Organized Crime in the U.S.?" March.

19. Klebnikov, Paul. 2000. *Godfather of the Kremlin: Boris Berezovsky and the Looting of Russia*. Friedman, Robert I. 2000. *Red Mafia: How the Russian Mob Has Invaded America*. Granville, Johanna. *Demokratizatsiya*. 2003. "'Dermokratizatsiya' and 'Prikhvatizatsiya': The Russian Kleptocracy and Rise of Organized Crime." Summer, pp. 448–57.

20. As of this writing, 24 years later, Belarus still suffers under the vestiges of the "last dictator in Europe," Alexander Lukashenko. *Criminal Organizations*. 1996. "New Russians, Old Cons, and the Transition to a Market Economy: Reflections From Abroad." vol. 10, no. 2.

7

Preventing Fraud 3000 Miles Away?

It was 1998, and the Northern Irish government earlier had reached an agreement that allowed for sharing governance with the British. Referred to the "Good Friday Agreement," the Irish Republican Army (IRA) dismantling was about to become a reality. But with this Agreement, another form of criminality was emerging.

Faced with the likelihood that its sources of revenue were drying up, remnants of the IRA decided to ply its trade—extortion—on the construction industry.

The government was aware of the inroads made by former IRA members into the building trades. Retaining the services of Ronald Goldstock, the pioneer who invented the Independent Private Sector Inspector General or IPSIG, Goldstock suggested that the government embark on an experimental project. Insert an IPSIG in every state-funded construction project. Goldstock defined the scope of services and designed an RFP or Request for Proposals which was advertised worldwide.

Essentially, the government of Northern Ireland would support the integration of a private inspector general in a construction company of a publicly bid project. The government would underwrite the costs associated with retaining the IPSIG.

At the time, I was working for Thacher Associates, a private investigative firm headquartered in New York City. One aspect of our business portfolio was integrity monitoring. Having just completed the most intensive integrity monitoring project in the nation, the rescue and recovery efforts at the site of the World Trade Center after 9-11, Thacher Associates was in the most advantageous position to export its knowledge to the European Union.

However, lacking a physical presence in Ireland would prove detrimental unless we could partner with a firm or company that performed similar tasks to those advertised in the RFP.

Years earlier, I had met and became quite friendly with Martin Kenney, a solicitor from Canada. He would attend the annual conference at Cambridge University every September, as would I.[1] Kenney was considered one, if not the premier, fraud investigator in the world. He had received the prestigious Donald Cressey Award from the International Association of Fraud Examiners.[2] Kenney was living in the Republic of Ireland. He had partnered with a firm in Northern Ireland to monitor the construction of a soccer stadium.

I contacted Kenney and asked him to partner with Thacher Associates and respond to Northern Ireland's RFP. He agreed. Enlisting the skills of Colm Morgan, a certified public accountant and attorney headquartered in Northern Ireland, we submitted a proposal delineating what steps we would take mitigating corruption on construction sites selected by the government of Northern Ireland.

In partnership with Kenney and Morgan, Thacher was chosen to transfer our expertise to the government entities that would eventually police the publicly-funded construction projects that were part of significant infrastructure investments by the British government.

The initial proposed site was in Derry, or Londonderry, depending upon whether you were a republican or a unionist.[3] While working on this project, I was instructed time and again by Colm to choose my words carefully, particularly when referring to [London] Derry. I learned pretty quickly that not only a new series of linguistic rules were to be

---

1. *Cambridge International Symposium on Economic Crime.* Jesus College. Cambridge University, Cambridge, England.

2. Martin Kenney & Co. Solicitors. Tortola, British Virgin Islands. Kampa, Dana. *BVI Beacon.* 2020. "Special Report: Lawyer claims he forgot getting $100,000 from BVI Airways." October 5th. Ryan, Nick. Boswell Group. 2014. "The Man Who Makes the Fraudsters Pay."

3. Muholland, Marc. 2002. *The Longest War: Northern Ireland's Troubled History.* pp. 54–55.

applied, but our efforts to mitigate corruption on these sites would be different from the challenges we confronted in New York City.

For example, the rules of non-engagement by the racketeers with the authorities, to put it bluntly, were off the table. Threatening or imposing physical punishments on contractors, government officials, and those (and their families) who cooperate with the authorities was fair game.

Furthermore, allowing the government to audit and compel the books and records for a particular project would be perceived as an intrusion of the contractor's proprietary information. Simply put, it was not graciously accepted and vociferously opposed.

Assigned with me on this project was Martin Aronchick. He brought a real dry sense of humor to the project. His legal skills were superb. He understood the construction industry, inside and out. And we worked well together.

But Aronchick, like me, came to the project with a New York "state of mind." Our questions and answers applied to the New York milieu. They indeed were not reflective of the environment during "The Troubles." Contractors knew the consequences of not paying off the local racketeers who controlled a geographic locale. They knew that family members were not safe if they informed the authorities of incursions by organized crime elements. They knew that projects could be closed down by unions they had to employ. And most of all, they learned not to trust the government to do the right thing.

Arriving in Belfast and escorted to the offices of the Secretary of State, Department of Finance for Northern Ireland, we met with several government officials and the contractor, Finley. Martin and I regaled them in our efforts to rid the construction industry in New York of organized crime influence. We discussed our successes in implementing integrity controls at the former World Trade Center site after 9-11. And our attitude was, "if you can make it in New York, you can make it anywhere."

The lone construction company owner, Finley, was far from impressed or receptive to our presentation. Intently listening, his first question was, "When you go back to New York, who's protecting me?" Naturally, we punted and handed the question off to the government officials sitting around the table. Regardless of how confident the government officials were in ensuring the safety of the construction owner, his family, and workers, Finley was not convinced.

As the meeting was about to end, my colleague, Martin Aronchick, began giving his professional calling card to those sitting around the table. It was classic New York. Perhaps it would generate more clients and, in turn, more billable hours?

Finley suggested that Martin retrieve them quickly. They would be in the hands of former IRA members before we departed the building. Then in the next breathe, Finley unflinchingly said, "it doesn't matter, I'm sure they knew you were here when the wheels touched down."

If there was one redeeming aspect to the meeting that introduced some humor in what was a challenging sales pitch, it was when Finley referred to my colleague, Aronchick, as "some Hollywood movie star . . . Al Pacino?" The debate centered on whether Aronchick resembled Pacino or Robert DeNiro, bringing a bit of levity to the issues not likely to be overcome by our reassurances or that of the Northern Irish government. The group settled on DeNiro.

All departed amicably, except for Finley. He now realized that he was to play a central role in what was likely to be a precursor to the not yet released movie, *American Hustle*.[4]

Implemented for twelve months, we audited the books and records of Finley's company. We interviewed contractors and sources. Nothing was amiss. No fraudulent payments to sub-contractors. No ghost employees were detected. No threats of violence or efforts to extort the contractor. No payoffs to public officials.

The project was an overwhelming success. But the government never implemented it on a grander scale.

As the saying goes, "maybe if it was too good to be true, it wasn't."

---

4. In 2013, the *American Hustle* was released in which DeNiro made a cameo appearance. The movie was a fictional take on the ABSCAM probe (1978-1980), in which the FBI establishes a front company to induce payoffs to politicians, gangsters, and extortionists.

8

The Globalization of Crime[1]

In 1979, I was introduced to David Powis, the Deputy Assistant Commissioner/Crime of Scotland Yard.[2] He had been visiting the United States collecting information on our domestic law enforcement intelligence systems. Finding his way to the New Jersey State Police Intelligence Bureau, Capt. Justin Dintino summoned me to his office. We discussed our intelligence program and our analytical training with Anacapa Sciences.[3]

Replicating what we had learned, I instructed two intelligence analysts, Paul Andrews and Paula Carter, to implement a comparative training program. It would be taught at the State Police Academy in Sea Girt, New Jersey. When discussing this with Powis, he asked whether he could send two Scotland Yard detectives to the training course.

In October of 1980, Frank Pulley and Alistar Graham of Scotland Yard arrived in the United States. Housed at the Academy facilities in Sea Girt, they attended a two-week course on organized crime intelligence analysis procedures and techniques. On the weekends, I entertained them

---

1. Martens, Frederick T. *International Journal of Comparative and Applied Criminal Justice.* 1991. *Transnational Enterprise Crime and the Elimination of Frontiers.* vol. 15, no. 1. Sterling, Claire. 1991. *Octopus: The Long Reach of the International Sicilian Mafia.* February. Sterling, Claire. 1994. *Thieves' World: The Threat of the New Global Network of Organized Crime.* June.

2. Global Image Works. "Deputy Assistant Commander David Powis, armed robbery, robbery, flying squad, metropolitan police." 1984. Powis, David. 1977. *Signs of Crime: A Field Manual for Police.* January 1st. Kelland, Gilbert. 1987. *Crime in London: From Postwar SOHO to Present-Day Supergrasses.* pp. 361-362.

3. Anacapa Sciences, Inc. Law Enforcement and Intelligence Analysis Training. Santa Barbara, California.

with my family, developing what proved to be a forty-year relationship with Frank and his family.

Frank, as I would later learn, was a hero in his own right. Pulley disarmed an armed robber, earning him the Queen's British Empire Medal awarded to him personally.[4] He never once mentioned this to me during our decades of friendship, simply indicative of his understated humility. Nor did he tout his many accomplishments investigating organized crime and corruption that had infected the sterling reputation of Scotland Yard.[5]

As a consequence of this fortuitous meeting, I traveled to London in 1981. There I met with Martin Short, a friend of Pulley. Short had been working for Thames Television at the time. He was selected to initiate a seven-part series of organized crime in the United States.[6] We had many discussions over Sheppard's Pie and pints of Guinness, developing the program's agenda and those who could be resourced to bring the spoken word to the visual medium.

At this point, Pulley and I discussed whether he would consider retirement to become a consultant to the program. At first, Pulley was reluctant. But as we would discuss the rich and untouched material that existed in the United States and how it would expand his horizons, he became increasingly intrigued. Once he agreed, the next task was selling Pulley to Thames management.

Pulley had no experience in the television industry, nor was he an authority on American organized crime. Self-educated, well-read, and highly skilled at writing the Queen's English, Pulley was a brilliant storyteller and historical encyclopedia of crime and vice in London's inner-city. His command of the vice rackets in the disenfranchised communities, often the melting pot for all sorts of criminal activities, was second to

4. *Second Supplement to The London Gazette.* 1968. December 24th.

5. Cox, Barry and John Shirley, Martin Short. 1977. *The Fall of Scotland Yard.* Kelland, Gilbert. 1986. *Crime in London.* Kelland, Gilbert. 1986. *Crime in London: From Postwar Soho to present-day Supergrasses.* pp. 83–84. British Broadcasting 3 Part Series: *Bent Coppers: Crossing the Line of Duty.* April 14, 21, 28, 2021.

6. Short, Martin. 1984. *Crime, Inc.* January 1st. Boardman, David. *The Guardian.* 2020. "Martin Short: Television journalist whose films and books exposed police corruption and the covert world of Freemasonry." September 20th.

none. Referred to by Sir Gilbert Kelland, deputy commissioner for crime at Scotland Yard, as "one of the most outstanding operational officers the force has ever known . . . he became something of a legend."[7]My job was to convince the program's management that Pulley would have a wide swath of law enforcement sources available to him that only someone with a law enforcement background would be able to access.

I appeared before the organizing committee that was responsible for the program's execution. Championing the skills that Pulley brought to the table and the reluctance of law enforcement to make time for journalists, Pulley proved to be the perfect antidote. They were convinced. Pulley was offered a position as a consultant.

Thus, I began my indoctrination into organized crime in Great Britain as well. Meeting with Pulley over the years, I was afforded his passionate insight into the various schemes engineered by Caribbean drug dealers, the Italian Mafia, Albanian gangsters, Nigerian fraudsters, and the Irish Republican Army. We established a symbiotic relationship. And one that to his dying day only sharpened and broadened my horizons when it came to an understanding the global networks that penetrated the political economies the world over.[8]

In 1987, while attending one of the earliest conferences hosted by Jesus College, Cambridge University, I was introduced to an emerging scholarly endeavor—the globalization of crime.[9] There I met Barry Rider, the organizer of this symposium, and Michael Levi, who started educating me on this relatively new and scantily-researched phenomenon.[10] It began my journey into intrigue and deception on a scale often found in spy novels.

Later in the year, I was elected President of the International Association for the Study of Organized Crime (IASOC). Initiated to provide a

---

7. Kelland, Gilbert. 1986. *Crime in London: From Postwar Soho to Present-Day Supergrasses.* p. 83.

8. Frank passed away on April 30, 2019. *International Journal of Comparative and Applied Criminal Justice.*1984. "Cross-Cultural Reflections of Organized Crime." vol. 8, no. 1–2., pp. 63–74.

9. Cambridge International Symposium on Economic Crime.

10. Levi, Michael. *Cardiff University. School of Social Sciences.* Wales. Rider, Barry. *University of Cambridge, Centre for Development Studies.* Cambridge, England. Mitsilegas, Valsamis, et. al. 2019. *Research Handbook on Transnational Crime.*

forum for both academics and practitioners to address organized crime, IASOC was at the forefront of what is today called transnational organized crime, or TNOC.

Recently IASOC merged with the Global Initiative against Transnational Organized Crime located in Geneva, Switzerland.[11] This Initiative represents the continuing evolution of what began in 1967 with the publication of *Task Force Report: Organized Crime* and Cressey's pioneering study, *Theft of the Nation,* in 1969.[12]

With the demise of the Soviet Union in 1989, an entirely new form of organized crime had emerged. Russian organized crime had become the fresh flavor of the day.[13] The movement of assets and capital from Russia was now on law enforcement's radar. The so-called *Bratva,* the *OPG,* and *Vorovskoy Mir* were the latest forms of criminal enterprises that would transform how organized crime was perceived globally.[14]

While our domestic forms of organized crime were undoubtedly enough food for thought, international and transnational organized crime opened up a new genre for academic study and criminal investigation.[15] With the lighting speed of a computer keystroke, racketeers and dictators could deposit millions of dollars in Cyprus, Lichtenstein, or Andorra from anywhere in the world. Ill-gotten proceeds of crime could be disguised in any number of ways, avoiding detection by traditional

11. A decision among the members of IASOC was made in November of 2019 at the ASC meeting in San Francisco, California to transfer all the records to the Global Initiative, which agreed to host the organization and advance it to the next level. Also see *European Consortium of Political Research: Standing Group on Organized Crime.*

12. Presidents Commission on Law Enforcement and Administration of Justice. 1967. *Task Force Report: Organized Crime.* National Institute of Justice, Washington, D.C. Crossey, Donald R. 1969. *Theft of the Nation.* Catino, Maurizio. 2019. *Mafia Organizations: The Visible Hand of Criminal Enterprise.* pp. 237–243. von Lampe, Klaus. 2016. *Organized Crime: Analyzing Illegal Activities, Criminal Structures, and Extra-Legal Governance.* p. 41.

13. Finckenauer, James O. and Yuri A. Voronin. *Issues in International Crime.* 2001. "The Threat of Russian Organized Crime." June. Martens, Frederick T. *Crime and Justice International.* 1999. "Is There Russian Organized Crime in the U.S.?" March. pp.11–12.

14. Shelley, Louise. *Studies of Organized Crime.* 2004. "Contemporary Russian Organized Crime: Embedded in Russian Society.in Organized Crime in Europe." pp. 563–84.

15. *Global Initiative Against Transnational Organized Crime.* 2021. "The Global Illicit Economy: Trajectories of Organized Crime." March 11th. Bradford, Ben., et. al. *The Sage Handbook of Global Policing.* Ochoa, Rolando. 2016. "Local Dynamics of a Global Phenomenon: Policing Organized Crime." June 21st. pp. 463–78.

law enforcement methods and means. For the young detective, an entirely new and dynamic field of criminal investigation was about to open up—cyber-crime.

Throughout the next decade, I traveled the world. Much of this travel was under-written by Dick Ward, who had established the Office of International Criminal Justice at the University of Illinois, and Margaret Beare, the Director of the Nathanson Center at York University.[16] It certainly allowed me to meet with many more prominent law enforcement officials and academics who were embarking on this new and exciting adventure.

More importantly, it convinced me that the threat of transnational organized crime was not temporary but represented an existential threat to not only democracy but the administration of justice everywhere in the world.

Recognized by the United Nations as an ongoing threat to government institutions, they initiated a game-changing project, *SHERLOC*. Designed "to facilitate the transfer of information on transnational organized crime," this project provides both researchers and practitioners with a global database.[17]

Today, we witness Russian oligarchs, international racketeers, world leaders, and prominent international businesses laundering their illicitly derived monies through real estate purchased in London, Paris, New York, Hong Kong, and other major world financial hubs.

Banking institutions are undoubtedly amenable to accepting this illegal or dirty money, with few if any questions asked.[18] Cash is king, as the saying goes.

The consequences of this explosion have been the implosion of political institutions that have denied the people of their respective countries

---

16. Beare, Margaret E. and Frederick T. Martens. *Journal of Contemporary Criminal Justice.* 1998. "Policing Organized Crime: The Comparative Structures, Traditions, and Policies within the United States and Canada." November. vol. 14, no. 4, pp. 398–427.

17. United Nations office of Drugs and Crime (UNODC). SHERLOC.

18. O'Brien, Timothy L. *The New York Times.* 1999. "Russian Says Officials Funneled Cash to Bank in Laundering Case." August 28th. Hilzenrath, David S. *The Washington Post.* 1999. "Russians Use Tiny Island to Hide Billions." October 28th.

an honest government. In scandal after scandal, the world witnessed governments turned into kleptocracies.[19]

Natural resources plundered. In South Africa, Venezuela, Russia, or Brazil, global inequality has been exacerbated on a scale never before seen.[20] The less resilient sovereign countries have been rendered helpless, ill-equipped, and incapable of addressing the political and economic turmoil that transnational gangsters have visited on the body-politic.

Even in countries with robust civil institutions, a resurgence of criminal organizations and the attendant corruption are a perennial challenge.

In the late eighties, an Australian Royal Commission inquiry into corruption once again reinforced the adage, "power corrupts, and absolute power corrupts absolutely."

Tony Fitzgerald, Q.C. from New South Wales, was called upon to investigate the police practices in Queensland—a province dominated by the National Party of Australia for three decades. Fitzgerald exposed systemic corruption that infected all branches of government. It had undermined the rule of law and perverted the administration of justice.[21] It resulted in the Premier resigning, three former ministers and the police commissioner sent to prison, and an established independent crime commission.[22]

It was November of 1990 that I received a call from Jack Morris. Morris was working as a consultant to the newly-established Criminal Justice Commission in Queensland. I knew Jack through my relationship with the California Department of Justice. Jack was a true believer in the intelligence process and promoted it throughout the country and the world.[23] He had struck up a relationship with the Commission's

19. Bullough, Oliver. 2018. *Moneyland: The Inside Story of the Crooks and Kleptocrats who Rule the World*. September 6th.

20. Milanovic, Branko. 2018. *Global Inequality: A New Approach for the Age of Globalization*. Stiglitz, Joseph E. 2002. *Globalization and Its Discontents*.

21. *The Conversation*. 2019. "Thirty Years On, the Fitzgerald Inquiry Still Looms Large over Queensland Politics." June 30th. *Crime and Corruption Commission* (Queensland). 1989. "The Fitzgerald Inquiry." July 3rd.

22. Established by the Queensland Criminal Justice Act 1989, it has undergone several reiterations, and now is called the Crime and Misconduct Commission.

23. Morris, Jack. *Criminal Intelligence File: A Handbook to Guide the Storage and Use of Confidential Law Enforcement Materials*. 1992. Palmer Enterprises.

Chairman, Sir Max Bingham.[24] Preparing to return to the United States, Jack suggested his replacement be someone who knew how to advance the intelligence capabilities of the Commission to the next level. Jack asked me if I would be interested in applying for this position. Naturally, I agreed to participate in the interview process.

Sir Max had been a former Attorney General of Tasmania. Both political parties respected him. His integrity was beyond reproach. As the Commission's first chairman, Sir Max proved a breath of fresh air to a morbid and corrupt criminal justice apparatus that ruled for decades over Queensland. But he was also an outlier, seconded from Tasmania. His unfamiliarity with the toxic culture deeply embedded in the body politic had him walking a political tightrope.

In December of 1990, I traveled to Brisbane, Australia, to interview for Morris's position. A board of five commissioners interviewed me, Sir Max being the chairman. After the interview, Sir Max had invited me to join him for dinner.

We discussed many things. Sir Max's fondness for America was captivating and overwhelming. He was a true patriot. He credited America with saving Australia from the Japanese during World War II—one that had escaped me in my history classes.

Sir Max, over dinner, offered me the position of intelligence supervisor with the Commission. It was undoubtedly an exciting offer and challenge. But living on the other side of the world, with three school-age children on this side of the world, would prove problematic.

In addition, I had just settled into my position with the PCC, which afforded me a host of opportunities that would not be available "Down Under." Fortunately, a situation developed in Australia that precluded my retention—and allowed for a graceful exit.[25]

Again, as luck would have it, I was in Shanghai, China, in 1991 lecturing at one of Dick Ward's seminars when I met Jim Litster, a member of the South Australian Police. Navigating the streets and alleyways

---

24. Wikipedia: Sir Max Bingham.

25. Letter from Sir Max Bingham dated 10 January 1991. "Since our conversation of yesterday, matters have arisen which make it impossible for this Commission to proceed as we had planned with your proposed appointment. The Commission will not be filling the vacancy at present. I am personally very disappointed. Yours Sincerely, Sir Max Bingham Q.C. Chairman."

of Shanghai, we traded war stories about the Sicilian Mafia, the Calabrian 'Ndrangheta, and the Chinese Triads. This ancient port city was known for its century's long history with organized crime and political corruption.[26]Shanghai was beginning to emerge from its feudal origins, transforming itself into what has become a world-class destination.

Policing and investigations in Australia were not much different than in New Jersey or the United States. Politics, policing, and prejudices were universally similar. Besides his investigative acumen for uncovering the traditional and more complex crime of South Australia's landscape, Lister was an authority on crime and social dysfunction in the Aboriginal outback. He understood the abject poverty that had been inflicted on the original settlers of Australia and made no excuses for the government's failure to address the issues that destined this community to a life of non-relevance.[27]

Had I not known better, I would have thought he was speaking of our Native-American reservations.

Jim understood the nuances of policing in a multi-cultural environment. He was not wedded to worn-out and ill-advised policing strategies merely because of the past. He believed in progressive policing—anticipating crime problems and preventing both their intended and unintended consequences.

In speaking with Jim, he pointed out a visceral reaction to any outsiders coming into Australia, especially among the police. The police union was politically powerful. It would resist a foreign interloper with whatever means it had at its disposal.

Two decades later, contracted by the State of New York, I traveled to Australia to investigate a Melbourne-based casino company seeking a coveted casino license. Teamed up with my Australian colleague, Anthony Romeo, we met with the principals of the gaming enterprise seeking a lucrative New York casino license. Searching through their financial records and assessing their propriety for being awarded a gaming license in New York state, we would often question why an Australian casino

---

26. Martin, Brian G. *The Journal of Asian Studies.* 1995. "The Green Gang and the Guomindang State: Du Yuesheng and the Politics of Shanghai, 1927-37."

27. ABC NEWS. 2004. "SA appoints new body to oversee Pitlands." March 16th.

company would want to taint its sterling reputation in the epicenter of organized crime? But the return on investment was worth the risk.

Fortunately, this assignment allowed me to meet up with Jim and his lovely wife, Suzanne, in the City of Churches—Adelaide. Traversing the idyllic countryside, we nostalgically ruminated about our careers and the state of organized crime in our respective countries and globally. It was a refreshing interlude to an exhausting trip.

Upon my return to the states, I detoured to Japan. Fortunately, I was introduced to an authority on Japanese organized crime through my association with Alec Dubro, who researched the Japanese Yakuza.[28] There I was treated to several tutorials on how Japan dealt with organized crime. I was given photographs of an actual Yakuza ceremony and the rituals associated with becoming a member—including a video that visually depicted the disciplinary tradition requiring the severing of a finger. It was certainly unlike anything I had experienced in the west.

If travel and interfacing with law enforcement from other cultures teach you nothing more, there is no universal logic nor strategy to address organized crime. Every country handles it differently. Japan, until recently, licensed the Yakuza. Germany, Australia, the Netherlands, and Portugal have legalized certain vices or regulate their activities, mitigating organized crime's harms inflicted on society.

On the other hand, subjected to the predatory elements of the invisible hand for centuries, Italy's approach has resulted in massive police raids and judicial inquests. Whether it be the Mafia, N'Drangheta, Camorra, or the lesser-known Apulian criminal groups, *Organized Crime* has been a shadow government, immune from government suppression or control.[29] The violence associated with this underground culture certainly hit home on May 23, 1992.

Giovanni Falcone, the judge who courageously challenged the Sicilian Mafia, his wife, and three police officers were assassinated in Sicily. The repercussions of this assassination were felt worldwide. Two months

---

28. Kaplan, David E. and Alec Dubro. 1986. *Yakuza: The Explosive Account of Japan's Criminal Underworld.*

29. Allum, Fella, Isabella Marinaro, Rocco Sciarrone. 2019. *Italian Mafia's Today: Territory, Business, and Police.* Europol (The Hague). 2013. "Threat Assessment - Italian Organized Crime." June 24th.

later, the assassination of Paolo Borsellino, another Anti-Mafia judge, and five police officers enraged both the Italian government and the international community.

Attending a conference in Rome, Italy, three months later, the shock and fury was unmistakable.[30] Throughout the two-day conference, discussions regarding the successful use of RICO in addressing *Cosa Nostra* were all-consuming and relentless. There was an irrepressible desire to wreak havoc on the Mafia and avenge their assassinations. It was increasingly apparent that the laws of Italy addressing the Mafia were not as effective as the American RICO statute. Moreover, *Organized Crime's* influence on Italy's political and legal systems has compromised and diminished the political will to address its "eternal presence in Italian society."[31] Its' tentacles continue to strangle economies, not only in Italy but throughout the world.[32]

With the fall of the Berlin Wall in 1989 and *perestroika* opening up the former Iron Curtain, the evolution of Russian organized crime had taken on a new urgency. I was subsequently invited to present the findings of our tri-state Russian organized crime report at a conference in Moscow, followed by a trip to what was now an "independent" country, Belarus.

Accompanied by one of the foremost academic experts on Russian organized crime, Louise Shelley, we met with the Russian government and academic representatives. How privatization resulted in the evolution of a kleptocracy engineered by the political elites who emerged from the ruins of the former Soviet Union was the primary topic of many conversations.[33]

30. UNICRI: Crime and Justice Research Institute: 1st Meeting of Police and Criminological Experts. October 12-13, 1992.

31. Scotti, Benjamin. Loyola Marymount University and LMU Loyola Law School. *Loyola of Los Angeles International and Comparative Law Review.* 2002. *RICO vs. 416-bis: A Comparison of U.S. and Italian Anti-Organized Crime Legislation.* December 1st. pp. 143–64.

32. Calderoni, Francesco, et. al. *European Journal of Criminology.* 2015. "The Italian Mafias in the world: A Systematic assessment of the mobility of criminal groups." pp. 413–33. December 31st. Marshall, Jonathan. 2021. *Dark Quandrant: Organized Crime, Big Business, and the Corruption of American Democracy.* April 9th.

33. Granville, Johanna. *Demokratizatsiya.* 2003. "'Demokratizatsiya' and 'Prikhvatizatsiya': The Russian Kleptocracy and Rise of Organized Crime." pp. 449–57.

Explicitly addressing the use of our racketeering and corrupt organizations statute to contain organized crime and our citizens' privacy
protections was alien to our Soviet colleagues.[34]

It was apparent that the legal protections afforded United States citizens were not relevant nor understood by our Russian counterparts.

Clearly, in a few short years, globalization had enveloped the underworld. No longer were arbitrary geographic borders sufficient to impede
the flow of crime. Frontiers that once contained crime had collapsed. A
new breed of international racketeers and gangsters migrated to weak
and vulnerable economies whose civil institutions were easily compromised. It was the beginning of a new "war on transnational organized
crime" and one that few nation-states were prepared for nor capable of
addressing.

Invited to discuss the obstacles to investigating political corruption,
the Nathanson Centre for the Study of Organized Crime and Corruption
hosted a conference in Santiago, Chile. After describing the events that
led up to and resulted in the dismemberment of the Crime Commission,
I met several political activists or dissidents, as the case may be. They
were pursuing ideas and strategies to redress the atrocities of the Pinochet regime. They discussed the so-called "Dirty Wars" that Pinochet had
inflicted on those who opposed his rule.[35] Their interest, of course, was
how they might use the racketeering laws in the United States to uncover
the crimes committed at the behest of the C.I.A and repatriate property
that Pinochet arbitrarily confiscated?[36]

These discussions reminded me of my 1975 interview with Frank
Mallamaci, a member of the Bonanno Mafia family. Educated by a
mobster regarding the C.I.A's role in shipping arms and munitions to

34. Galeotti, Mark. *Global Crime*. 2004. "The Russian 'Mafiya': Consolidation and Globalization." February. pp. 54–69. Shelley, Louise. *Demokratizatsiya*. 1995. "Transnational Crime: The
Case of Russian Organized Crime and the Role of International Cooperation in Law Enforcement." p. 63. Martens, Frederick T. and Steve Roosa. *Journal of Contemporary Criminal Justice*.
1994. "Exporting RICO to Eastern Europe: Prudent or Irresponsible?" December 1st.

35. Slattery, Gram. *Reuters*. 2015. "Chile Doubles Down on Prosecutions for Pinochet-Era
Crimes." November 1st.

36. Bonnefoy, Pascale. *The New York Times*. 2020. "'An End to the Chapter of Dictatorship':
Chileans Vote to Draft a New Constitution." October 25th.

the Dominican Republic in the sixties, the so-called "Domino Theory" played out in Chile and South America.[37]

Again, what it taught me is that "everyone has a story to tell" and "no one has a monopoly on history or truth." There's knowledge to be gained from an array of commoners, gangsters, prostitutes, and yes, even political dissidents if we are curious, open-minded, and patient enough to listen.[38] Contemporary and self-indulgent historical narratives often ignore that which exposes the underbelly and illicit economies of the host society.

Of course, there was a substantial difference between how the west addressed transnational organized crime and how it was addressed in the Pacific Rim, especially China. Let there be little doubt, under Communist regimes, surveillance on a 24/7 basis is the norm. Little escapes the authorities. Whether I was in Beijing, Hanoi, Moscow, or Minsk, the Communist Party was well aware of my presence as I was of theirs. This became seemingly evident in Guangzhou, China, in June of 2005.[39]

Attending a conference organized by Dick Ward, a speaker from Hong Kong rudely insulted the Chinese premier in a public forum. That night, he was whisked away, never to be seen again during the conference. It served as a poignant reminder that freedom of speech and academic freedom is fleeting.

Later, escorted to the police station that housed the "steel ring," I observed hundreds of closed-circuit cameras strategically located throughout the city. No one could escape the "steel ring" and its prying eyes. It was a sober reminder that crime control has no limits in China. Social order took precedence over civil liberties. The rule of law was as ambiguous as it was amorphous.

---

37. For a detailed treatment of this arrangement see Marshall, Jonathan, *Journal of Global South Studies,* 2018. "The Dictator and the Mafia: How Rafael Trujillo Partnered with US Criminals to Extend His Power." p.63. Martens, Frederick T. 2015. *We'll Make An Offer You Can't Refuse: A Primer on the Investigation of Public Corruption.* pp. 18–19. Short, Martin. 1996. *Crime Inc.: The Story of Organized Crime.* pp. 108–31. Webb, Gary. *San Jose Mercury.* 1996. "Dark Alliance." August 18th-20th. Scott, Peter and Jonathan Marshall. 1998. *Cocaine Politics: Drugs, Armies, and the CIA in Central America.* pp. viii.

38. Martens, Frederick T. *Organized Crime Digest: Reflections of a Mob Boss.* 1997.

39. Hangzhou City, PR China. 2005. Sam Houston State University Conference on Intelligence in Collaboration with MPS. June 17th.

Having made several trips to China in the ensuing years, my last trip proved to be one of the most memorable. Duke University School of Law had arranged for a joint Asia-America conference on transnational crime in Hong Kong.[40]

Asked to present a paper, *Is the Upper-World Much Different from the Underworld?* I compared and contrasted organized crime operations to totalitarian and non-totalitarian regimes, being careful not to (in) cite China as an example. Of course, the metaphor was not lost on the students who were in attendance. With Hong Kong having reverted to control by the People's Republic of China, there was no need to embarrass or inflame our hosts.

Fortunately, through a series of intermediaries, I met with businessmen and bankers in the private sector. Discussing the movement of currency throughout Hong Kong and meeting with several casino executives in Macau, I concluded that China was one colossal washing machine.

Massive amounts of cash were laundered through vacant real estate, foreign trade, and casinos, than could ever be stopped, contained, or even mitigated by law enforcement. The term "investment banking" was simply a euphemism for money laundering. The scope and depth of money laundering were mind-boggling.

This realization led to the proverbial question: if you cannot outlaw money laundering—a crime that is in effect, consensual—should it too be stricken from our criminal code and be dealt with solely administratively or civilly?[41]

One of the principal critics of these money laundering laws is the distinguished organizer of the Cambridge Symposium on Economic Crime, Barry Rider. He contends, "The success of law enforcement agencies have

---

40. Robert Black College, Kong Siu Luey Lounge. 2012. Duke University School of Law. 2012. Asia-America Institute in Transnational Law. Seminar, July 9th.

41. Scheiber, Noam and Emily Flitter. *The New York Times.* 2020. "Banks Suspected Illegal Activity, but Processed Big Transactions Anyway." September 20th.

had around the world in 'taking the profit out of crime' is very limited and does not commend itself as a particularly efficient strategy."[42]

Applicable academic studies have examined this issue and could not make a strong case for their efficiency or effectiveness. When coupled with anecdotal evidence, there appears to be mounting evidence that these laws have had a negligible effect on deterring money laundering and arresting those engaged.[43]

Nonetheless, one thing is for sure. Laws proscribing money laundering and its attendant consequences have proven critical in investigating public corruption, crimes of the powerful, human trafficking, the illegal arms trade, and international terrorism.[44] Moreover, providing racketeers and gangsters with a distinct competitive advantage in the lawful marketplace undermines the principles of legal egalitarianism, never mind economic equity.

Transferring money from the bad guys to the good guys [the two perhaps indistinguishable] requires a level of transparency. Whether it's in the form of campaign contributions, real estate transactions, weapons sales, casino wagers, stock and options trading, or simply brown paper bags and unmarked envelopes, it leaves a trail. Even cryptocurrency is traceable and has proven to be vulnerable to law enforcement intervention.[45] Moreover, the filing of suspicious activity reporting may not be dispositive initially, but it certainly can lead to fruitful investigations.

In the final analysis, eliminating or scaling back laws that address these pernicious activities should *not* be evaluated *solely* based on their efficiency or effectiveness. Instead, these laws are simply another arrow in the quiver of law enforcement which is exceedingly underfunded to

---

42. Rider, Barry A.K. Opening Ceremony of the Centre of Anti-Corruption Studies and Seminar. 2009. "Accountability and Responsibility—Reinforcing the Criminal Law." February 20th. p. 211. Rider, Barry. *European Journal of Law Reform.* 1999. "The Crusade Against Money Launder—Time to Think!" p. 524.

43. Levi, Michael and Peter Reuter. *Crime and Justice.* 2006. "Money Laundering." vol. 34, no. 1, pp. 289–375. Savona, Ernesto U. 1997. *Responding to Money Laundering: International Perspectives.* October 1st.

44. Rider, Barry. A.K. and Li-Hong Xing and Bill Tupman. *Journal of Money Laundering Control.* 2015. "Organized Crime: Origins and Projections." June.

45. United States Department of Justice. 2021. "Department of Justice Seizes $2.3 Million in Cryptocurrency Paid to Ransomware Extortionists Darkside." June 7th.

address this activity. Money laundering investigations are likely to uncover the scope and depth of systemic corruption, human trafficking, and the exportation of violence and extortion.[46]

Following the money still represents an indisputable investigative strategy.

46. Rose-Ackerman, Susan and Bonnie J. Palifka. *International Economic Association Series.* 2018. "Corruption, Organized Crime, and Money Laundering." April 5th. pp. 75–111. Hallman, Ben, et. al. *International Consortium of Investigative Journalists.* 2020. "6 Money Laundering reforms that experts say need to happen now." October 19th. Taub, Jennifer. 2020. *Big Dirty Money: The Shocking Injustice and Unseen Costs of White-Collar Crime.* September 29th.

9

A Bold Visionary Takes Command
of the State Police

At the funeral of State Police Colonel Justin J. Dintino, former Governor James Florio, in his eloquent eulogy, called for a book be written about Dintino's extraordinary rise from the son of Italian immigrants to lead and transform the New Jersey State Police.[1] It was a moving send-off for my friend and mentor, who was instrumental in allowing me to investigate organized crime and public corruption.

While not the book Florio had called for, this last chapter will hopefully be a fitting tribute to *The Colonel*.

Regardless of one's career in either the private or public sector, mentors play a critical role. They serve as role models. They inculcate their reasoning processes into yours. They provide insights into the political minefields that confront their decision-making. And they are often critical to your career path. I was fortunate to have met Dintino in 1974, seven years into my State Police career.

The State Police is an organization that was and is wedded to seniority over meritocracy. Being mentored by a rough-hewed Trooper born in 1929 was the exception as opposed to the rule. That's called luck.

Dintino was from South Jersey, the less populated part of the state. I was from North Jersey, the most populous region of the state. He served in "A" Troop. I served in "C" and "E" Troop. He lacked a college degree.

---

1. On February 1, 2020, Colonel Patrick Callahan officiated over the funeral of Dintino.

I had two advanced degrees. He was 45. I was 30. He never served in the military. I was an Air Force veteran. Our backgrounds and differences were stark.[2]

Nonetheless, we bonded in ways that few of my colleagues could understand.

So what was it that brought us together?

Attending a seminar in Sea Girt, New Jersey, Dintino asked a relatively simple question. "If drug arrests continue to climb, purity increases, and demand is not diminished or declining, what does this tell us about the war on drugs?" I raised my hand. Dintino called upon me.

My answer was, "we have little impact. We are losing this war."

Afterward, Dintino approached me and asked where I was assigned. At the time, I just transferred into the Major Crimes Unit, which specialized in homicides and arson. He asked me if I was interested in coming to the Intelligence Bureau. I responded, "Definitely."

Months had passed, and the Criminal Investigations Section supervisor, Major William Baum, pursued the transfer of DSFC Jack Liddy from the Intelligence Bureau to his Section. Baum was assembling a team of detectives to investigate organized crime on New Jersey's notorious waterfront.[3] The Colonel saw an opening—Liddy for Martens, who at the time was simply a detective with no rank. Baum and Dintino agreed. The trade was initiated.

The Intelligence Bureau reported directly to the Superintendent of State Police. Col. Clinton L. Pagano was appointed, taking the reins from David B. Kelly and Eugene Olaff. All being ex-military, they understood the necessity and value of intelligence.[4]

They recognized that for intelligence to be relevant and practical, it must be actionable—tactical—and visionary—strategic. Simply arresting and prosecuting organized criminals or corrupt politicians would

---

2. Wren, George J. Jr. 2009. *Jersey Troopers II: The Next 35 Years (1971-2006)*. October 27th. pp. 107–21.

3. Delaney, Bob and Dave Scheiber. 2008. *Covert: My Years Infiltrating the Mob*. February 1st. Wren, George J. Jr. 2009. *Jersey Troopers II: The Next 35 Years (1971-2006)*. pp. 400–405.

4. While The Colonel never served in the military, he was one of the most ardent proponents of intelligence in addressing organized crime and terrorism.

not eliminate or contain organized crime or public corruption. Systemic reforms were needed to prevent its recurrence.

The total value of an intelligence product lies in the analysis phase, which was central to the process. Taking raw information and transforming it into a finished product used on a tactical and strategic level was the real trick.

Troopers and detectives as a whole were not receptive toward reading over reports and providing a finished intelligence product. Their skill-sets were more attuned to collecting and assessing the information. Massaging it and drawing relationships and inferences from the information required the skill sets of social scientists and perhaps analysts who worked for the Central Intelligence Agency. Dintino recognized this but was at a disadvantage in attracting the personnel needed to perform these tasks.[5]

Being one of the few who had an advanced college degree, Dintino made the risky decision to have me team up with DSG George Coyle in addressing this alien intelligence concept.[6] At the time, the Law Enforcement Assistance Administration (LEAA) provided grants to states to initiate the intelligence function in their respective agencies.

Dintino saw an opportunity to leverage the monies allocated by LEAA. Instructing Coyle to begin pursuing grants to implement the analytical function within the Intelligence Bureau, we met with Thomas O'Reilly of the Office of Attorney General. O'Reilly was the liaison at the time with the Department of Justice, which housed LEAA.[7]

Discussions were initiated with LEAA and O'Reilly. We subsequently met Charles H. Rogovin, the first administrator of LEAA and a law professor at Temple University School of Law.

Rogovin and Dintino struck up a relationship immediately.[8] In Dintino, Rogovin saw someone willing to take on a bold experiment.

---

5. Kelland, Gilbert. 1987. *Crime in London: From Postwar SOHO to Present-Day Supergrasses.* p. 362.

6. Dintino, J. J. and F. T. Martens. *Police Chief.* 1981. "An Enduring Enigma: The Concept of Intelligence Analysis." December. vol 48, issue 12, pp. 58-64. Dintino, J. J. and F. T. Martens. 1983. *Police Intelligence in Crime Control: Maintaining a Delicate Balance in a Liberal Democracy.* Martens, Frederick T. "The Intelligence Function." In Edelhertz, Herbert, ed. National Institute of Justice: Symposium Proceedings. 1987. *Major Issues in Organized Crime Control.* September.

7. Rutgers Institute for Secure Communities. "Thomas J. O'Reilly: Executive Policy Advisor of the Center on Policing."

8. See Appendix B regarding my eulogy to Rogovin.

Integrating civilian college graduates and former analysts of the CIA into a somewhat insular function—the Intelligence Bureau—was not enthusiastically welcomed.

Allowing outsiders to read reports with detailed information about corrupt politicians, mobsters, and the informants who provided this information would be perceived as occupational heresy, never mind a threat to the confidentiality and sensitive nature of the information and the sources contained in the reports.

Nonetheless, Dintino's strong personality prevailed. He instructed Coyle and me to pursue a federal grant and, if awarded, assemble an analytical staff made up of both sworn detectives and civilians. Unsurprisingly, most detectives had little desire to devour intelligence reports in an office setting.

With the awarding of the first grant, five civilian analysts, all college graduates, were recruited. The sixth, a retired veteran analyst of the CIA, was also part of this initial contingent. Training these analysts in intelligence techniques was accomplished by Anacapa Sciences, headquartered in California. They had an admirable track record educating both the civilian analysts and investigators in the role of analysis in the intelligence process.

Dintino's commitment to the intelligence process was unwavering. Demanding we continue to pursue federal monies to advance the analytical function, LEAA provided another federal grant for six additional analysts. The State Police now had a contingent of twelve civilian analysts, all with college degrees working side-by-side with detectives, most of whom did not have college degrees.

To say that this caused some resentment would be an understatement. Coupled with a starting salary that was equal to a trooper-recruit only exacerbated a contentious situation. Dintino would have none of it. Make it work was his mantra. Those who resisted fell out of favor with Dintino. And in the State Police, a quasi-military organization, that was a significant incentive to remain or appear to remain either neutral or supportive.

It was an experiment in the 1970s that has taken on a whole new dimension in the post-9-11 era. For those who may not remember, a CIA analyst identified the late terrorist Osama Bin Laden's secret hideaway in

Pakistan that ultimately led to his fortified compound and, finally, his *elimination*.[9]

Today criminal intelligence analysts are embedded in virtually every large law enforcement agency in the country. Courses are routinely instructed by many of the early pioneers of the analytical function.[10]

The International Association of Law Enforcement Intelligence Analysts (ILEIA) continues to advance the craft of intelligence analysis throughout the world. Without any doubt, Dintino and Rogovin are credited with instilling this function in many of our domestic intelligence bureaus.[11]

Under Dintino, the New Jersey State Police had developed a national model reviled throughout the country.[12] Naturally, with fame comes those wishing to capitalize on it.

Ronald Goldstock, a colleague of Rogovin's, had been appointed as the head of New York's Organized Crime Task Force (OCTF). He asked if I was interested in heading up his intelligence function. The salary offered significantly more, and the position was intriguing. Naturally, I considered it and went to Dintino and apprised him of the offer.

Dintino, not one to display his emotions, simply said, "Stay with me." He need not have said anymore, nor did he. The decision was obvious. Not interested.

That did not stop Goldstock from recruiting several analysts at higher salaries than New Jersey could provide. However, as Dintino would often say, "it's a form of flattery . . . other states looking to New Jersey for professionalizing their intelligence function is something we can and should be proud of . . . it's the consequence of being the best."

As Dintino advanced up the ranks of the State Police, from Lieutenant to Captain, to Major, to Lieutenant Colonel, to Deputy Superintendent,

9. *The Telegraph* (London). 2014. "The True Story of the CIA Analyst Who Hunted Down Bin Laden." December 20th.

10. Andrews, Paul P. Jr. and Marilyn B. Peterson. 1990. *Criminal Intelligence Analysis*. Peterson, Marilyn B. 1998. *Applications in Criminal Analysis: A Sourcebook*. Peterson, Marilyn B. and Bob Morehouse. 2000. *Intelligence 2000: Revising the Basic Elements*. Peterson, Marilyn B. 2018. *Applications in Intelligence-Led Policing: Where Theory Meets Reality*. August 2nd.

11. Dintino, J. J. and F. T. Martens. 1983. *Police Intelligence in Crime Control*.

12. Blakey, G. Robert, Ronald Goldstock and Charles Rogovin. 1978. *Rackets Bureaus: Investigation and Prosecution of Organized Crime*. January 1st.

he followed through on his promise—"stay with me." Advancing to Lieutenant with just twelve years in the State Police was unheard of at that time. Seniority usually trumped meritocracy, although there were exceptions.

With the State Police having one of the most aggressive organized crime and public corruption programs in the country, Dintino emerged as perhaps the country's most important law enforcement executive. When organized crime became the country's newly-elected President, Ronald Reagan's priority, Dintino was perfectly positioned.[13]

Chairman of the Law Enforcement Intelligence Unit (LEIU), Dintino, was often called upon to testify before Congress on intelligence and organized crime matters.[14]Reagan recognized him as a national leader, who in 1983 chose him to serve on his recently-formed Commission of Organized Crime.[15]

Known for its apolitical posture, the New Jersey State Police was an organization whose political neutrality was proudly and honorably respected. It prided itself on being a law enforcement agency that served *any* administration with dignity and professionalism regardless of political philosophy or ideology.

Dintino's appointment was not only a symbol of pride for the New Jersey State Police. Indeed, it was a recognition at the government's highest level—the President of the United States—of Dintino's professional stature as a leading authority on organized crime. Never before nor since has a President of the United States made such a coveted appointment for a member of the New Jersey State Police.

Of course, with Dintino's appointment to this Commission came additional responsibilities. He was obligated to attend hearings throughout the country. He read volumes of documents that the Commission's staff

---

13. Executive Order 12435—President's Commission on Organized Crime. 1983. July 28th.

14. House of Representative: Committee on Energy and Commerce. 97th Congress. 1981. *Organized Crime Links to the Waste Disposal Industry.* May 28th. Janson, Donald. *The New York Times.* 1982. "Crime Threat to Jersey Casinos Reported." July 12th. United States Senate: 98th Congress, Committee on the Judiciary. 1983. *Organized Crime in America.* p. 106.

15. Werner, Leslie Maitland. *The New York Times.* 1983. "President Chooses 20 As Members of Organized Crime Commission." July 29th.

disseminated, and in the end, voted on various aspects of the Commission's final report.

The Commission was chaired by a renowned and controversial former federal judge, Irving Kaufman, who presided over Julius and Ethel Rosenberg's trial. A friend of the infamous Roy Cohn and FBI Director J. Edgar Hoover, there was always a question of *ex-parte* communications between the three before, during, and after the trial?[16]

Kaufman's appointment by Reagan as Chair of this Commission was primarily a result of his presiding over the trials of the confederation of Mafia members who attended the now-infamous Appalachian Conference in upstate New York.[17]

Dintino, not one to involve himself in partisan politics, had no particular affinity toward, distrust, or dislike of Kaufman. He did not view the Commission as an instrument of partisan politics when he was initially appointed. It is doubtful whether anyone did.

While the Commission was in the process of examining the role of casinos in the scheme of money laundering, Dintino witnessed a distinct change in the attitude of the Commission. Until 1985, casinos were under no obligation to report suspicious financial transactions or what was then seen as structuring and laundering illicit monies.[18]

One of the principal casino operators in Las Vegas, Steven Wynn, had been the subject of an investigation in New Jersey involving the transfer of $1.1 million from Anthony Castelbuono to his casino in Atlantic City.[19] Dintino was aware of this and encouraged the Commission to investigate the circumstances surrounding this transaction. There was

---

16. History Channel. 2019. *Roy Cohn: From Ruthless 'Red Scare' Prosecutor to Donald Trump's Mentor.* March 12th.

17. Berger, Marilyn. *The New York Times.* 1992. "Judge Irving Kaufman, of Rosenberg Spy Trial and Free Press Rulings, Dies at 81." February 3rd. President's Commission on Organized Crime. Hearing before the Committee on the Judiciary, United States Senate. May 8, 1984. *United Press International, Inc.* 1983. "Personality Spotlight; Judge Irving Kaufman: Tough Jurist returns to the Spotlight." July 28th. *The Harvard Crimson.* 1960. "The Mob and the Law." December 5.

18. Government Accounting Office. 1996. "Money Laundering: Rapid Growth of Casinos Makes Them Vulnerable." January 4th.

19. Schmitt, Eric. *The New York Times.* 1985. "Allegations of Money Laundering Disputed by Jersey Casino Operator." June 27th. Smith, John L. 2001. *Running Scared: The Life and Treacherous Times of Las Vegas Casino King Steve Wynn.* January 31st. *New Zealand Herald.* 2000. "Wynn some, lose some." June 29th.

a reluctance that Dintino and subsequently other Commissioners did not understand.

Often the case, hindsight is 20/20. Years later, it became apparent to Dintino and others that Las Vegas casino executives had lobbied the Administration to reject any efforts to regulate money laundering by casinos.[20] Pursuing this case would only provide the impetus to include casinos in the money laundering statutes.

Released in 1986, the Commission's Final Report was rejected by nine of the Commissioner's, Dintino included. The official report was, in fact, the minority report, with the dissenting commissioners issuing a blistering retort. Kaufman's stewardship went down as a failure—a thud, much like his prison sentences in the Appalachian Mafia cases.[21]

With Dintino's career winding down and reaching the mandatory retirement age of 55, the Equal Opportunity Employment Commission (EEOC) flatly rejected mandatory retirement provisions *unless a BFOQ—Bonafide Occupational Qualifications—accompanied them.*

It affected many higher-ranking officers in the State Police. Dintino and Pagano, who, as Superintendent, were obligated to retire. Flying in the State Police helicopter to Nutley, New Jersey, Pagano and Dintino sought the intervention of then-Senator Carmen Orecchio, the President of the Senate. Pagano suggested that the State Police's mandatory age fifty-five retirement statute conform to the federal EEOC ruling. Essentially, it would have obliterated compulsory retirement at age fifty-five, allowing the upper echelon of the State Police to remain in office until, well, whenever?

The Senator agreed until the State Police Fraternal Association interceded and made its opposition known.

The Association's position was straightforward. By eliminating the age requirement for retirement, the ranks of the State Police would atrophy. The older officers would stay indefinitely. The younger troopers would be stymied in their quest for advancing to leadership positions. It would do a disservice to the citizens of New Jersey.

---

20. In 2007, Jim Mintz and I interviewed Steve Wynn, who had made application for a New York Casino license. When we inquired about the Castelbuono event, Wynn became quite animated and vociferously challenged the version of events surrounding this exchange of monies.

21. Ostrow, Ronald J. *The Los Angeles Times*. 1986. "Key Issues Not Dealt With, Half of Panel Says." April 2nd. Santos, Lori. 1986. *Crime Commission Wraps up work in Discord*. April 7th.

There was a division between the younger Troopers that I was a part of and the older Troopers, which Dintino and Pagano represented. It was a divisive and troubling issue for both sides, and certainly for me.

As a compromise, Pagano proposed to Orecchio that the position of Superintendent be excluded from the legislation. The logic was simple. The Superintendent was a political appointment by the governor. The governor should be able to appoint whomever, regardless of age. The State Police Fraternal Association and Orecchio agreed to this compromise.

This compromise, of course, caused dissension among the older officers. Realizing Pagano no longer had their backs, an ad-hoc association, State Police Against Age Discrimination (SPADD), was formed.[22] Major Louis Grossi led it.

SPAAD retained the legal services of Justin Walder, one of the more prominent criminal defense attorneys in New Jersey. Winding its way through the courts, SPAAD failed to convince the court that forcing retirement at fifty-five was age discrimination so long as the State Police adhered to the BFOQ.

Retirement of all those officers over the age of 55 was imminent—September of 1985.

Dintino retired from the State Police after a thirty-three-year career and just two months shy of his fifty-sixth birthday. Recognizing the impact of Dintino's retirement, Joseph Collum, who was instrumental in exposing racial profiling in the State Police, wrote,

> The ramifications of his [retirement] would take years to become manifest. No one in the State Police possessed a portfolio equal to his. Even Pagano couldn't ignore Dintino's reputation and moral authority. He was the man who could stand up to the Superintendent and challenge him . . . the day he walked out the door, he took with him any semblance of a check-and-balance at State Police HQ.

As his chief of staff, Colonel Pagano reassigned me to command the Narcotics Bureau, North Region, where I had worked undercover 14 years earlier.

---

22. Sullivan, Joseph F. *The New York Times.* 1984. "Troopers in Fight on Retiring." November 18th. Collum, Joseph. 2013. *The Black Dragon: Racial Profiling Exposed.* October 4th. pp.50–51.

With an opportunity awaiting me in Pennsylvania and the ability to retire in 1987 after twenty years of service and at the age of 43, I met with Dintino, who was then at New Jersey's State Commission of Investigation. We discussed my options, but he was reluctant to advise me to retire.

He had cautioned me, asking me, "are you prepared to walk into that den of iniquity . . . Pennsylvania's record investigating corruption is strewn with many bodies . . . Remember Freddy, the system will always outlast you . . . changing a political culture is nearly impossible . . . just look what it took to do in New Jersey, and we had all the tools and support."

At the time, The Colonel had no idea that he would be selected to head the State Police, nor did I. He was now at the New Jersey State Commission of Investigation, applying his knowledge and skill to investigate public corruption in my old stomping grounds, Paterson, New Jersey.

We discussed the political obstacles that stymied investigations of known racketeers and its corrupt vice squad. He was particularly interested in the illegal video poker enterprises run by the Mafia, especially Johnny Ventura. We discussed the DeFranco mob-hit, the Carter-Artis prosecution, and the influence of the Genovese and Lucchese Mafia Families with the Paterson Police Department. There was no doubt in my mind that systemic corruption had once again infected this chronically diseased police department.

Irony and *karma* can be and often is unrelenting and harsh.[23] James Florio was elected governor in 1989.

A Democrat and native to the rough-and-tumble politics of Camden County, New Jersey, clandestine efforts were made to taint Florio with the corruption that had permeated the Camden County political machine. Dintino was aware of these efforts. Through several confidantes and emissaries, he was able to get the ear of Florio.

Florio was exorcised by the negative publicity the State Police was receiving concerning racial profiling. Pagano had taken the position that it didn't exist.[24]

---

23. Collum, Joseph. 2010. *The Black Dragon.* p. 155.

24. Peterson, Iver. *The New York Times.* 2001. "State Officials Had Data on Profiling, an Aide Says." March 15th. Transcript of Deposition of Paul Zoubek before Senate Judiciary Committee. March 10, 2001.

Dintino met with Florio. He provided Florio with a detailed pro-active plan—a plan spontaneously hatched on napkins at Skeeters Pub in Blackwood, N.J.—that would return the State Police to the sterling reputation it once enjoyed.

Among the many reforms Dintino proposed to Florio was eliminat-ing the annual State Police golf tournament. Industries that the State Police policed "were asked" for "donations." Dintino saw this as a classic shakedown.[25] "It may not be illegal, but it sure as hell is unethical . . . We're in the law enforcement business, not the fundraising business," Dintino told Florio.

Minority representation at the higher echelons in the State Police was abysmal. Senior command staff was non-representative of the State's diverse population. Dintino took the position that all else being equal, minority troopers would be promoted over non-minority.[26]

Although Dintino, like most from his generation, were high school graduates, he recognized the need to impose a higher standard for incom-ing troopers. The relative absence of a military background—compulsory service was eliminated—and the legal age of enlistment was 18 made for less well-rounded, mature, and seasoned Troopers. Dintino would im-pose a four-year college degree on prospective applicants, or a two-year degree and two years of military service. This requirement would, in ef-fect, serve two goals. Accelerate the educational achievements of Troopers and re-impose an age of 21 or older on future applicants.

And racial profiling was to be eliminated. Absent a reasonable suspi-cion of a crime; there were no random searches of vehicles. Instinct would be replaced by the rule of law. As Dintino would often say, "I'd rather not another ounce of drugs were seized than witness another Trooper go to prison for a civil rights violation."[27]

Florio bought into Dintino's progressive agenda. Florio decided to replace Pagano. With Florio appointing Robert Del Tufo as his attorney

---

25. Collum, Joseph. 2010. *The Black Dragon*. p. 165.

26. My classmate, Valocean Littles, was promoted to Lt. Colonel by Dintino. He was the only Black in the 73rd Class that graduated in 1967. Collum, Joseph. 2010. *The Black Dragon*. p. 156.

27. Collum, Joseph. 2010. *The Black Dragon*. pp. 156, 165.

general, he would need or prefer a buy-in from Del Tufo, to whom Dintino would formally report.[28]

Del Tufo was reluctant to replace Pagano. Over the years, Pagano had built a relatively extensive bi-partisan political base, many of whom lobbied to retain Pagano as the Superintendent. As is often the case, political decisions are never entirely black or white.

In keeping Pagano, his allegiance would be to Del Tufo. Appointing Dintino, his loyalty would be to Florio. Age was no longer a factor. It was eliminated at the behest of Pagano and the State Trooper's Fraternal Association.

With Del Tufo not wholly sold on dismissing Pagano, he reached out to Edwin Stier, a close confidante. Stier had served as the Director of the Division of Criminal Justice. He had worked closely with Dintino and admired his judgment, investigative skill, and most of all, his uncompromising integrity.

Stier was adamant. Pagano had to go. He had become an embarrassment to the State Police—an organization that Stier admired and respected. A change was needed.[29]

Del Tufo finally agreed. But he felt that Pagano deserved a soft-landing. The Commissioner of Motor Vehicle position was available. Del Tufo met with Dintino and asked him if he could live with Pagano as its Commissioner. Dintino reluctantly agreed.[30]

Within a couple of months, Dintino admitted it was a wrong decision on his part. Dintino felt that Pagano was undermining his agenda and could not separate himself from the State Police. After one year at Motor Vehicle, Pagano "retired" from his position as its' Commissioner.

Dintino moved quickly. Racial profiling was front and center on his reform agenda. Meeting with the American Civil Liberties Union (ACLU) and other interested parties such as the Black Ministers Council, lawmakers, and the Trooper's Fraternal Association, Dintino made the bold announcement. "Not one drug arrest is worth a trooper going to jail."

28. Collum, Joseph. 2010. *The Black Dragon*. pp. 151–56.
29. Conversation with Edwin Stier, October 30, 2019.
30. Collum, Joseph. 2010. *The Black Dragon*. pp.154–55.

So much for the misdirected and ill-conceived policy that championed racial profiling as an anti-drug enforcement methodology. Dintino put an end to it, only to see it return after his resignation.[31]

Legislative hearings conducted years later elicited testimony that exposed a widespread practice of racial profiling routinely engaged in "by the unconscious attitudes of nonracist law enforcement professionals as well as deliberate actions by a few rogue officers."[32] Entering into a consent decree with the United States Justice Department, the State Police hopefully has eliminated once-and-for-all racial profiling from its ranks after ten years of oversight and reforms.[33]

The finely-calibrated and tempered response by the State Police to the demonstrations that roiled the state after the death of George Floyd bodes well for these reforms and the current leadership of the State Police under Col. Patrick Callahan.[34]

On October 30, 2019, Colonel Callahan hosted a celebratory 91st birthday party for Colonel Dintino at the State Police Academy in Sea Girt, New Jersey. The *Justin J. Dintino Repository of Organized Crime Literature* was established in his honor. With over one hundred active-duty Troopers attending the annual in-service training, Dintino addressed the Troopers, reflecting on his career in the State Police. Former Governor Florio, former Chief Justice James Zazzali, former Acting Attorney General Fred DeVesa, and former Division of Criminal Justice Director Edwin Stier attended. All touted Dintino's legendary contributions to the State Police.

---

31. McFadden, Robert D. *The New York Times*. 1999. "Whitman Dismisses State Police Chief for Race Remarks." March 1st. *The News Journal*. 1999. "Whitman Fires state police superintendent." March 1st. p. A3. *The Courier News* (Bridgewater, NJ). 2000. "Troopers Want Case Thrown Out." August 1st. Collum, Joseph. 2010. *The Black Dragon*. Hogan, John I. 2005. *Turnpike Trooper: Racial Profiling and the New Jersey State Police*.

32. Hardy, Benjamin H. *Office of Legislative Research*. 1999. *New Jersey Report on Racial Profiling*. May 11th. Gormley, William L., et. al. 2001. *Report of the New Jersey State Senate Judiciary Committee's Investigation of Racial Profiling and the New Jersey State Police*. June 11th.

33. Megerian, Chris. *The Star-Ledger*. 2009. "Judge Terminates decade-long federal oversight of N.J. State Police." September 21st.

34. Juxtaposed against the 1967 Newark riots, the State's response was not only remarkable but commendable. Tully, Tracey and Kevin Armstrong. *The New York Times*. 2020. "How a City Once Consumed by Civil Unrest Has Kept Protests Peaceful." June 1st.

Florio regaled Dintino as "the right man at the right time." Zazzali referred to Dintino's knowledge of organized crime as an eye-opener that guided him in addressing union corruption.[35] Stier made a moving tribute to Dintino, referring to his storied career as one of "extraordinary courage, integrity, skill, and resourcefulness."

Colonel Callahan focused on Dintino's exceptional skill in investigating organized crime. "His informant development skills were renowned . . . he would mentor new Troopers and freshly-minted detectives in the art of soliciting sources of information, making the tasks of solving crime look easy. In many respects, his approach was visionary, realizing that community policing was and is the answer to crime control."

You could tell from Col. Callahan's infectious smile and Col. Dintino's strained grin, they connected. Ironically, Callahan graduated from the Academy on October 30, 1995—the day of Dintino's 66th birthday. As we say, "Once a Trooper, Always a Trooper." It was a remarkable and generational tribute to and for both Colonels.

As we retired to Fratello's in Sea Girt, N.J., I could sense that time was running out for The Colonel. His mind was still sharp, but his body was frail and tired. In his younger years in the State Police, a multi-mile distance runner and prodigious tennis player, his legs barely carried him now. His arms were thin. His face was gaunt. He would repeatedly say, "I'm old Freddy . . . It's not fun . . . from 80, it was downhill." In retrospect, he was preparing me for what he was confronting—death.

I knew The Colonel's way of doing and saying things. He was matter-of-fact, often perceived as cold and distant. He was not one to lament the negative. Few would ever be able to cut through what many saw as a foreboding and stern exterior.

But for one that knew and worked for and with The Colonel over forty-five years, I recognized that beneath that hardened and callous shell was a person who believed in justice and fairness. He despised prejudice. He never disparaged the less fortunate. He believed that every person deserved to be treated with dignity and respect no matter their status in life. He admired those who pulled themselves up from their bootstraps.

---

35. Chief Justice Zazzali's private legal practice essentially entailed representing both private and public unions in the State.

He was everything a young trooper could want in a mentor, a boss, a friend, and a person.

I often say how fortunate I was to have been mentored by this man. What he taught me and what I learned could never be replicated in a classroom.

When detectives bemoaned the fact that they were required to meet with the investigating attorney on a complex investigation, The Colonel would say, "At least you know when, not if things go bad, you have good legal representation." Point well taken.

And when things went off track, he would say, "learn from it, it won't be the last time, but don't make the same mistake again . . . if you do, it becomes a habit . . . habits lead to mistakes . . . so don't get trapped into making it a habit. "The Colonel only needed to tell you once. He was not in the habit of repeating himself.

Despite what many saw as a hardened exterior, underneath was an empathetic and non-judgmental soul. When his friend Joe Salema was indicted in a corruption probe, he felt disappointed and saddened.[36] He understood the frailties of the human character, regardless of his code of personal integrity.

Too many, he was a maze of contradictions—no formal higher education, yet wiser and more brilliant than those who had advanced degrees. A product of rural culture, Troop A, yet steeped in the complexities of investigating organized crime and corruption. A disciplined gambler himself, he saw the corruption that illegal gambling wreaked on society and, against all odds, did something about it.

Born in 1929, when segregation in the military was practiced, he promoted racial diversity and equity in a quasi-military organization. Graduating the Academy in 1952 when women need not apply to the State Police, he championed the inclusion of women within the enlisted ranks. Recognizing the futility of arresting and prosecuting drug users/couriers, the so-called low-hanging fruit, he accentuated the demand side of the equation, investing in the DARE program and any effort to dissuade drug use and abuse.

---

36. Hassell, John. *The Home News* (New Brunswick, NJ). 1995. "Florio's Top Aide Indicted." February 24th.

To put it bluntly, The Colonel defied and deplored the stereotypes that so often crudely define the law enforcement profession. To "The Colonel," it was more than a job, a career. It was a calling.

The week of January 13, 2020, I received a call from Dennis "Denny" Dintino, the Colonel's son. "Freddy, my Dad would like to see you . . . do you think you could come down to see him?" I thought that is an unusual request, but I had better take the time to see him. His time is precious, insofar as I had seen him in October of 2019. Then I was not particularly thrilled about his health. I could only imagine how it may have worsened.

I told Denny that I would come down on the 21st of January, believing he was at his home in Turnersville. "No," Denny said. "He had taken a fall and was undergoing rehabilitation in a facility in Blackwood, N.J."

"Ok, I will go there."

Arriving in his room where he was convalescing, he was asleep. He had looked so much older and frail since October. I knew these were not going to be pleasant conversations. We greeted one another, but I could see he was in pain.

He had demanded to go home. Denny, his son, tried his best to console him. I could see this was not going well. I nodded to Denny to leave the room, de-escalating what was becoming a contentious situation. There was no way "The Colonel" was going home. He was much too frail and, at times, a bit disoriented. He would doze off periodically. When he was lucid, his memory was still sharp.

"Who was that Captain in charge of R&I?" "Capt. Barry," I responded. "No, not him . . ." I could see he was fading in and out, so I just let him ruminate.

We spoke about his time on the President's Commission, Charlie Rogovin, Phil Manuel, and others. He lamented on what a disappointment the Commission was and how it could have done great things.

He was particularly chagrined at [Senator] Sweeney's [President of the New Jersey Senate] refusal to give [Colonel] Callahan a hearing and confirm him to Superintendent. "I like Callahan . . . he treated me with respect . . . we seemed to hit it off . . . I think he liked me."

I reminded him that Col. Callahan's father, Mickey was a State Police Major. "Yeah," he responded, "a true gentleman . . . I liked him too . . . when I get out of here, I'm going to see to it that Callahan is confirmed as Superintendent."

Of course, we discussed how he and I became so intertwined in each other's professional and personal lives. He reiterated the so-called "trade . . . Liddy for Martens . . . how he and [Major] Baum got along so well (not quite as keen as he seemed to remember) . . . and all the great work the State Police did in addressing organized crime and corruption."

My sadness deepened as it was now after four o'clock, and I was preparing to leave. He grabbed my hand. I said, "I love you, stay safe, and I will see you next week at your house . . ."

He said, "I don't think so . . . Freddie; you were always loyal to me . . . I love you." I left with tears in my eyes, knowing I would not see him again.

I met Eileen, his daughter, who was just arriving to attend a meeting in the parking lot. The rehabilitation facility was no longer willing to extend his physical therapy. They felt that he was unable to continue and make progress. "The Colonel" was unable or unwilling to cooperate. He no longer had the will to live. Eileen was resigned to the fact that "The Colonel's" days were dwindling.

On January 24, 2020, I received a call from Denny. "My father passed away." I, of course, gave Denny my condolences and told him to call Col. Callahan. A State Police funeral befitting of a retired Colonel and Superintendent was awaiting him. And Colonel Callahan did not disappoint.

On February 1, 2020, before the pandemic struck New Jersey with a vengeance, Colonel Dintino received a funeral that the pandemic would have denied one month later. Much like his career, "The Colonel" went out in grand style, his dignity eulogized, his integrity championed, and his devotion to his wife, Doris, of 71 years praised by his son, Denny.[37] [See Appendix A.]

---

37. Johnson, Brent. *The Star-Ledger*. 2020. "Former N.J. State Police Leader who took on racial profiling and organized crime dies." January 25th.

No one makes it alone in this life. We all have a friend, a teacher, a partner, a spouse, a colleague, or a mate to support us, give advice, open up doors, and guide us. I had several, starting with my mother and father and ending with my beloved and most dedicated and loyal mentor in 2020.

It was a hell of a run and one that I will always cherish. And it would not have been possible had I not met an obscure Lieutenant in 1974, who became not only a mentor but a friend, a confidante, a teacher, and a role model.

RIP, my friend!

APPENDIX A

Remarks at the Dedication of the Col. Justin J. Dintino Repository of Organized Crime Literature[1]

Edwin H. Stier

Colonel Callahan, Governor Florio, Chief Justice Zazzali, Attorney General DeVesa, current and former retired State Police leaders, law enforcement colleagues, friends, and most importantly, Colonel Justin Dintino and his family.

It is easy to recount Justin Dintino's many achievements in law enforcement and the national recognition he earned during his long career. He is, of course, most closely associated with exposing and investigating organized crime in New Jersey, culminating in a well-deserved appointment by President Reagan to a panel of experts charged with reporting on the structure and the threat of organized crime across the nation.

But there is a deeper level to the story of Col. Dintino. It has to do with his character and the organization to which he devoted his professional life. For he defined what it means to be a "Trooper." If we leave this place today having honored a great leader of this organization only for his achievements, we will be missing the most crucial lesson his life can teach us.

So please indulge me while I give you some historical context to understand better what kind of man Col. Dintino is and the role he played in the history of our state.

---

1. In excess of 300 books, documents, and personal papers were dedicated to the New Jersey State Police Academy for the future education of State Police recruits and those embarking in a career investigating organized crime and public corruption.

When Trooper Justin Dintino, badge #1152, fresh out of the farm fields of South Jersey, graduated from the State Police Academy on December 2, 1952, he could not have understood the hidden political culture of this state and how it would challenge his integrity. During the early years as a road Trooper, he displayed tenacity and skill as an investigator in Troop A and gradually, almost reluctantly, gravitated toward detective work. In the early 60s, when he began to investigate illegal gambling in South Jersey, he collided with the tremendous power of New Jersey's political corruption.

Long before Trooper Dintino came along, it was widely understood that New Jersey political power was concentrated in the urban counties. Hudson, Essex, Passaic, Middlesex, Atlantic, and Camden Counties were the centers of power where candidates for office were selected, and favors were exchanged.

At the same time, New Jersey was home to every organized crime group operating in the New York and Philadelphia metropolitan areas. From colonial days, when Benjamin Franklin described New Jersey as a "kegged tapped at both ends" by New York and Philadelphia, our state seemed incapable of resisting exploitation by outsiders. During Prohibition, we gave free rein to bootleggers and their criminal enterprises. When Prohibition ended, those groups expanded into gambling, prostitution, drug dealing, loan sharking, cargo theft, and many other crimes, creating a flourishing illegal economy parallel to legitimate commerce.

We failed to recognize the extent to which county machine politics had become captive to organized crime? There was virtually nothing at any level of government out of the reach of criminals. In fact, in the darkest days of the 1950s and 1960s, racketeers had so infested government institutions that they were able to name a State Police superintendent to whom they paid a regular salary alongside a government check.

So when Investigator Dintino, operating out of the Turnersville Station, decided to lock people up for illegal gambling, he was confronted by a delegation from Division Headquarters. They told him in no uncertain terms to lay off gambling. Most of us would have failed that moral test. After all, there was plenty of other crime to deal with, and he could have accepted their enticing rationale that gambling was to be policed by headquarters units, not the troops.

But Investigator Dintino was not built to accept such deception. He knew that Trenton was conducting no gambling raids and that the racketeers behind the gambling were thumbing their noses at law enforcement absent his efforts. And so, convinced that it was his duty to enforce the criminal laws and at significant personal risk, Investigator Dintino persisted.

In those days, a handful of Troopers like Dintino could not abide by the affront to their duty as law enforcement officers and their pride. They were typically passed over for promotion and transferred to remote outposts where they couldn't pose trouble. They felt isolated and frustrated but could not conform to the corrupt culture that had grown like cancer from within the organization from which they had sworn their loyalty.

They had no way of knowing that during this period, a transformative figure in State Police history, David B. Kelly, had maneuvered himself into the position of Deputy Superintendent and was secretly being fed information by the FBI to stem corruption within the organization. By 1965, Kelly could muster enough political support to become Superintendent but was concerned that any sudden change in policy toward organized crime would end his administration. So in 1966, Col. Kelly secretly brought together the core members of the future battle against organized crime and their corrupt political friends in the basement of his home. Five Troopers were quietly transferred to a newly created Intelligence Bureau, assigned to collect information about the structure and membership of organized crime, their illegal enterprises, and their sources of protection. Based on his record of resistance to corruption, determination to enforce the law against criminal enterprises, and resourcefulness, Justin Dintino was a charter member of Kelly's team of revolutionaries.

Detective Sergeant Dintino flourished in the new environment that Col. Kelly had created. He built relationships with the FBI in Philadelphia and Camden, earning their trust and overcoming the stigma of past corruption. During his gambling investigations, he had developed organized crime informants to whom he now turned for intelligence on a full range of organized crime activities from murders to political payoffs.

As the Intelligence Bureau was getting on its feet, something happened that would change law enforcement history forever.

In 1967, frustrated with the growing power of organized crime nationally and the unwillingness of the then US Attorney General to unleash the full resources of the Department of Justice to fight against it, the FBI leaked records of extralegal electronic surveillance installations they had been operating for several years to Life Magazine. Those bugs revealed, in graphic detail, the inner workings of the mob nationally. Based on that information, Life Magazine ran two articles exposing the links between racketeers and politicians throughout the country, emphasizing New Jersey. Details of discussions between high-level mobsters about the sources of their impunity, including their State Police connections, dropped like a bomb in New Jersey. Kelly and his team took full advantage of the shockwave. Working with a courageous legislator, Senator Ed Forsythe, a set of robust new laws were pushed through a stunned legislature. For the first time anywhere in the country, they created a grand jury with statewide jurisdiction, and along with it, legalized court-authorized electronic surveillance and the power to grant witness immunity. These were tools essential to penetrate the layers of insulation protecting the most powerful racketeers and corrupt politicians.

But Kelly and his team were not satisfied to have a few new laws on the books. They pressed the Attorney General into giving the State Police the resources to implement those laws. And so, in 1969, a new unit was created within the Intelligence Bureau, made up of experienced prosecutors, to work alongside Troopers like Lt. Dintino to transform raw intelligence information into successful prosecutions—the first such program in the country.

Over the next ten years, hundreds of mobsters and corrupt politicians were brought to justice. All of the mob bosses identified with Life Magazine were brought down. County political leaders, legislators, mayors, police chiefs, prosecutors, and even judges were convicted. And the New Jersey State Police became a national model of integrity and effectiveness in the fight against organized crime.

Major Dintino could have rested on those achievements as he rose through the ranks to fill the newly created position of Lieutenant Colonel.

But here is where the story of his character deepens. For many years the State Police had been targets of accusations of abusing minorities by civil rights organizations. By the time Gov. Florio was elected in 1989, the State Police had been barraged with lawsuits, and in some cases, Troopers had been convicted of civil rights violations and even imprisoned. At the outset of his administration, Gov. Florio turned to Col. Dintino as his new Superintendent, demanding that the problem be assessed and fixed.

We all know that law enforcement tends to rely on statistics to measure itself. The number of arrests, drug seizures, weapons recoveries, and the like gives us a sense of comfort that society is being protected. Col. Dintino saw through the deception in numbers. His policy was straightforward—protecting the rights of all citizens is the highest priority of the State Police. For emphasis, he instructed his troops that he would prefer that not another ounce of drugs were seized to witnessing another Trooper going to prison for a civil rights violation.

The troops came to understand that Col. Dintino was serious. They followed his lead so scrupulously that the New Jersey State Police received the unqualified praise of the American Civil Liberties Union for the first time in its history. During his tenure, racial profiling ended.

To understand the real significance of this, I need to tell you one final story. It is not about sweeping policy change or law enforcement splashed across the media. At best, it is a footnote in the history of Col. Dintino's tenure. But I witnessed it, and I want you to understand its profound implications.

In the early 1990s, Newark's most dysfunctional, crime-infested neighborhoods conducted a community policing experiment. With no fanfare, a unit of Troopers and Newark Police Officers were assigned to patrol on foot from an apartment that had been converted into a mini-precinct. Not since the 1967 Newark riot had residents encountered Troopers in their community, and the distrust was palpable. But within a mere couple of months, dramatic transformations began to occur. The police started to recognize law-abiding community members as individuals, forming trusting relationships among them. The police began to respond to neighborhood priorities, providing safety for residents to emerge from their homes to shop and interact with neighbors. Children were free to play without fear of being caught in a crossfire between rival gangs. Residents began to give police information about the locations of drug dealers and organize to clean up their neighborhood. Fundamental social values incompatible with drug use, thievery, and violence began to take hold in the neighborhood—all because of the intimate connection that grew in a few short weeks between the police and the community they served.

What are the lessons that Justin Dintino can teach us? They are defined by the State Police motto: Honor, Duty Fidelity. But to whom do we owe these obligations? Co. Dintino's story tells us the public. Regardless of the differences among us, individually, we are entitled to the loyalty and protection of law enforcement. Col. Dintino did not simply preach those values. He fought against overwhelming obstacles with extraordinary courage to live by them and lead the New Jersey State Police by his example. Let us never forget.

Edwin H. Stier
October 30, 2019
Sea Girt, New Jersey

APPENDIX B

A Tribute to My Friend and Mentor: Charles H. Rogovin

Frederick T. Martens

Asked to speak at this memorial service for my dear friend and mentor, Charlie Rogovin, I only had seven minutes. What can you say about Charlie that wouldn't take seven days or seven months? Charlie's resume alone would take seven minutes.

Indeed, Charlie's championing the 1968 Omnibus Safe Street Act, which established the Law Enforcement Assistance Administration, said it all. Appointed by the late President Lyndon Baines Johnson to be its first Administrator, Charlie's efforts educated hundreds of thousands of police officers throughout the nation. Yes, hundreds of thousands, no exaggeration, received college and advanced professional degrees due to this Act alone.

As Charlie would often say, "The police have a tremendous amount of discretion and the absolute authority to impose the death sentence with no judicial review, and yet all we require is a high school diploma to be a cop."

As a consequence of Charlie's vision, a requirement in many police departments require a college degree. This vision, I believe, will reign as Charlie's most significant accomplishment.

But it doesn't stop there.

Charlie was responsible for stewarding what would prove to be one of the most controversial legal enhancements in the "war against organized crime." Court authorized electronic surveillance was the subject of polarizing debates among good governance groups, the American Civil Liberties Union, law enforcement, and civil rights organizations.

In 1967, Charlie singlehandedly recruited and coaxed six consultants into contributing their time and expertise to writing *Task Force Report: Organized Crime.* The final report made a case for Federal and state statutes regulating electronic surveillance, among other reforms.

Getting this through Congress was no easy feat.

Tapping the phones of corrupt politicians and putting listening devices in their offices and homes would not endear you to the political elite. Yet Charlie, against impossible odds, lined up an array of advocates who championed transparency in government. His efforts ensured the passage of a statute that provided judicial oversight of "unauthorized but not illegal" electronic surveillance.

Make no mistake about it. The 1967 *Task Force Report: Organized Crime* changed the landscape of proactive law enforcement against organized crime.

Simply put, it was revolutionary.

Charlie also understood the value of integrating the academic disciplines in the "war against organized crime." He was, without question, the most forceful advocate for civilian intelligence analysts educated in the social sciences—sociology, psychology, history, political science, organizational research.

And if you think it was easy integrating civilians into quasi-military organizations populated by crusty old, stuck in their ways bosses of yesteryear, think again. That was no small endeavor.

Charlie convinced even the most obstinate and skeptical opponents through his profound sense of humor and perfectly reasoned logic. Ultimately civilians were allowed access to raw, unedited, and sensitive police intelligence files that contained the identities of highly confidential sources.

Today, law enforcement agencies throughout the country and the world employ thousands of civilian intelligence analysts.

As we all know, Charlie was a most articulate and entertaining raconteur. Why didn't he do stand-up comedy and commercial voice-overs and make millions of dollars still baffles me?

Who could tell a joke better than Charlie?

Indeed, no one, and I mean no one, could tell the "Flying Scotsman joke" like Charlie, applying the British accent and Queens English flawlessly.

He used this skill that he honed to perfection to win over those curmudgeon police administrators and arrogant prosecutors who endured Charlie's pitch.

No one, and I mean no one, could capture and enthrall an audience like Charlie. This skill allowed Charlie to establish a rapport with some of the most ardent opponents of implementing sophisticated intelligence-driven policing strategies.

And it made him one of the most sought-after speakers on the law enforcement circuit in this country and the world stage.

In 1983, President Reagan chose Charlie to serve on a commission to re-examine the "war against organized crime." Charlie once again distinguished himself as the leader of the "Gang of 9". They took issue with the Commission's final report. Too much time had been spent on the Mafia. Not enough focus was directed at the newer forms of organized crime that were emerging throughout America.

Again, Charlie's commitment to "telling it like it is" was what made Charlie the crème-dele-crème of law enforcement educators and professionals.

On a personal note, I was most fortunate to have Charlie as a friend and a mentor.

We began our journey in Colorado in 1983 when the late Gov. Richard Lamb asked Charlie to examine the workings of the Colorado Bureau of Investigations. He chose me to assist him in this inquiry. You indeed get to know someone when you spend 24/7 for two weeks with them. I then developed a personal relationship with Charlie that carried me to the day he passed away.

And when the Pennsylvania Crime Commission was obligated to investigate the corrupt Attorney General of Pennsylvania in 1992, Charlie stood tall in the face of a hostile and defensive Legislature that was intent on protecting the way business was done in Pennsylvania.

Accused of every form of ethnic and political bias, undertaking a witch hunt, and engaging in a political vendetta, Charlie confronted the political elites who ruled Pennsylvania head-on. He never shied away from the job he swore to do: investigate and expose public corruption and organized crime.

We were, of course, abolished, but as Charlie would say, "what better way to enshrine your legacy than to be abolished by corrupt politicians."

As many of you know, many of our adversaries served time in Federal prison—not state institutions.

As an:

- Assistant and Chief District Attorney
- President of the Police Foundation
- Assistant Attorney General
- Administrator LEAA
- Assistant Director of Johnson's Task Force on Organized Crime
- A Commissioner on Reagan's Commission on Organized Crime and
- Vice-Chairman of the Pennsylvania Crime Commission,

Charlie was an iconic figure in the world of law enforcement.
As he would often quip, "Ok, so I couldn't hold a job."
Always Charlie was:

- Meticulously dressed and groomed
- Tenacious
- Scholarly
- Cerebral
- Confident
- Ethically beyond reproach
- Self-deprecating
- and a GIANT among his peers

But in my world, Charlie had one more trait that made him much more than a giant among his law enforcement peers.

As you have heard, he rubbed shoulders with:

- Presidents
- United States Senators, Congressmen, and women
- Governors
- Attorneys General
- Federal and State judges
- Mayors and a host of appointed and elected public officials

He was both secure and comfortable in that rarified world.

But what made Charlie so special to me, and I suspect many of those here today, was his humility and humbleness when educating, befriending, and investing in those who did not have the stature nor the titles that were so much a part of Charlie's other world.

Titles and stature meant very little to Charlie. Instead, Charlie passionately embraced and relished mentoring and shaping the minds of ordinary people—cops, police executives, prosecutors, judges, and most of all, fledging students.

It's what made Charlie "One of a Kind" and "Kind to Everyone."

Charlie lived a whole and rich life, one that took advantage of all the possibilities, obstacles, and challenges that came his way.

Indeed, he prevailed in leaving this world a better place from whence he found it in 1931. We will all miss Charlie in our unique ways.

But in the words of President Lincoln, whose birthday happens to be today but whom Charlie never met nor worked for, "It's not the years in life that count [but] the life in your years."

God Bless You, Charlie, and Rest in Peace. Know that you left an enduring legacy among the many people that were privileged to have graced your worn path.

Frederick T. Martens
Executive Director/Retired
Pennsylvania Crime Commission
Delivered at the Temple University School of Law
Memorial Service Honoring Professor Charles H. Rogovin
February 12, 2016

About the Author

FREDERICK T. MARTENS is a re-tired New Jersey State Police Detective/Lieutenant. He was the Executive Director of the Pennsylvania Crime Commission. Martens has worked undercover during the 1970's, conducted investigations of organized crime and public corruption, has been qualified as an expert on organized crime in both federal and state courts, and has served as an integrity monitor during the search and recovery efforts at the site of the former World Trade Center and its rebuilding. He has been con-
tracted by the City of New Orleans to investigate fraud and procurement abuse post Hurricane Katrina and served as a monitor on a construction project in Derry, Northern Ireland.

Martens is a charter member of the Vidocq Society, former President of IASOC, and has taught at Pennsylvania State University and The College of New Jersey. He has lectured throughout the world on organized crime, racketeering, and public corruption. He has master's degree from Fordham University and John Jay College of Criminal Justice. He is a prolific book reviewer for Rutgers University School of Criminal Justice. *Police Intelligence in Crime Control*, which he co-authored was recognized by IAELIA for its outstanding contribution to the advancement of the intelligence profession. He is the author of *We'll Make You An Offer You Can't Refuse: A Primer on the Investigation of Public Corruption*.